(7/12)

Hertfordshire
COUNTY COUNCIL
Community Information

17 SEP 2003

Norfolk

22/4/04

2 9 APR 2000

2 4 JUL 2000

1 5 APR 2004

1 6 AUG 2004

2 5 AUG 2000

- 7 JUL 2005

- 6 MAY 2003

- 6 SEP 2005

1 5 JUL 2003

12/11

L32a

Please renew/return this item by the last date shown.

So that your telephone call is charged at local rate,
please call the numbers as set out below:

	From Area codes 01923 or 0208:	From the rest of Herts:
Renewals:	01923 471373	01438 737373
Enquiries:	01923 471333	01438 737333
Minicom:	01923 471599	01438 737599

1987

1987

L32b

D1437234

1991

JLP 1991

2

PORTRAIT OF
LINCOLNSHIRE

Portrait of LINCOLNSHIRE

by

Michael Lloyd

ROBERT HALE · LONDON

Robert Hale Limited
Clerkenwell House
Clerkenwell Green
London EC1R 0HT

Photoset by Rowland Phototypesetting Ltd
Printed in Great Britain by
St Edmundsbury Press, Bury St Edmunds, Suffolk
Bound by Woolnough Bookbinding Ltd

Contents

List of illustrations

PICTURE CREDITS

Nos. 7, 17, 27, 41, 42, by C. J. Lloyd; the rest by the author.

Introduction

In 1959, when I went to work in Lincoln, my uncle remembered attending the Royal Show there in 1906. His main recollection was that, from Shropshire, he had crossed the sea to get there, by train admittedly. This typifies, in extreme form, the remoteness of the county in the eyes of inhabitants of many other parts of England.

Two hundred years ago they had some excuse. From London a traveller wealthy enough to hire horses and a post chaise would probably reach Lincoln after three days on the road. His journey was long and perhaps uncomfortable, but at least he would, with luck, arrive dry shod and without undue danger. Had he come from East Anglia, however, he would have crossed the tidal estuaries of the Wash, where a guide was usually considered necessary and where the famous story of King John's baggage train was a reminder of potential disaster. The approach to the county from the north, as well, was by a sometimes hair-raising ferry over the Humber, and ferries were also the only means of crossing the Trent above Newark before the river was bridged at Gainsborough in 1791. Once inside the county, distances were enormous. Travellers by mail coach from London to Barton-on-Humber were only half-way to their destination when they entered Lincolnshire at Market Deeping. The roads, too, were nothing but mire and misery in many parts of the county in winter, and cross-county communication could be very slow and difficult. In 1772, for instance, George de Ligne Gregory was faced with the problem of transporting a pointer bitch from Grantham to Grimsby. He decided to send the animal by stage wagon to Gainsborough and on from there by river; the whole journey was likely to take nine days.

The eighteenth-century picturesque tourist, therefore, would approach Lincolnshire often with some difficulty, perhaps also with some caution, and returning he would report on the most unusual features of the area to the exclusion of all others. Thus was born the stereotype of a flat expanse peopled by strange men on stilts, where there was nothing worth looking at but large numbers of magnificent churches. To some extent this image has survived, although there is no excuse for it now when London, the industrial Midlands and North and many other parts of England are within three hours' travel.

Lincolnshire has another problem to cope with, in that it cannot properly be labelled either a northern, a midland or an East Anglian county. In many ways it shares characteristics with all three. Holland is East Anglian; South Kesteven has many features in common with the limestone belt which stretches southwards through Northamptonshire towards the Cotswolds; the western lowlands similarly belong to the midland plain; in northern Lindsey there is little doubt that one is in the north of England. Lincolnshire has always been too large a county to be classified conveniently within one geographical area; too large also for its name-town ever to have been looked upon with total commitment as the county capital. Distances and centrifugal forces were too great. In fact, in the administrative sense of a unit of local government, Lincolnshire never has been a 'county'. Before 1974 three separate county councils administered the Parts of Holland, Kesteven and Lindsey. Since 1974 the old divisions have been abolished, and there is now a united Lincolnshire, shorn, however, of a large chunk of the old Parts of Lindsey which has been incorporated into the new county of Humberside, whose boundary follows a somewhat erratic and inconsequential course across the map south of Grimsby and Scunthorpe.

Lincolnshire's position as debatable ground between North and South goes back as far as its first colonization by the Anglo-Saxon tribes, when the area was divided between the kingdoms of Lindsey and Middle Anglia. The latter was soon swallowed up by Mercia, but Lindsey preserved a separate identity until late in the eighth century, although for much of the time it was an uncomfortable buffer state between the much more powerful Mercian and Northumbrian kingdoms, regularly and alternately conquered by the armies of their kings. The arrival of the Danes in the mid-ninth century altered the situation dramatically; the invaders established themselves early and strongly in Lincolnshire, and from it they launched attacks on the now retreating forces of the adjoining kingdoms. Lincoln and Stamford were two of the Five Boroughs from which an expanding Danish area was ruled; and the Scandinavian settlement was so thick that no later English reconquests could erase its influence on local administration and institutions. Nowhere in England are the Danish place-name endings of *by* and *thorpe* so frequent as they are in Lincolnshire.

For much of its history the county has been one of England's great food-supplying regions. In the eighteenth century the fat beef and mutton produced in its extensive areas of rich grazing land were perhaps the chief exports to other parts of the country. Grain, however, was always important in the local economy and became more so after the enclosures of the late eighteenth and early nineteenth centuries. Lincolnshire became once more what it had been in Roman times, one of the great corn-producing areas of England. It still is, and its agriculture is diversified by large acreages of potatoes and sugar beet and by the widely grown vegetable crops of the fenland. Stock-raising is a much less widespread feature of the scene than it once was; the long-wooled Lincolnshire sheep which once whitened whole areas of pasture are a rare sight. Herds of Lincoln Red cattle, large, well built and a deep reddish brown in colour, are more frequently seen.

It is best when passing through the Lincolnshire countryside to put aside all bucolic idylls and to think of the journey as a tour through an enormous food-factory. To a great extent the landscape has been moulded by the hands of men, its sole function the efficient production of crops. After centuries of gradual reclamation, the needs of the time caused an enormous burst of activity to bring land into cultivation between about 1750 and 1850. It suited men's farming techniques to lay out whole landscapes of scattered farmsteads and neat enclosures where previously there had been vast open fields. Fens and marshes were drained, upland wastes and sandy lowlands enclosed and made fertile. This was a revolution in the countryside probably even more dramatic than the more recent one which has seen the disappearance of thousands of miles of hedge and re-creation in many areas of an open-field landscape, where great armies of enormous machines are almost constantly at work ploughing the land or breaking it up, spraying or harvesting. Richard

Jefferies once commented upon the easy life of the 'idle earth'. The soil of Lincolnshire no longer enjoys much rest. As soon as one crop is harvested, it is time to prepare for the next.

This, therefore, is essentially a working landscape; but it is by no means one without beauty. There are many parts of the county which have been consciously beautified with hedgerow timber and shelter belts and parkscapes. Elsewhere the view may be almost treeless, but there is still an attraction to be found in the great rolling cornfields of the wolds and heath and even in the almost aggressive flatness of the fens under an enormous sky.

The county's geological make-up is typified by a series of bands running from north to south. This is particularly marked in Lindsey where the lowlands of the Vale of Trent are succeeded by a ridge of limestone, a central clay vale, an upland area of chalk wolds and finally a low-lying coastal marsh. In the southern half of Lincolnshire the limestone ridge spreads westward to the county boundary near Grantham, and the central clays slope gently into the fenland at their eastern edge. Bands of different building materials follow the lines of geological structure; brick is most common in the western vale, stone almost universal in all but recent housing on the limestone belt, its normal colour varied in places by golden ironstone. East of the limestone belt brick is the main material again; the chalk of the wolds is used occasionally, and the green sandstone which underlies the chalk is seen frequently in the churches of the area but not so often in the domestic architecture. Most of the villages in the county underwent a great rebuilding in the nineteenth century when brick replaced the much less permanent materials with which many of the farms as well as the houses of the poor had been constructed. This rebuilding was perhaps less marked on the limestone belt, where the villages usually seem to have rather more surviving houses of the seventeenth and eighteenth-centuries. Away from the centres of settlement almost all the outlying farmsteads were erected among their fields during and after the great period of enclosure in the late eighteenth and early nineteenth centuries.

In my description of the regions of Lincolnshire I have started in the south-west, with Kesteven, and followed an anticlockwise route around the county, ending with Lincoln itself. It was obvious from the start that any conscientious attempt to describe every one of over seven hundred ancient parishes in this enormous area would be pointless. A couple of sentences for each of them would have been all there would have been space for and would have left none over for more general themes. I have tried therefore to combine some of the features of a guidebook with more general descriptions of the landscape, which guidebooks often lack, and with enough background information about the county's past to set the present scene in its historical context. Anyone who wants to study the architecture of Lincolnshire, in particular its numerous magnificent churches, in greater detail will take Sir Nikolaus Pevsner as his guide. Anyone who wants to know more of its history can turn to the publications of the Society for Lincolnshire History and Archaeology, in particular to the volumes in the History of Lincolnshire series, and for editions of archive material to the publications of the Lincoln Record Society.

This book, therefore, is an uneasy marriage of history and descriptive guide. It has also been impossible to prevent frequent descents into the realms of pure anecdote, for the county's past abounds in good stories. 'Gossiping Guides' were popular in the nineteenth century; if this twentieth-century version proves to be at times more of a gossip than a guide, I offer (limited) apologies.

1

South Kesteven

Stamford

There is no better approach to Lincolnshire than that of the north-bound traveller on the Great North Road. The modern bypass descends into the valley of the Welland to the west of the 'very fair, well-built, considerable and wealthy town of Stamford', affording an entrancing view of the town itself, rising gently in the distance above its water-meadows, a harmonious composition of mellow stone in a setting of green. Such is the view glimpsed momentarily by the hastening motorist. The more leisurely traveller can follow the old North Road as it skirts Burghley Park wall through the trees into High St, St Martin, which curves down past St Martin's Church to the Welland bridge. This part of the town, Stamford Baron, contains a fine, light and spacious, mainly Perpendicular church and some fine domestic architecture, including the George Hotel and the Burghley Almshouses down by the river. Among the Cecil monuments in St Martin's Church, Lord Burghley, Queen Elizabeth's minister, lies in state, his feet resting on a lugubrious-faced lion. The large monument to John, fifth Earl of Exeter, who died in 1700, shows him comfortably half-reclining with his wife like guests at a Roman banquet. At a modest distance from the great is the 1885 memorial to Thomas Cooper Goodrich 'a rare cricketer and a good man'. The medieval glass in the chancel windows was brought from Tattershall in the eighteenth-century.

The importance of the crossing of the Welland which joins St Martin's to the rest of Stamford was a major element in the making of the town. Here the river was comparatively easy to ford, and an important prehistoric trackway and the Roman

Ermine Street cross it within a few hundred yards of each other. The name Stamford implies a ford with a firm, stony bottom, quite different from the miry going which must have existed both to east and west where the valley bottom broadens into alluvial, once marshy, land. Even so, there is little sign of settlement in Stamford itself in either prehistoric or Roman times. The Roman station was a little to the north, at Great Casterton in Rutland. Stamford was perhaps an early Anglo-Saxon settlement, in which case its rise to pre-eminent importance as one of the Five Boroughs of Danelaw was a rapid one.

The Middle Ages saw both the peak of Stamford's greatness and the beginnings of decline. It stood on an important north-south link, which became *the* most important link once the Trent was bridged at Nottingham in the late twelfth century. It also stood astride the River Welland, which gave navigation to the sea, and between the great wool-producing areas of South Lincolnshire and Leicestershire. Its wool-merchants were predominant in the medieval period. Many ventured overseas to the great wool-mart of Calais and returned to endow almshouses or 'Callises' for the good of their souls and the support of the aged and infirm. Economic wealth brought spiritual welfare also in the multitude of churches and religious communities and in the fame of its medieval schools, which at one time threatened to rival Oxford and Cambridge, when in the early fourteenth century a group of disaffected Oxford masters seceded to Stamford and for a short time a quasi-university flourished.

The decline of Stamford's wool trade, the silting up of the Welland and, ironically, its position on the Great North Road (which encouraged a passing Lancastrian army to sack this firmly Yorkist town) all contributed to some measure of decay in the fifteenth and sixteenth centuries. The population was more or less static until the late seventeenth century. The number of parishes was reduced from eleven to six in 1548. An ordinance of 1574 forbade the employment of outsiders so long as townsmen were out of work. The occasional observer described it as a 'poor decayed town'. Gradually, however, new enterprises began to flourish: leatherworking, weaving and, after the reopening of the Welland in about 1678 provided easy water transport for barley, the malting trade. By now Stamford combined the position of an important local market and small manufacturing

town with an ever-increasing importance to the growing number of travellers who frequented its inns, its shops, its assemblies and its theatres and provided trade and employment for
many of its citizens. The eighteenth and nineteenth centuries
saw the heyday of Stamford as the staging post. Enormous
numbers of coaches, private carriages, horse and foot-passen-
gers passed through: the 'Rockingham' to Leeds, the Highflyer'
to York, the 'Wellington' to Edinburgh, and the 'Alexander' to
Leicester and Cambridge, are a few only of the coaches named in
the 1826 Directory.

Travellers at this period saw a town of fine medieval churches,
some good public buildings, great inns and a variety of well-
built domestic architecture. They could also see yearly the
Stamford 'Bull Running', an extraordinary example of the
power of local custom to withstand the forces of progress, law
and order and humanitarianism. Described as early as 1646 as
'a sport of no pleasure except to such as take pleasure in
beastliness and mischief', it consisted of a mad dash round the
town in hot pursuit of a bull provided yearly by the local
butchers. 'The gates all shut up, the bull is turned out of the
Alderman's house, and then hivie, skivy, tag and rag, men,
women, and children of all sorts and sizes, with all the dogs of
the town, promiscuously running after him with their bull-clubs
. . . that one would think them to be so many furies started out of
hell.' By 1788 the corporation was somewhat ashamed of the
custom and proclaimed it unlawful and punishable by *death*.
However, threats, special constables, the First Dragoons and
the Earl of Exeter combined could not prevent the 'bullards'
from having their sport. In 1789 the Second Dragoons were
outwitted by a female bullard, and the soldiers joined in the fun;
in 1790 the Third Dragoons were equally powerless. Authority
now left the bullards in peace for a number of years, and
parliamentary candidates curried favour with the electorate by
subscribing a bull from time to time. But national opinion was
turning against such manifestations, and in 1833 the Society for
the Prevention of Cruelty to Animals made a determined
attempt to get the custom suppressed; unabashed, the inhabitants baited both the bull and the Society's inspector. In 1837
some of the bullards were prosecuted for riotous assembly; large
numbers of special constables were sworn in in 1838, and the

dragoons were called in; and equally large forces were called upon in 1839 and were successful in curtailing the sport though not in preventing it completely. However, as if satisfied with outwitting the authorities on a number of successive years, perhaps also somewhat worn down by the cost of the policing operation, the inhabitants entered into a sort of gentlemen's agreement with their corporation, and 1840 saw neither special constables, nor dragoons nor bull.

Kindness to bulls was one manifestation of the nineteenth century's march of progress: railways and rampant industrial development were another. These latter fell more gently upon Stamford than on many towns: most industrial development was on a comparatively small scale, the Great Northern main line passed by some miles away, and the borough expanded little beyond its ancient bounds. Critical voices then and later saw in this a sinister plot by the Marquesses of Exeter who, owning much of the land, could hamper industrial development, improvement in communications and even increased housing provision. Certainly the Cecils were a paramount influence in nineteenth-century Stamford (Gladstone described the town as a Tory fortress used from time to time to accommodate a wandering Tory official of whom some other constituency had grown weary), but it was not an unchallenged influence. For much of the century the *Stamford Mercury* was a liberal paper, and briefly in 1831 one of the town's parliamentary seats was won for the radical cause by Charles Tennyson (the poet's uncle) who was then challenged to a duel by his fellow member, Lord Thomas Cecil. Tennyson himself underwent the ordeal with some philosophy, recording that the duel was expected to be the first of a series arising in the heated political atmosphere of Reform agitation in which it was only reasonable that he, holding the post of Clerk to the Board of Ordnance, should fire the first shot.

All the periods of Stamford's history have contributed to making the town which we see today; so also has the geographical accident which places it within easy reach of a number of sources of good stone: Ketton, Barnack, Clipsham and Weldon are all close by, and the town itself had several quarries in the medieval period and perhaps later. No one building dominates, as the cathedral dominates Lincoln; instead, a host of different ages, styles, sizes and shapes mingle to form one of England's most beautiful towns, in which every corner and every narrow alley provides some fresh vista to delight. The harmony of the whole is produced by the blend of many-shaded stones in the walls and in the roofscape of Collyweston slate. The details of the individual buildings forever offer some new pleasure to the eye; nowhere can there be more variety of gable, pediment, chimney, bay, doorway or window.

The student of medieval domestic architecture in Stamford may pursue his interest in the undercrofts of shops, in the occasional archway and in many scattered fragments; he must even venture, according to reliable authority, into both the gentleman's toilet and ladies' powder-room of the George Hotel. Also from this period are one fragment of the castle and one or two other pieces of the medieval defences. The town is rich, on the other hand, in medieval ecclesiastic buildings. One of the six churches, the now redundant St Michael's, is almost entirely a nineteenth-century rebuilding; the others belong mainly to the thirteenth and fifteenth centuries. The Early English tower and spire of St Mary's are the focal points of the view of the town as one descends through St Martin's. All Saints is also a largely thirteenth-century church, much enlarged in the Perpendicular period at the expense of various members of the Browne family including that merchant 'of very wonderful richnesse', William Browne, who can be seen among several memorial brasses to the family, his feet resting on the woolpacks which produced his wealth. His other great monument is close by in Broad Street, Browne's Hospital, often described as one of England's finest surviving examples of a medieval almshouse. In spite of restoration and additions in 1870, there is still much of the medieval building surviving, including the chapel and the audit room.

For the later architectural development of Stamford there is abundant evidence in almost every street. Houses and public buildings of every period from the sixteenth-century onwards abound. Above all it is a marvellous place for aimless wandering (with some caution, though, for the traffic through the narrow streets, in spite of the A1 bypass, is very heavy at times).

The South Kesteven Landscape

What shire is there can show more valuable veins
Of soil than is in me? or where can there be found
So fair and fertile fields, or sheepwalks near so sound?

So brags Kesteven in Michael Drayton's *Poly-Olbion*, when the personification of the division is countering the boasts of Holland about the riches of the fenland. In Camden's *Britannia* also the area is compared with Holland, though rather more cautiously, as being 'happy in the possession of an air much more wholsome and a soil no less fruitful'.

South Kesteven is an area whose undulating landscape, plentiful woodlands and pleasant villages of mellow stone are immediately easy on the eye. It is also the area which by all the rules of accessibility ought to have given past travellers their first and lasting impression of Lincolnshire. England's main north-to-south routes by both road and rail passed through it, over its broad uplands and wooded valleys, in cuttings through its limestone bones. The nature of the country made this stretch of the Great Northern line by far the most expensive to construct on the whole of the route from London to York. It is manifestly far from flat; but travellers had heard all about the fens, and it was the fens they were determined to remember.

Geologically South Kesteven is an area of greater complexity than any other part of the county. South of Grantham the limestone Heath and its attendant marlstone skirt fan out westward to join the Leicestershire uplands. In many parts, particularly in the south east of the region, the limestone is covered by a layer of clay. In turn, here and there patches of gravel cover the clays, and there is a band of gravel soils of varying width between the eastern edge of the claylands and the Fens. (In his work on the place-name evidence for Scandinavian settlement in Lincolnshire, Professor Kenneth Cameron has pointed out the vital importance of these gravels in the settlement pattern of the area.) The district is well

watered. The Witham rises on the Rutland border and flows
northwards; to the centre of the district two parallel valleys are
formed by two streams (which the Ordnance Survey now calls
the West and East River Glen though the eastern one once
combined official anonymity with the unofficial title of the
Eden) which flow southwards for some twenty miles before they
unite and swing north-east through the fens to the Wash.

South Kesteven has by Lincolnshire standards an abundance
of woodland. The very name seems to be derived from a British
word *ceto*, meaning 'wood', and the Old Scandinavian *stefna*,
'meeting place' or 'administrative district'. The title of 'Woodlands District Council' is a possible modern paraphrase which
fortunately escaped the attention of those who christened the
new administrative area in 1974. The extent of the ancient
forest of Kesteven can be traced in a number of place-names
which include elements like 'field', from the Old English 'feld',
an open area in a forest, 'ley', from Old English 'leah', a clearing,
or in such names as Lound, meaning a grove. Some of the
occupations of the inhabitants of a forest country are to be found
in names like Colsterworth, the hamlet of the charcoal burners,
and Swinstead, the homestead where pigs were reared. Domesday Book records areas of woodland in many of the parishes;
1,100 acres in Corby, 1,250 in Bitchfield, for instance. The
pannage of these woodlands was valuable in supporting large
herds of pigs which wandered the forest floor picking up a living
from beech mast and acorns. Domesday bacon from these
energetic animals was perhaps very lean and a little stringy,
but it may well have been tastier than ours.

The forest of Kesteven was neither trackless nor impenetrable. Both the prehistoric Jurassic way and the Roman
Ermine Street ran northwards from Stamford; King Street, also
Roman, entered the county at West Deeping and ran through
Bourne to Sleaford. Another Roman route joins King Street
near Bourne to Ermine Street south of Ancaster. Salters Way
started probably from some unknown site on the coast, followed
the line of the present A52 Donington to Grantham road for
some distance, crossed the Witham at the important Roman
settlement of Saltersford in Little Ponton and joined the Fosse
Way in Leicestershire. Water communication along the southern boundary was provided by the River Welland; along the

eastern edge ran the Roman Car Dyke which runs fifty-six miles from Peterborough to Lincoln. Archaeologists have disagreed as to whether this was built as a canal or as a catchwater drain which may also have been used for transport.

Pre-Roman settlement is particularly thick in the Welland valley. The distribution map of Roman finds and the sites of major Roman settlements and villas are naturally enough to be found near the lines of their roads and of the Car Dyke. When the Anglo-Saxon settlers arrived, their two main needs were sources of water and an easily worked soil not too deeply covered with woodland. They picked out the more fertile stretches of upland, the less impenetrable clays and the gravels; the place-names on the Welland valley, for instance, are all of English origin, as are the majority of names of the fen margin from Deeping up to Horbling. Onto the pattern of the Anglo-Saxon settlement that of the Danes was later superimposed, filling in the spaces left by the former on the gravels, pushing up the Roman roads (not Ermine Street – they disliked limestone) and river valleys, making clearings in the more impenetrable wood-land, taming the less hospitable clays. South Kesteven is one of the areas most richly endowed in Danish place-names in Lincolnshire.

The continuing bosky appearance of many parts of South Kesteven testifies not so much to the extent of the original forest cover as to the tree-planting activities of its many resident landed families in the eighteenth and nineteenth centuries. This was and is the part of the county which is nearest to the main routes of north-south communication, nearest to London, nearest to what many would call 'civilisation'. It was also an area of attractive undulating countryside, ripe for landscaping and improving with plantations, avenues and vistas. To what extent all these considerations were conclusive is doubtful; so many factors, notably the places where land was available for purchase at a particular time, played their part in deciding where a family settled. What is certain is the great number of estates large and small in this area, all with their houses and surrounding parkland and plantations of greater or lesser extent, which stretch from Uffington and Casewick in the south, through Irnham and Grimsthorpe, to the great cluster around Grantham. It is also noteworthy that a number of families who had estates scattered over several parts of Lincolnshire chose this area for their main residence. The Dukes of Ancaster preferred Grimsthorpe to Eresby House near Spilsby, where they had enormous estates. The Turnors settled at Stoke Rochford, the Cholmeleys at Easton, both in preference to their equally broad acres and alternative houses to the north and east of Lincoln.

The Southern Triangle

A tour of South Kesteven could well begin with the triangle bounded by Stamford, the Deepings and Bourne. This coincides roughly with the old administrative area, the Wapentake of Ness. The name means a headland or cape, and one can apply it, according to taste, to a promontory jutting eastward into the fens, or jutting south and west between Rutland and the Soke of Peterborough.

All but one of the roads out of Stamford plunge immediately over the boundary and out of Lincolnshire. The one exception runs due eastward along the Welland, which here forms the boundary between Lincolnshire and what is now Cambridgeshire. To the south cattle graze under the willows in waterside pastures; northwards corn lands on gently rising ground merge into the distant woods. Soon the willows give way to the more formal plantations of Uffington Park. Uffington village lies almost entirely on the north side of the road, its seventeenth- and eighteenth-century houses a delight in Stamford stone. The south of the road is taken up with the big house, or what remains of it: ornate gates open (or remain closed) upon a yew alley leading nowhere. A little farther and the ruin of the late seventeenth-century house of the Earls of Lindsey can be seen, standing as it must have done more or less untouched since it was gutted by fire in 1904.

The Berties of Uffington were a younger branch of the Grimsthorpe family, who succeeded to the title of Earl of Lindsey on the death of the last Duke of Ancaster in 1809. Charles Bertie, the founder of the Uffington family, lies buried in the church under a monument which records in detail his noble descent, his services to the Crown at home and abroad and his many virtues.

Eastwards from Uffington the road continues its level course in a well-wooded countryside through cornfields which slope gently down to the Welland. Beyond Tallington the ground seems completely flat; some brickwork begins to appear among the stone, and the hedgerow timber gives way to rows and clumps of poplars and willows. Vast gravel workings dominate the landscape near West Deeping, whose charming village street runs down to a bridge over the river at the county boundary. At Uffington and to a lesser extent Tallington, the stonework takes on some of the grandeur of Stamford; West Deeping seems simpler, smaller in scale, the product more of vernacular tradition than of the builder's pattern book.

Market Deeping, on the other hand, was and appears a place of some consequence. Here the east-west road crosses the north-south route (the A15) which was for many years the principal route to the south for much of Lincolnshire. The direction 'Turn at Stilton' on the Lincoln mails in the eighteenth century meant that the Lincoln mail coaches left the Great North Road and continued their journey through Peterborough, Deeping and Sleaford. The Car Dyke, the Roman canal from Peterborough to Lincoln, also passes here. Thus Deeping and its sister village, Deeping St James, which merge into one to form a single small town, have always enjoyed good communications by Lincolnshire standards, with the alternatives at most periods of both road and water transport. Even in the mid nineteenth century Deeping St James had a boat-builder, and no doubt the Welland was the principal means of transport for the stone of which most of its buildings are constructed. The scale of Market Deeping is almost consciously urban, with imposing Georgian (and earlier) houses and definite signs of the nineteenth-century age of improvement, which brought to the town the benefits of a gasworks, a stone bridge to replace the old wooden one and a town hall. One or two inns of some size betoken the importance of the coach traffic of former years when the 'Mail' from Lincoln left for London from the Bull Inn at seven each evening and the 'Imperial' from Stamford departed for Boston at three in the afternoon from the New Inn.

The name Deeping signifies 'deep meadow', and we are here at the very edge of the fenland on land much of which has been reclaimed from the marsh. Traditionally, according to the dubious testimony of Crowland's apocryphal chronicle, the late eleventh-century lord, 'a person much devoted to agricultural pursuits', enclosed a large tract of marsh, built an embankment to keep out the Welland and formed a large vill of tenements and cottages. The details of the story may be a fable, but there is evidence which seems to point to a considerable expansion of population between Domesday Book and 1282, when a survey of the manor of Deeping records twenty-five free tenants who rented land from the lord, ninety-four bond tenants who held their lands by rent and by labour services (one day's ploughing at the winter sowing, one day's ploughing and two of harrowing at the Lent sowing, and twenty-three more days in winter, summer and autumn) and 137 cottagers who held their cottages, some by rent alone, some by rent plus nine days' autumn work (worth only a penny per day to the lord, because he had to feed them). It is tempting to identify these cottage holdings with the long row of house plots which follow the course of the Welland between Market Deeping and Deeping St James.

The church at Market Deeping is dedicated to St Guthlac, the patron saint and legendary hermit of Crowland. This did not prevent frequent friction between the Lords of Deeping and their tenants on the one hand and the abbey on the other, mainly over their rights in the fenland. The evil deeds of the 'men of Deeping' figure prominently in the chronicle of the abbey, as in the 1380s, for instance, when, following the settlement of a boundary dispute, the Deeping men tore down the boundary crosses, tore up the abbot's fishing-nets, detained his provision wagons, beat up his servants and threw his boatmen into the river. Like 'roaring whelps of lions' they lay in wait to break their malice on any monk of Crowland incautious enough to pass their way. Only a rumour that the Earl of Derby had given orders to burn Deeping to the ground and slay all the inhabitants reduced them temporarily to quiescence.

The Deepings have spread considerably of recent years; many new houses have been erected for Peterborough commuters, but the main streets of the villages still remain a harmonious composition of mellow stonework, most pleasant to behold.

East of the Deepings the fen proper begins, a vast, open plain where the boundary between Kesteven and Holland (that boundary which caused so much discord between the men of Deeping and the monastery of Crowland) follows no clearly visible landscape features. The fenland will be discussed elsewhere in this book, so for the moment we will follow the main road northwards from Deeping. At first the land is so flat, as well as being well wooded, that the distant gentle slope upwards on the west and the slope down to the Fens on the east are more or less imperceptible. But they exist none the less; the line of villages is set back a short distance from the Car Dyke which marks the edge of the Fen. At Langtoft and Baston stone is still the predominant building material. Both these villages were Crowland manors in the Middle Ages, their tenants harassed and their animals driven off by the Deeping men in times of ill feeling. Later owners of Langtoft lie buried in the church. Bernard Walcot mourns his wife Sarah:

> Thou bed of rest reserve for him a roome
> Who lives a man divorced from his deare wife.

Two William Hydes were buried in 1694 and 1703, the latter 'beautiful in his person . . . of great sence and learning . . . he labour'd the greatest part of his life . . . under the most exquisite torments of the gout, in hope of a blessed resurrection'.

At Thurlby stone has given place to brick as the most frequent housing material. The road climbs slightly, and the eastward view opens out. Brick is also predominant in the small town of Bourne.

As we now see it, Bourne is mainly an eighteenth- and nineteenth-century erection. The simple basic layout is of four main streets leading from a central crossing, the angles filled in by smaller streets. The main crossroad broadens out to form a small market-place, and here are the main inns and the town hall erected in 1821 with an ornate portico and staircase which do not protrude but are recessed into the building. The appearance is of a comparatively modern, business-like town with few airs and graces. Above their modern shop fronts some of the buildings on the main streets display fine eighteenth- and nineteenth-century features, but there is not a great deal of domestic architecture which is earlier, apart from a row of cottages of dubious age, labelled incongruously 'Tudor Cottages 1636', and the Red Hall. This grand early seventeenth-century mansion has had a chequered career: once the residence of a branch of the recusant Digby family (whence it became erroneously etched in local legend as the place where the Gunpowder Plot was hatched), it had been reduced by the nineteenth-century to the level first of a young ladies' academy,

then of station master's house. The Beeching axe of the early
1960s, apart from depriving most of Lincolnshire of railways,
almost deprived Bourne of its Red Hall, but the building was
saved and its future now seems secure.

The history of Bourne dates back to a far earlier period than
the surviving evidence above ground would suggest. It owes its
early importance and settlement (from at least the Roman
period) to the copious supply of water issuing from the spring
which gives its name. In the Middle Ages it possessed a large
castle, of which only earthworks survive, and an abbey of
Augustinian canons founded in 1138, of which the parish church
is the one remaining building, with traces of work of all periods
from the mid-twelfth century, through an ambitious rebuilding
in around 1200 to the fifteenth century. Among the memorials
are those to the last of the Digbys of Red Hall who died in 1811
and to Eleanor Pochin who 'in the charitable distribution of an
ample fortune . . . appeared to consider herself as the delegate of
Heaven'.

Historical evidence enables us to penetrate behind the
façades of the eighteenth- and nineteenth-century shops and
houses and to people them with some of the men and women who
walked Bourne's streets. Almost everything necessary for the
life of its people could be obtained in a small market town such
as this, a fact illustrated by the lengthy inventory drawn up
after the death of Francis Dawkins, grocer and mercer of
Bourne, in 1734. The valuers spent two November days in
recording his shop goods, household furnishings, stock and
crops. The housewives of Bourne had an enormous choice of
materials: camlets, calamancos, Scotch plaid at 14d a yard,
black flowered damask at 2s, prunella, shalloon, serge, Bella-
dine silk, kerseys, broad cloth, white drill, mohair, green grogram at 1s.4d and serge denim at 3s.4d a yard. Silvered coat
buttons lay on the shelves side by side with penny hornbooks,
primers plain or gilt, testaments, coffin handles at 3s a dozen,
locks, hinges, nails and knitting pins, fenugreek and gall,
verdigris and aloes, brandy at 1s.10d a gallon and writing paper
at 6s a ream. His warehouse was filled with sugar at about £1
per hundredweight, tobacco at 11d and 1s.2d a pound, pepper,
saltpetre, nuts, treacle, brimstone, cloves at 9s a pound, sassa-
fras chips, gunpowder, pitch and rape oil.

Behind the shop the Dawkins family lived in some comfort, with silver plate, blue and white china, and Delft-ware in the dining-room, not to mention an old gun and thirty pictures. Upstairs in the best chamber was a bed with its bedding curtains and valance valued at £17.10s.0d. On the top floor James, perhaps a shop assistant, shared his garret with a 'parcel of cheese'. As well as his shop goods the grocer had a few acres of corn, some cattle and over fifty sheep, six 'cart jades' worth £20, an old black mare and other horses. All were turned out in the field except for the 'black poney' who shared his stable with three calves.

The limited area served by the town as a shopping centre is well illustrated by the list of debtors. With one exception all are from within a ten-mile radius, the vast majority from Bourne itself, most of the others from neighbouring villages such as Thurlby, Rippingale, Edenham and Ryhall, just over the Rutland border on the Stamford road.

This road completes the perimeter of the Stamford-Deeping-Bourne triangle. It mounts quickly above Bourne to the last slopes of limestone as they descend towards the fen. To the east there are wide views over the town and beyond. Ash, often stunted, half dead but indomitable, is the principal hedgerow timber around the mainly arable fields. To the west the ground is often set off by a backcloth of woodland. Toft, a stone-built hamlet sheltered by steep slopes rising above the East Glen River, alias the Eden, is one of a number of outlying hamlets of the large parish of Witham-on-the-Hill which itself lies back from the road. The main village is of Anglo-Saxon origin within whose territories the Danes settled in the outlying hamlets of Bowthorpe, Manthorpe, Toft (the 'homestead') and Lound (the 'grove') on the far side of the river; Witham church has a tower rebuilt in 1738 following a collapse. The story is told in White's 1856 *Directory of Lincolnshire*: 'The spire with a great part of the tower fell down in 1738, whilst the ringers, having rung some merry peals, were regaling themselves in a neighbouring inn. The steeple was rebuilt in a plainer but more substantial manner.' According to the same source, Witham's misfortunes continued in 1773 when the inn, the vicarage, the tithe barn and other buildings were burned down. The Victorian school close to the church is inscribed with the excellently authoritarian motto: 'Train up a child in the way he should go and when he is old he will not part from it.'

In an ode to his native village published in 1834 in a volume entitled *The Village Muse*, C. W. Friend commented on the comparative prosperity of the inhabitants:

> In thee no half-starv'd families are seen
> No ragged youngsters lounge about the street
> All are well fed, their clothing neat and clean
> And they with ev'ry needful good replete
>
> If we survey with an attentive eye
> The cots of those who're termed the lab'ring poor
> We find a pig in almost every sty
> And in each hovel one milch cow or more.

This prosperity and some good examples of nineteenth-century estate cottages may have been due to the practical benevolence of the resident squire, General William Augustus Johnson. Born in 1777, he served in the Peninsular War and served as Member of Parliament for Boston and later for Oldham and as Chairman of Kesteven Quarter Sessions for over thirty years. A 'radical Tory' in politics and an able and progressive magistrate, he detested the new Poor Law of 1834 which exiled paupers from their native villages to the new Union workhouses. The Johnsons had been Witham's main landowners for about a century. The Reverend Woolsey Johnson built Witham Hall, now a school, between 1752 and 1756. He was also the prime mover in the enclosure of the open fields of the parish in 1752.

All the remaining villages in this area took their sites from the proximity of one branch or other of the River Glen. All are predominantly stone-built. Carlby stands on the limestone on the Rutland border; the others lie mainly on gravel. Greatford means 'gravel ford'. It is a charming village of water in the cedar-shaded moat of the Hall, and has trees and stone houses and a most extraordinary congregation of carved obelisks, mushrooms, coronets, elephants and other strange objects scattered around, all carved apparently for exhibition as garden ornaments at the Chelsea Flower Show in the 1930s to drum up custom for their creator. At Greatford and at Shillingthorpe in the adjoining parish of Braceborough the Willis family, the 'mad doctors', had their private lunatic asylums. Monuments to the Reverend Francis Willis, his wife and his sons Robert and John are to be found in the church. Francis Willis's monument records his 'natural taste and inclination' towards medicine and his continuance in practice until the last hour of his life, in 1807, in his ninetieth year. 'Initiated early into the habits of observation and research he ... was happily the chief agent in removing the malady which afflicted his present majesty in the year 1789.' George III's next attack in 1801 was treated successfully by Robert and John Willis, as the former's memorial records: 'a benefit incalculable to the country at a moment pregnant with doubts'.

Greatford and its former hamlet of Wilsthorpe lie in a flat land of dykes and willows and cornfields. Barholm a little to the south is another stone village with roofs of thatch and Collyweston slate. The church has Anglo-Saxon and Norman work, and a spire rebuilt in 1648 with the inscription

Was ever such a thing since the creation
A new steeple built in the time of vexation.

Grimsthorpe Country

North and west of the Stamford to Bourne road is a wooded, undulating area through which the Northern main line keeps company with the River Glen. Limestone and clay dominate the soils. Stone as a building material is interspersed with brick from the nineteenth-century brickyard of Little Bytham, which also boasted its Adamantine Clinker Works. Grimsthorpe Park dominates the landscape of much of the area.

In the mid-twelfth century a community of Cistercian monks settled on a site given by William, Earl of Albemarle, in the thickly wooded hamlet of Grimsthorpe on the western edge of the large parish of Edenham. They quarried the local stone for the building of their house, which they named Vaudey, 'God's Vale'. Gradually the community prospered on grants large and small from local benefactors, some of them specifically for the upkeep of the gatehouse, the wool house, the mill or the tannery. No trace of Vaudey now remains above ground, though nineteenth-century excavation discovered the site on the south side of the lake in Grimsthorpe Park. Half a mile north of Vaudey, in the thirteenth century, Gilbert de Gant built a castle, in four ranges round a central courtyard. The present Grimsthorpe Castle incorporates parts of this building, but almost every succeeding century has also left its mark. Charles Brandon, Duke of Suffolk, made hasty additions for a royal visit in 1541; Vanbrugh rebuilt the north front in the 1720s; Lord Gwydir had the west front replaced in 1811.

The story of Grimsthorpe is part of the story of a family, or rather a group of families, who have played a vital role in Lincolnshire history. They originated at Willoughby, in the coastal marsh near Alford, taking their name from their native place. Over the succeeding centuries a series of profitable marriages and an ever-ramifying network of younger sons spread the family name throughout the county and beyond. The ninth Baron, William, Lord Willoughby, married Maria de Salinas, lady-in-waiting to Catherine of Aragon. The King's gift on their

wedding was a grant of lands which included the future ownership of Grimsthorpe on the death of the then tenant. He died in
1526, leaving as sole heir a daughter, Catherine, about five or
six years old. Her wardship was granted by Henry VIII to
Charles Brandon, Duke of Suffolk, one of the King's most
trusted favourites and the husband of his sister Mary (always
referred to as 'the French Queen' from her brief marriage to the
elderly Louis XII of France, whose ailing constitution was
thought to have been given its *coup de grâce* by his necessary
attentions to his young bride). In July 1533 the French Queen
died; in September the Duke, aged forty-eight, married his
ward, now aged about fourteen. Their marriage lasted, with
apparent regard and contentment on both sides, until his death
twelve years later. The shower of royal favour which fell upon
Charles Brandon like autumn leaves included a grant of the site
and lands of Vaudey after its dissolution, a gift essential to the
further development of Grimsthorpe's parkland.

The young widowed Duchess with her great estates was one of
England's greatest catches; matchmakers even gossiped about
the possibility of her supplanting her friend Catherine Parr to
become Henry VIII's seventh bride. She remained single,
however, until 1553, when she married a man of comparatively
humble origins, Richard Bertie, her gentleman usher and
trusted adviser. The story of their strongly Protestant beliefs, of
their flight on New Year's Day 1555 from the Marian per-
secution, first to the Low Countries, then to the Rhineland,
finally to Poland, forms one of the most Hollywood-like sections
in Foxe's *Book of Martyrs* and has often been told.

The daily life of Grimsthorpe shortly after Richard Bertie's
triumphant return from exile with his Duchess is vividly illustrated in an account book of their household expenditure which
has survived for the years from 1560 to 1562. Grimsthorpe was
an enormous household; the list of those 'such as dayly remayne'
in it includes a preacher, steward, cofferer, comptroller, master
of the horse, gentlemen ushers, gentlemen waiters, clerk of the
provisions, yeomen of the wardrobe and yeomen of the cellar. An
army of more menial servants, including cook, children of the
kitchen, grooms of the stable, gardeners, labourers and retain-
ers brought the total to well over a hundred, not including the
twenty women who 'did weede the gardin and cortes' for 2d a

day. The children of honour included the children of some of the
gentlemen ushers as well as 'Master Peregrine' and 'Miss Suzan'
Bertie. Payments were made for their clothing, for their school-
ing, for a lute at £2.6s.8d for the two Bertie children, for
playthings which they bought from a pedlar at the gate, and to a
man who celebrated his marriage by giving a banquet for them
in the park.

The park was also the setting for various other entertainments and sports such as archery, apparently with small bets
laid on the result. Richard Bertie gambled mildly on these
sports; he also lost regularly at cards, never more than 2s. He
liked fine clothes such as the 'hatt of thrummed silke garnished,
and a bande of gold, for my master at his coming to Grimsthorpe', which cost 18s. The Duchess also gambled occasionally, as when Bertie dished out a shilling for her in single pence
to play at tables when she was ill, when the wind was whistling
round Grimsthorpe and the crannies in her room had to be
stopped up with brown paper. When they travelled, for instance
to their London house at the Barbican, they journeyed with a
great company of followers. Once 'my master' travelled to London with eighteen men and horses, 'besydes strangers'; the
Duchess had to feed twenty-four on a visit to Court.

The enormous household consumed enormous amounts of fish
and meat (and, apart from bread and a few oranges, apparently
very little else) at tables arranged, and supplied, in order of
precedence. Great quantities of beer were brewed; the cellar was
stocked with claret and 'elegante' (Alicante) and Rhenish wine
under the charge of Father Frier, the yeoman of the cellar, who
obviously kept strict control of the keys. When he could not be
found, even the Duchess in her sickness had to send out for a pint
of claret, which cost her 2d. A large and frequently mobile
household needed a large number of horses; there are no figures
for 1560, but the Duchess had 135 in 1546. Henry Naunton, the
master of the horse, was a man of great importance in the
household who was given £6 to buy 'a gown of grogram and a
doublet of satin against his marriage', performed by the vicar of
Bourne, when a juggler and his musician received 10s for
providing the entertainment.

There was a constant stream of visitors. Some came for alms,
some came with gifts, some came for temporary work, like the

Scotsman who worked nine days in the stables and then moved on. A poor man who had been in Bedlam was given a shilling; a man from Bourne brought 'a bayting bull'; a 'moresse dawncer' of Little Bytham was given 2s; two men came with puppets; the Queen's players gave a performance for 20s; Lord Robert Dudley's players, 'which offered themselves to play but did not', received 10s. Other 'gyftes and rewardes' were given to numerous servants of neighbours who came bearing presents, to the mowers and haymakers, when the Duchess and her husband were walking in the park, and to Mrs Brodbank for killing forty-four rats at Vaudey. Another visitor was a 'fetherbedddryver' from Lincoln, who appeared occasionally to blow a current of air through the beds to keep them sweet and fluffy. To judge by the number of beds, many of the household slept on feathers, but not all; the children of the kitchen had beds of straw.

The Duchess of Suffolk died in 1580, Richard Bertie two years later. Their son Peregrine, so christened on account of his birth in exile, became the 'Bold Lord Willoughby of courage fierce and fell' beloved of Elizabethan balladeers. He commanded Elizabeth's armies in the Netherlands and in France and died in 1601 as Governor of Berwick-on-Tweed. His son Robert, created Earl of Lindsey, was a trusted commander of Charles I's armies killed at Edgehill in 1642. Later generations served the Crown in more of a ceremonial than a military capacity and were rewarded with the marquessate of Lindsey in 1708 and finally with the dukedom of Ancaster in 1715.

Edenham's fine church contains the imposing monuments of the first four dukes, as well as that of Robert, Earl of Lindsey. Scheemakers portrays the first Duke as a Roman senator; he is described as an 'equal asserter of the Rights of the Crown and the Liberty's of the People' who 'when Parliaments were up resided in this County where he lived Hospitably and had a Good Interest'. His successors surround him, including the short-lived fourth Duke, who died of scarlet fever at the age of twenty-three after serving as a volunteer against the rebellious American colonists. According to malicious gossip, his will included a legacy to 'a very small man', used by the Duke as a sort of human Rugby-ball, whom he used to fling across the table to the companions of his drinking bouts. Among the mighty lie the remains of the Reverend John Bland MA, chaplain to the third Duke, who died in 1761. 'He lived many years with his truly noble patron and received signal marks of his favour, friendship and confidence, and desired this inscription to perpetuate his grateful sense of the favours he was honoured with.'

Robert, fourth Duke of Ancaster, was succeeded by his uncle, Brownlow Bertie, on whose death, in 1809, the dukedom became extinct. The title of Willoughby, however, continued in the female line in the form of Priscilla Barbara Elizabeth Bertie, Baroness Willoughby de Eresby, whose husband, Sir Peter Burrell, also received a title, that of Baron Gwydir, from the great Bertie estates in North Wales. Another failure of the male line, on the death of Alberic, twentieth Baron Willoughby, in 1870, produced another baroness in her own right, who married Gilbert John Heathcote, Baron Aveland, and whose son was created Earl of Ancaster in 1892. This Heathcote marriage was important in that it added to the original Bertie estates not only extensive lands in Rutland but also considerable property to the west and north of Grimsthorpe.

Grimsthorpe dominates the countryside today almost as pre-eminently as its owners dominated the lives of chaplains and servants, tenants and labourers. The house itself is grandiose, whether it is seen close at hand or as a prospect along an avenue of trees or as a view of distant towers rising above cornfields and plantations. The park is enormous, and estate buildings and estate plantations stretch far beyond it. Oaks line the approach roads in all directions before they give way to the ashes which seem to be the principal hedgerow trees of South Kesteven. It is a working landscape but one created also to delight the eye.

One such tree-lined road from Grimsthorpe leads through cornfields on a gentle slope to Swinstead. Vanbrugh is said to have built a large house here for the first Duke of Ancaster before he commenced work at Grimsthorpe. Traces of his hand are to be seen here and there, notably in the square towers of a pavilion which rises to the east of the village. The village itself is a delight of grey stone, tinged with gold, fine, steep-roofed seventeenth- and eighteenth-century vernacular architecture and a church whose slightly squat tower has the most splendid gargoyles at its corners, including what seems to be a mouse of enormous proportions and somewhat sinister leer. The fifth

Duke, as befits a younger son who succeeded by fortunate chance, is buried here away from his predecessors at Edenham; his severely classical monument contrasts admirably with the Gothicism of that to his niece, Priscilla Barbara Elizabeth, Baroness Willoughby.

From Swinstead the B1176 crosses open country southwards to Creeton, then follows the West Glen River and the main line towards Stamford, the slopes on the east bank well timbered by the edge of Grimsthorpe Park. A little westward another line of villages is linked by a minor road which alternates between upland views and the narrow valleys of the Glen's tributary streams, between an open table-land and the woodlands which surround Holywell on the Rutland border. The 'considerable village' of Castle Bytham slopes upwards from a stream and a pond with swans; opposite, the steep motte of the former castle gives superb views over a red-tiled roofscape. The land is very choppy in this region: narrow, quite deep valleys and folds; undulating fields where lots of good hedges have survived; little roads meandering through meadowsweet, cranesbill and wild roses. There is a good deal of pasture with sheep in the landscape between Bytham and Swayfield, summarized by a nineteenth-century observer as 'soil various, uphill and down, very unusually so'.

The Northern Section:
Heath, Claylands and Fen Edge

The A151 which pursues a winding eastward course from the
Great North Road near Colsterworth to Bourne makes a convenient division between the southern and northern sections of
South Kesteven. The limestone landscape of the Heath dominates the western side; heathland pure and simple along much of
Ermine Street and near Ropsley, 'a considerable village remarkably situated as it were in a bason with hills all round'.
Elsewhere the pure heathland gives way to a more undulating
wooded countryside, as it does around Boothby Pagnell on the
west branch of the River Glen. At Bitchfield the valley is narrow
and more bare, and a little to the west the hills are barer still.
Bassingthorpe is the perfect picture of a little hillside settlement: large farm, small church and the beautiful manor house
built by Thomas Cony in 1568 and very much out of fashion in
the early nineteenth century, when it was described as, 'a plain
strong stone edifice not at all ornamental as a gentleman's seat'.
This tiny settlement was creaking at the seams with navvies in
1851, when its population had swollen to 487 during the cutting
of the main railway line.

Corby Glen was endowed with the second element of its name
in recent years to distinguish it from the Northamptonshire
town, a rather touching act in Lincolnshire where innumerable
place-names are duplicated both within the county and among
its neighbours. As plain Corby, the little town was described in
1856 as 'small but ancient and improving'. Its October fair was
one of the largest in the county, for sheep, cattle and horses and
great quantities of grain from the surrounding area were de-
spatched from its station on the Great Northern line. The town
rises gently above the river. Particularly striking among the
stone buildings is the grammar school founded under the will of
Charles Read in 1671 for the instruction of the inhabitants in
reading, writing, the casting of accounts and as much Latin 'as

the occasion shall require'. Part of the endowment was for the free education of the poor sons of clergy and decayed gentlemen.

East of Corby the land flattens into an area of plateau between the two branches of the River Glen; hedgerow timber thickens into the plantations which surround Irnham Hall. With Corby, Irnham was one of the great centres of Roman Catholicism in Lincolnshire from the sixteenth century to the nineteenth. The estate belonged successively to the Thimbleby family, to the Conquests, to the Barons Arundell of Wardour and finally to Baron Clifford of Chudleigh, before it was sold in 1854 to William Harvey Woodhouse, a London wine-merchant. Irnham stands out even among the many fine villages of Kesteven; the early Tudor hall, gutted by fire in 1887 but still immensely picturesque when glimpsed across the park or from the church-yard, and the church itself, large and of all periods from Norman to Perpendicular, are set in a village full of trees and fine greystone houses of all periods from the seventeenth century onwards. Some of the story of the descent of the estate can be followed in the array of monuments in the church. Sir Andrew Lutterell, an owner who died in 1390, is commemorated by a brass. In his will he left instructions for a modest funeral. No one was to be invited, but such as came of their own free will were to be given food and drink. During the funeral service thirteen wax torches were to be held around his body by thirteen poor men. John Thimbleby, 'the last heir male of his ancient family' who died in 1712, is commemorated, as is Benedict Conquest who died in 1753. The absentee owners, the Arundells and the Cliffords, are represented by Maria Christine Arundell who predeceased her parents in 1805. William Hervey Wood-house, who lived only five years to enjoy the estate after his purchase, is relegated to a Grecian sarcophagus in the church-yard but is also commemorated in the sombre colours of an impressive crucifixion scene in the east window of the chancel.

Nearby the eastern branch of the River Glen flows down towards Edenham through an undulating clay landscape where wide views over open country alternate with great patches of woodland, and pasture alternates with broad fields of corn. A twisting, narrow road keeps approximate company with the windings of the little river through a series of tiny hamlets such as Bulby, whose moated site in a wood was, according to tradition still alive in the early nineteenth century, the site of a mansion house 'burnt down and destroyed by the owner, one of the Lutterels, in a rage of vexation against his lady for certain misconduct towards a male servant'. This rivals another tradition which attributes the round earthwork at nearby Ingoldsby to Oliver Cromwell's having constructed a battery here 'to destroy down two halls'.

Remoteness is the overpowering impression given by this 'cold clay country' of sparse settlement, a remoteness out of all proportion to its actual distance from busy main roads and railway line. Farther north the small villages of Braceby and Sapperton seem to have expanded little if at all since about 1850; they are full of good stonework of the seventeenth and eighteenth centuries. Nearby the church of Pickworth is well known for its medieval wall-paintings. The Last Judgment, the Weighing of Souls, the Ascension and other scenes can be made out, rather faintly in some cases. On the outside wall of the chancel is another monument to change and decay in the shape of a plaque recording the bequest of 40s for the perpetual upkeep of an adjoining monument; beneath it the monument in question moulders away and lichen obscures the wording. It is impossible even to read whose tomb it is.

Farther east brick becomes the main building material as the clays descend towards the fen edge. The A15 climbs gently from a flat landscape near Bourne to a series of shallow hills and valleys down which streams flow eastwards to the fen. The church and houses of the village of Aslackby in one of these valleys make a perfect picture when viewed from the main road. Folkingham lies on the slope of another little valley. The road broadens into what was once a market-place lined with houses of the seventeenth and early eighteenth centuries, dominated at the north end by the impressive façade of the Greyhound Inn, 'brand new' when John Byng was here in 1791 and 'an inn worthy of the Bath Road, but here sees not 2 post chaises a day'. Like several of the small towns of Lincolnshire, Folkingham probably gained more advantage from its use as a local administrative centre than from its strictly limited importance as a market. 'The town possesses but little trade,' says the 1826 county directory. By then it had also ceased to be used as a meeting-place for Quarter Sessions, but its new gaol erected in

1808 and recently enlarged brought in trade of a sort. The stately entrance lodge still survives, on the site of the lost medieval castle.

At Aslackby the Roman road, Mareham Lane, diverges from the A15 and follows an up-and-down course through dips and water-splashes. A mile or so to the east of Folkingham it passes the site where Stow Green Fair was once held. In 1268 Henry III granted to the prior and convent of Sempringham a yearly fair at their manor of Stow on the vigil, the feast and the morrow of St John the Baptist. Stow was a thriving settlement in the Middle Ages, with a church and at least thirty-five families in Domesday Book, but by the eighteenth century it was a lonely spot, as it still is, with all its houses and even the remains of the church gone. The fair continued, however; John Byng saw the skeletons of the booths by the roadside. By the middle of the nineteenth century it still survived with a horse fair in June and a pleasure fair, a sort of saturnalia for the labourers of the surrounding countryside, in July. 'Many publicans erect booths on the green for the sale of beers and spirits; and the fair has usually been visited by so many gipsies, pedlars and other disorderly persons, that the magistrates have found it necessary to send a number of constables to keep the peace.' There was talk of suppression, but it was not suppressed; Stow Green Fair died a natural death in the present century.

The village of Threekingham is a little to the north of Stow Green at the point where Mareham Lane crosses the A52. It is set back from the road among pastures, the tall spire of its large church rising above surrounding trees. Legend finds the origin of its name in the death here of three kings in a battle between Danes and Saxons. Place-name scholars find it in the settlement of a tribe called the Threckings. The present spelling, which replaces the historically more correct one of Threckingham, gives undeserved authority to the legend.

Eastwards the A52 descends almost imperceptibly to a wide fenland landscape of scattered farms and roadside dykes; the predominant cornfields are set off by occasional pieces of ancient pasture whose hedges are the only ones to be seen. The road is banked up above the level of the surrounding land. At Bridgend in the parish of Horbling, a small priory was founded in the twelfth-century with the specific purpose of maintaining

the causeway which carried the road over 'deep miry fens' to
Donington-in-Holland. A farmhouse now stands on the site by
the roadside. At this point the B1177 runs southward to follow a
line of fen-edge settlements towards Bourne.

These villages at the edge of the fen are often large, a
reflection of the large populations which their unstinted pastures could support. A description of Billingborough in 1739
says that it is 'environ'd with fertile fields and pleasant
meadows . . . . The fields are commonly sown with wheat, barley, peas and beans, all which they bear very good; . . . the fields
have a good sort of sheep in them . . . but sometimes they are
subject to take the rott. Horses thrive and grow fatt in the fenn,
of which they have plenty. Ash and willow grow plentifully, but
want more planters . . . . The buildings are some very good, some
very bad'. By the nineteenth century its bad housing had been
replaced to make it 'one of the neatest built and best situated
villages in the county', with 'several inns and well-stocked
shops'.

As all this suggests, Billingborough is a place of some size and
consequence, certainly as large as a number of the smaller
places in the county which once earned the title of market
towns. A certain amount of imported stone appears among the
predominant red brick of its houses, which include several large
ones of the seventeenth and eighteenth centuries. The church is
a fine, large, spired one, mainly fourteenth century. In fact there
are good churches to be seen along the whole row of these
fen-edge parishes. Perhaps of greatest interest because of its
historical associations is the fine Norman one at Sempringham ,
set back along a rough track nearly a mile from the road and
easily missed. (It is shown but not named on the modern OS
map.) This is the one surviving piece of the first foundation of
England's only native monastic order, formed by St Gilbert of
Sempringham in the mid-twelfth century. The foundations of
the priory, of the noble house which the Earls of Lincoln built on
the site and of the medieval village lie beneath the surrounding
fields.

The founder was a local landowner, unfit for a military life,
who took up what was almost the only possible medieval
alternative, the life of a cleric. His new monastic order arose
piecemeal, almost unwillingly on his part, but once in existence

it was very popular, and other foundations quickly followed Sempringham, about ten of them in Lincolnshire before the death of Gilbert in 1189, apparently at the enormous age of one hundred. The order was almost unique in that its houses contained both canons and nuns, served by lay brothers and sisters, though strict segregation of the sexes was observed.

At Haconby, a splendidly Scandinavian place-name, the B1177 joins the A15 on the way to Bourne. The small, compact settlement of Haconby contrasts with the undisciplined spread of its neighbour, Morton, whose long main street stretches for a considerable distance on each side of the main road. To the Reverend Samuel Hopkinson, responsible for the cure of souls in the two parishes in the early nineteenth century, the contrast between the firm landlord control of the former and the rampantly open society of the latter influenced the characters of the people. At Morton seven or eight inhabitants had been transported in the last thirty years; ninety sheep had recently been slaughtered or stolen, 'frequent housebreaking attended with open and outrageous violence by a gang of masqued thieves, who came armed . . . mischievous acts cruel to both man and beast, kept the public and private mind in continual alarm'.

The Great North Road and the Grantham Area

Late in the nineteenth century, when the railway had finally brought about the death of the great coaching routes, the North Road was almost deserted. Only carriers' carts and farm wagons shared it with the few members of the leisured class who preferred still to do their touring by carriage or on horseback. The stone pits which had provided materials for repair were overgrown with vegetation; many of the coaching inns had lost all trade and were inns no longer. Some recovered to become road-houses in the age of motoring; others remained as private houses. One such is the 'Bull' on Witham Common, a small house occupied by a cobbler in 1730, 'now a spacious building and an excellent inn' by about 1800. It still stands, a fine Georgian house at the junction of the road to Lobthorpe and Castle Bytham.

The A1 enters Lincolnshire from Rutland about ten miles north of Stamford, following a limestone ridge which slopes gently down to the west towards the line of villages in the valley of the River Witham. At North Witham the church has a fine assembly of monuments to the Sherards. Richard Sherard, who died in 1668, reclines in full wig, his elbow on a pile of books, his hand fondling a skull. Sir Richard, who died in 1730, is surrounded by cherubs of lugubrious aspect. Stone is the almost universal building material in these South Kesteven villages; at Skillington even the Methodists, notable throughout the county for their implantation of brickwork on the stoniest of ground, erected an impressive stone chapel in 1847. It dominates a fine village centre of seventeenth- and eighteenth-century houses. Higher up the slope one looks down from the churchyard over grey walls and red roofs to the green fields beyond, scarred in places by the traces of former ironstone workings which are plentiful in this area.

At Colsterworth the long, narrow village street was already a problem for traffic when the parish was enclosed in 1805, so a bypass was actually set out at that time. The stone here has a slightly yellower tinge than in some of the other villages around. Nearby, in the hamlet of Woolsthorpe, is the small seventeenth-century manor house where Sir Isaac Newton was born, with a direct descendant, it is said, of the world's second most famous apple tree (after Eve's) growing in the garden. At Colsterworth the A1 crosses the Witham and is bounded on the east and west by parklands as it proceeds towards Grantham. Magnificent grounds surround Stoke Rochford Hall, designed by William Burn in 1841 for Christopher Turnor. The house itself has survived, converted to a teachers' training college and now to a National Union of Teachers' conference centre. The influence of the grounds spills over into the village, which lies in a beautiful tree-filled valley. The church stands on the slope of the valley, its exterior decorated by superb gargoyles with frog-like faces; it is of all periods from Norman to Perpendicular and is a treasure-house of monuments to the Cholmeleys, the Turnors and others. One medieval couple lie under a blanket which is too small for them; their feet are sticking out. There is another fine church at Great Ponton where passers-by on the A1 look down over the village to the rising ground beyond the river and the main line. On the great tower, built by Anthony Ellis, merchant of the Staple of Calais in 1519, an inscription bids those who read it to 'Think and Thank God of All'. Nearby is the house which he also built. Below them the village street is lined by grey stone walls covered with lichens and stonecrop.

Grantham is surrounded by hills in almost every direction. The A1 bypasses it now, but travellers on the old road had to negotiate a steep slope down into the town, then up again to the top of Gonerby Hill and down the other side. This latter was the worst hill on the Great North Road between London and Edinburgh. The opening of canal navigation to Nottingham and the Midlands at the end of the eighteenth century brought increased trade to a town already important as a local market and a centre of road communications. Later the railway came and heavy engineering, and with them a considerable increase in size.

One of the town's nineteenth-century historians complains of the loss of many medieval buildings and their inferior replacements when 'Grantham town took to bricks and lost its good looks'. But there are still a number of fine medieval survivals, notably the 'Angel and Royal' whose fifteenth-century façade fronts one of England's best surviving medieval inns on the grand scale. Appropriately enough, the property was charged by a Mr Solomon with the payment of a rent-charge of 40s to endow the preaching of an annual sermon against drunkenness, 'I looking upon that sin to be the inlet of almost all others'. Nearby is the large and magnificent parish church of St Wulfram, whose spire, 270 feet high, dominates the whole town. There are some bits remaining of a late twelfth-century building, surrounded by evidence of a large-scale rebuilding in the late thirteenth, followed by further work in both the Decorated and Perpendicular periods. In the narrow streets near the church are further surviving fragments from the Middle Ages, part of the King's School and the core of Grantham House, with large sixteenth- and eighteenth-century additions grafted on. Nor was all architectural distinction lost when Grantham town took to bricks; 'the houses generally are of a superior kind', says an 1836 guidebook, and the eighteenth- and nineteenth-century façades which line many of the streets bear out this observation. No such claim, alas, can be made for the rather grim-looking housing estates which now spread out to the bypass and leapfrog over it towards Barrowby.

The attractions of its countryside and its comparative ease of communication with the great world made the area around Grantham into what has been described as 'the only truly gentrified region of Lincolnshire' by the early nineteenth-century. To the south lay Stoke Rochford of the Turnors and the Cholmeley seat at Easton; north was Belton House and the seat of the Thorolds at Syston; westward was the Welbys' house at Denton and Harlaxton Manor, an extraordinary fairy-tale palace designed in the 1830s by Anthony Salvin for the owner, George de Ligne Gregory. At the beginning of the century Harlaxton was described as 'a very remarkable neat built village', but that was before Gregory set to work upon it. For he rebuilt the cottages as well as the big house in a glorious mixture of styles culled from his large library of architectural books and his study of examples all over the country.

At Denton the earlier house has been replaced by a modern

one, but this is set in a magnificent parkscape which provides a rich green setting for this village of golden ironstone. This undulating countryside on the Leicestershire border is full of trees, avenues and plantations and great screeds of timber surrounding Belvoir Castle, which is itself glimpsed from time to time through occasional gaps in its woodlands. The ground falls north of Denton to the Grantham canal, then rises again to the great barrow-shaped hill which gives Barrowby its name and which gives sweeping views out over the Vale of Belvoir. Farther north still the land around Allington and Sedgebrook is rather flat, a flatness which gives emphasis to the stately westward march of an army of electricity pylons. Brick, sometimes stuccoed and colour-washed, is the main building material in these two villages; by contrast Allington's fine seventeenth-century manor house is of ironstone with dressings of lighter stonework.

North of Grantham, Syston Hall was demolished in the 1920s, and its parklands have largely been ploughed up. But Belton House still stands, after Grimsthorpe (or perhaps equally with it) the most magnificent of Lincolnshire's great houses. Sir John Brownlow laid the first stone in 1685, and by 1695 it was finished enough to entertain King William III in grand style. Sir John killed five fat oxen and sixty sheep, and when the King reached Lincoln the next day, 'he could eat nothing but a mess of milk'. Inside and out, Belton retains much of its original form, though there is evidence also of the facelift which it was given by James Wyatt in 1777 as well as of interior alterations carried out for Viscount Tyrconnel, the last of the Brownlows, in the 1720s. After his death it passed by marriage to the Cust family who were advanced to the peerage as Barons Brownlow in 1776 and Earls in 1815.

The monuments crowd the small church which adjoins the house. Hope leans upon a medallion where Lord Tyrconnel is represented; a long inscription records his loyalty to the monarch, his inflexible attachment to the true interests of his country and his retirement to the seat of his ancestors where, 'tho' willing to be at ease he scorned obscurity'. Sir John Brownlow is here, who built the house, and Sir John Cust, with the Speaker's chair, mace and journals testifying to his holding the Speakership for nine years from 1761 until he died in 1770, his life shortened, it was said, by the ardours of office, particularly the necessity of remaining in his seat during the longest of debates, unable to leave it even for the most urgent of bodily needs.

2

North Kesteven

The Western Lowlands

North of Grantham both the main line and the Great North
Road swing westwards to shake off the dust of Lincolnshire and
to cross the Trent at Newark. Between the rising ground of the
Heath and the Nottinghamshire border lies a broad plain of
mainly clay soils, interspersed here and there with beds of sand
and gravel. Through them the River Witham follows a winding
and largely canalized course towards Lincoln. The little River
Brant runs parallel and joins it near the city. The villages are
set on the gentlest of slopes above the predominantly flat lands,
safe from the extensive flooding which once characterized the
area.

Long Bennington is one of the finest of Lincolnshire's brick
villages. Assuming an original settlement around the church, it
appears to have expanded northward in an eighteenth-century
or earlier ribbon development. For over a mile a succession of
elegant, façades in red or dappled brickwork looked out upon the
busy traffic until the show was withdrawn a few years ago onto a
bypass to the west of the village. Beyond Bennington the main
road soon leaves the county. To the east the stately march of
pylons is the dominant vertical feature of the plain, dwarfing
the distant churches. In the predominantly bare landscape a few
elms struggle for survival in the hedgerows, and willows grow
along the streams and drainage channels. Far away the gentle
slope of the Heath can be seen.

The graceful spire of Claypole's fine church stands up from
this 'very cold clay dirty country', its stone contrasting with the
brickwork of the village. Like so many settlements in Lincolnshire, Claypole seems to have undergone a great rebuilding

after enclosure. A visitor in about 1800 commented on the improvement not only in the roads but 'also the buildings of the village; now brick and tile where formerly almost all stud mud and thatch'. Signs of enclosure are plain to see along the straight, broad-verged lane to Dry Doddington; the original layout of closes remains, a nice mixture of arable and pasture, divided by neat hawthorn hedges. Dry Doddington lies at the top of a low ridge commanding enormous views across to Belvoir Castle. It probably gets its name from the dryness of the site; in the early nineteenth century water had to be fetched from the Witham. It is a village of farmyards and good, honest mud with a decayed and slightly tottering church standing in a long disused churchyard. At Westborough, a mile to the south, along another wide-verged road descending through neat closes, some fine eighteenth-century houses are to be seen among the plentiful trees.

Along the Witham to the east of Westborough Arthur Young found Marston, 'a populous village, every cottage has half an acre or an acre with a garden and a little haystack, plus four or five acres beside for their cow in summer. They have besides a pig, and some sheep'. The river winds pleasantly among willow trees; above it rises the graceful spire of a predominantly Early English church with a good series of monuments to the Thorold family.

A minor road runs northwards from Marston to Lincoln through the heart of the clays; most of the villages in the area are easily accessible from this road. The limestone heath lies two or three miles to the east, a gentle rise of alternating pasture and corn with here and there the green of parkland and occasional glimpse of some of Kesteven's innumerable spires. Immediately to the north of Marston the limestone throws out a spur, culminating in the tree-topped eminence of Loveden Hill. This is a landmark for the whole of the surrounding country, in early times a place of meeting for the whole of the Wapentake, to which it gives its name, and a burial place in early Saxon times. In a dominating position in the choppy countryside between Loveden Hill and the Heath proper stands the aptly named village of Hough-on-the-Hill. Limestone and brick mingle here among oak and ash trees.

Hough's striking church tower, like that of Broughton-by-

Brigg in the north of the county, combines several stages of Anglo-Saxon work with a fifteenth-century top and has the unusual feature of a semi-detached circular turret joining the west wall of a square tower. The body of the church is mainly thirteenth century, extending upwards to a fifteenth-century clerestory. Here are several marble sarcophagi with lions' paws in memory of members of the Paine family, including Edward Paine, 'who early engaged in the Cause of Liberty and . . . in a Meeting of the Gentlemen and Clergy of the County (being High Sheriff) declared he would stand and fall with the Prince of Orange'. Sir John Cust succeeded to the Paine estates after his marriage to Ethelred Paine in 1743, a marriage preceded by a somewhat timid courtship during which he seemed to his friends as if about to 'cleave a giant or to throw his cap over the moon' rather than wait on a gentle, willing young thing who longed to hear him talk love. The combined charms, however, of his person and his settlements proved in the end stronger than the drawbacks of his timidity.

Below Hough a winding lane leads past corn and bean fields, a few fox coverts and roadside ash to the hamlet of Brandon. Here, as in Caythorpe and a number of the villages of the area, one encounters seventeenth- and eighteenth-century building which uses the two local stones available, a light-coloured limestone and dark golden ironstone in bands, to produce a sort of layer-cake effect. Farther west at Stubton stone gives way to brick, and the wood in the landscape is augmented by the plantations of varied timber which surround Stubton Hall. Fenton presents a good ensemble of church, farmhouse and duckpond. This is the house which, in 1684, was conveyed with its lands by George Lucas to his son in return for £280 a year, meat, washing and lodging for himself, his servant and such agents and friends as should visit him, and two horses and their keep 'fit for a gentleman's riding of his degree'.

Beckingham, on the A17 from Newark to Sleaford, has a fine towered church with Norman doorway and some splendid eighteenth-century houses including an imposing old rectory. Three miles to the east the A17 crosses the road from Marston to Lincoln. Close to the crossroads lie on one side Brant Broughton, one of the county's finest brick-built villages, on the other Stragglethorpe, with one of the most delightful of its smaller

churches. It has an Anglo-Saxon west wall, Norman and Early
English features and a Norman font, and a splendid interior
crowded with old woodwork, probably seventeenth- or early
eighteenth-century carpenter's work. There are box pews and a
double-decker pulpit and crowning all an enormous wall monument erected by his mother to Sir Richard Earle who died in
1697. Surrounded by cherubs, busts of youthful faces with
flowing hair, hang draperies which are pulled back to reveal
memorial verses recording the virtues of 'a morn that promised
much, yet saw no noon'. By the early nineteenth century little
remained but a stone gateway of the mansion where the Earle
family once lived. It was re-erected early in the present century,
however, and stands a splendid *pot pourri* of late medieval and
Elizabethan survivals, brought here from a number of sources,
surrounded by a vineyard.

In about 1800 Brant Broughton was described as 'a very
considerable and respectable village in a flat-country soil, sandy
loam excellent either for corn or pasture. Many respectable
freeholders reside here in genteel houses of brick and slate.'
These houses, of all dates from the seventeenth century to the
nineteenth, still give visual delight to the main street, and more
are to be found along the little lanes which run into it. The
church is magnificent: a soaring spire of the Decorated period
crowns a spacious nave of the same period to which a Perpendicular clerestory and angel roof were added somewhat later.
The exterior is rich in decoration, particularly the two splendid
porches with friezes of beasts and faces and roof-bosses where
the lamb and the pelican are symbolically displayed.

The road from Brant Broughton to Lincoln follows the River
Brant, now dredged and banked, looking like a canal, to prevent
flooding. The river forms the boundary between the line of
clayland parishes and the 'Low Fields' of the row of villages
which can clearly be seen along the steep western edge of the
Heath. Here, in Boothby Graffoe Low Fields, are the towers of
Somerton Castle, erected in the 1280s by Anthony Bek, the
warlike Bishop of Durham and the son of a Lincolnshire landowner. John I, King of France, spent part of his English captiv-
ity here, following his defeat at Poitiers by the Black Prince in
1356. His household of forty or more, apart from his English
captors, included two chaplains, secretary, clerk of the chapel,

physician, *maître d'hôtel*, three pages, four wardrobe men, three
furriers, six grooms, two cooks, a fruiterer, a spiceman, a barber,
a painter, a tailor, a 'king of the minstrels' and the court jester.
Wine in enormous quantities was shipped from Bordeaux to
Boston, partly for the use of the household but partly also so that
King John could sell it to his captors to raise funds for his needs.

These needs were considerable. Enormous sums were spent
on clothing; the royal tailor actually hired a workshop in Lincoln and employed a number of hands full-time making gar-
ments for the King. Jewels were bought, plate for the table,
service books for John's devotions and romances for his entertainment. A minstrel was rewarded with 3s.4d for singing him a
funny song about a dog and a monkey; on other occasions he
whiled away the time by playing chess or backgammon or
watching cock-fights. The King's son Philip kept dogs for coursing on the Heath and falcons. The churches of the neighbourhood benefited regularly from the captive King's benevolence,
as did some of the poor of the district when they ventured to call
with gifts of pears or white pigeons.

In February 1360, after a stay of six months, King John was
once more moved southwards to London, and ultimately home to
France. His baggage left Somerton in twelve wagons. Surplus
items were sold: a lady of Navenby buying two chairs for 20d,
William Spaign two trestles, two forms and the King's own
bench. The half tun of wine remaining in the cellars was politely
left as a gift for the wife of his custodian.

Between the Brant and the Witham a line of villages is joined
by a network of narrow lines wandering inconsequentially
round sharp corners. There is an almost imperceptible rise and
fall from the lowlands of the Brant up to the villages. It is an
area of early enclosure, and in places the surviving hedgerow
timber and the remaining pattern of small closes cannot have
changed greatly in the last three centuries.

The enclosure of these parishes appears to have taken place in
the early seventeenth century. A document survives in which
the inhabitants of Bassingham petition the chief landowner
that their parish, like Brant Broughton and Carlton-le-
Moorland, should be enclosed. Their account of their present
state is a pitiful one. Their commons are stocked with so many
cattle that many of them starve; the poor multiply among them

by reason of the large numbers of houses which have been erected; the cattle constantly break into the cornfields and devour them; the ground is subject to flooding and so overrrun with weeds that many farmers, 'beinge wearied with the un-answeared chardges of orderinge theire arable grounde, leave their lands unploughed'. The poor, who now perhaps keep two or three 'starvelinge cows' in summer and need poor-relief in winter, would get more milk and more profit from one cow properly nourished in a close allotted for the use of cottagers. An enclosure would also prevent the daily trampling of five or six hundred cattle on a trek of several miles across the fallow field down to the pastures by the Brant and would prevent the constant attention needed to stop them straying; now, it is said, from every household at least one person is so occupied every day, including Sundays, and absence from church occasions rudeness in youth, ignorance in manhood and discomfort at the latter end.

Bassingham has a number of good seventeenth- and eight-eenth-century farmhouses. The church, Norman and Early English with a fifteenth-century clerestory and some good gar-goyles, over enthusiastically restored in the 1860s, stands on the banks of the Witham, bereft now of windings, of willow trees and (usually) of floods. Near to the church the monstrous shape of the old rectory presents its backside to the world, all red brick and drainpipes like the rear of a Victorian hospital. It was rebuilt in the 1870s by the first resident rector for a century; he built on the grand scale, intending, it is said, to fill his house with a large family. The family, however, did not materialize, and within a few years he exchanged livings with another clergyman who was more amply provided with offspring.

A mile to the north of Bassingham, Aubourn has a fine Elizabethan, or possibly Jacobean, hall, the spire of a Victorian church left as a landmark when the rest was pulled down and the chancel of the preceding old church now once more in use for worship. The array of Meres and Nevile family memorials in this small building is almost sufficient to crowd out the worship-pers. On the west bank of the Witham a small oasis of trees surrounds the tiny village of Thurlby with its eighteenth-century hall and a church with one of the most beautifully kept churchyards in the county. Norton Disney is full of roadside timber, merging into extensive woodlands; in its church are medieval memorials to the Disneys and a Flemish sixteenth-century brass re-used and re-inscribed in memory of William and Richard Disney and their wives, 'commendable amongest their neighbours, trewe and faithfulle to their prince and country, acceptable to th'almighty'. Woodlands, mainly conifer plantations, continue on what were formerly the extensive moorlands of the parish of Stapleford on the Nottinghamshire border, and the roads are a mass of colour when the rhododendrons bloom in early summer.

When William Cobbett travelled along the Roman Fosse Way between Newark and Lincoln in 1830, he found, it is true, smaller fields and thinner sheep, less obvious agricultural riches than in other parts of Lincolnshire, but also 'a pleasant country, a variety of hill and valley'. Such quotations, together with place-names like Thorpe-on-the-Hill (or even more its earlier version of 'Thorpe super Montem'), might give an exaggerated idea of the undulations of the area. The slopes are in fact very gentle and the heights very low. But there are a number of very definite gravel rises, on one of which, running northwards from Norton Disney across the Fosse Way, most of the villages in the area stand. It is a countryside where bare stretches mingle with areas of deep woodland. Most of this is modern plantation, however, rather than a survival of the Domesday woodlands where, for instance, Countess Judith held two woods, one eight, the other fourteen furlongs long by four broad among her lands at Eagle. Place-names such as Eagle (from 'ac leah', the oak wood) are reminders of the former state of much of the landscape. Eagle still has its woods, from which Lincolnshire's most suicidal pheasants emerge to plague passing motorists. Nearby a farmhouse stands on the site of the former preceptory of the Knights Templar.

Across the border in the Nottinghamshire villages of the Newark area there is a good deal of building in a local ragstone mingled with the brick, but apart from a few houses in North Scarle there is little evidence of this material in Lincolnshire. The Lincolnshire parishes were that little bit farther away from the River Trent, and transport would have been more difficult. So this is an area of many-shaded brick, looking at its best when the low, slanting western sunlight picks out the flecks of varied colour. The winding village street of Swinderby passes a good series of eighteenth-century houses, and the early seventeenth-century enclosure of the parish has left a landscape of small closes with plenty of hedgerow oaks. Small, early enclosures and thickening woodland continue for some distance to the north of the village. In contrast the former moorlands along the top of the ridge near Eagle were enclosed much later; the fields are larger; the views on both sides are immense.

The Fosse Way reaches Lincoln in an area of bungalows and gravel pits. The city's most extensive urban sprawl has been achieved in this direction. Farther to the west vast stretches of woodland, mostly nineteenth-century plantations, surround the overgrown village of Skellingthorpe and the small one of Doddington. Doddington Hall is one of Lincolnshire's finest houses, designed in the late Elizabethan period, possibly by Robert Smithson, for Thomas Tailor, the registrar of the bishopric of Lincoln. The interior was almost completely altered in the eighteenth century, but the exterior appearance, with fat-domed cupolas rising above the surrounding countryside, is very much as it was when the house was first built.

The Sleaford Area

John Byng found Sleaford 'truly melancholy' and its church 'a cumbrous pile, crowded with niches'. In fact it is one of the most attractive of the smaller Lincolnshire towns, and the church, where a marvellously ornate rebuilding in the late Decorated and Perpendicular periods has far from obliterated some fine Early English work, is one of the most interesting. It stands beside its fifteenth-century timber-framed vicarage, looking out over the small market square where Byng watched a hatter take enormous trouble to set up his stall and lay out his wares, only to pack them all up again within a few hours, and mused on the vanity of human life, 'not long enough, or too long for such nothingness'. Gothic, or Tudor, or a combination of the two, continues in the nineteenth-century Sessions House on the corner and in Carre's Hospital another nineteenth-century building, which replaced that set up in 1636 on the site of the Carre family's house for the maintenance of twelve poor men. They were endowed with £10 a year each, including the cost of a new gown each year at Whitsuntide.

Throughout the town the nineteenth-century stonework of Messrs Kirk and Parry, local architects and building contractors, mingles happily with houses of the seventeenth and eighteenth centuries. In Westholme House, now the County Library, we find their style at its most cheerfully inventive; a miniature Loire château rises above the red-tiled roofs of a Lincolnshire town. Equally imposing is their Gothic entrance to the gas works; far more so than the rather miniature gas-holder behind.

The original settlement of Old Sleaford lay about half a mile to the east of the present town centre, on the Roman Mareham Lane. The modern town, which retained its full title of 'New Sleaford' until comparatively recent times, grew up on bishopric lands around the castle of the bishops of Lincoln, which has long since disappeared. The opening of the Sleaford Navigation to the River Witham near Tattershall in the 1790s gave considerable impetus to the expansion of the town. By 1856 it was described as 'flourishing and important' and 'so much improved and beautified during the present century that it is now one of the handsomest towns of the county, and has been styled "the flower of Lincolnshire" '.

Sleaford lies in a land of spires, of magnificent churches and of delightful villages, where the main building material is the Ancaster limestone, plentifully supplied from quarries only a few miles away. Ewerby, to the north-east of the town, where the land is gently sloping down towards the fens, is perhaps the most spectacular of these churches, all of a piece of the fourteenth-century, with soaring broach spire and finely carved rood screen. In the chancel is the tomb of the twelfth Earl of Winchilsea, who died in 1898, his monument in pleasing imitation of medieval style, with the Earl lying in his robes, a dog at his feet. Nearby, among the trees of Haverholme, gardens and a fragment of the house remain of the nineteenth-century residence of the Winchilseas.

South of Sleaford, Mareham Lane follows the claylands near the fen edge, through a predominantly flattish and open countryside dominated by the enormous silhouette of Sleaford's maltings built by Bass & Co in the early years of the present century. A little farther west the A15 pursues a parallel but much more winding course towards Folkingham and Bourne. Among the villages on or near this road, all have good churches, that at Aswarby making a delightful picture when viewed through the oaks of the park. Osbournby is a particularly attractive village and one likely to be missed. Its street lies at right angles to the main road and presents a fine array of local vernacular styles from the seventeenth century to the nineteenth. Here are brick and stone houses with hipped roofs, houses with mullioned windows, large houses and small. The church is large and, for a change, has a tower not a spire. The chancel is long and full of light, its sedilia ornamented with odd heads and crouching figures, including a slightly mad-looking lady in a floppy head-dress. In the nave, rather dark in contrast to the light of the chancel, is a splendid set of bench ends, by no means a usual feature in Lincolnshire, where medieval woodwork is far from plentiful in the churches. Among them a rather small dragon is engaged in unequal contest with a much larger St George; Adam and Eve cover their privities in a somewhat suggestive manner, and an eagle is surrounded by its babies. On the rough stone wall of the nave hang paintings of Moses and Aaron by T. Philips of Bourne, singled out, not without affection, in the *Buildings of Lincolnshire* as possibly the worst paintings in the county.

East of the A15 the ground sinks gradually downwards in a broad landscape of cornfields and coppices. Westward the rise towards the higher areas of heathland is interrupted by little valleys where there lie a number of delightful villages of mellow stone such as Culverthorpe, with a view across the lake towards its late seventeenth-century hall, and Heydour, whose church has a number of monuments to the Newtons, a family prominent in the county in the seventeenth and early eighteenth century. The direct male line died in 1743 with Sir Michael Newton, who had served as MP for Grantham in four parliaments, his judgement not misled, so his monument records, by the 'example of a corrupt and venal age, enslaved to ministerial influence'. He lost his only son in 1733 at two months old, according to tradition dropped from an upper floor by a pet monkey.

The country around here is well timbered with many small closes and roads which are narrow and sometimes winding. To the north and west the high heath is more open. Through this area the A153 follows the valley of the little River Slea towards Grantham, through Wilsford and Ancaster, where lay the important Roman settlement of Causennae on Ermine Street. The handsome main street of the village follows the line of the Roman road. At Rauceby the bare heath landscape is relieved by luxurious parkland, while a little farther north, beyond the A17, the village of Cranwell, with a nice little church in a grand *mélange* of architectural styles from Anglo-Saxon onwards, is dwarfed by the vast piles of Air Ministry neo-Georgian of Cranwell RAF College.

Lincoln Heath

The main road from Sleaford to Lincoln holds no terrors for the twentieth-century motorist, and the placid agrarian face of the countryside gives no hint of its former perils. To the eighteenth-century traveller, however, the name of Lincoln Heath was one which inspired terror. After he had safely negotiated Dunsby Hill, notorious for its highwaymen, he ran a great risk, particularly after dark, of losing his way in a vast and unlandmarked wilderness, 'wild, barren and naked, possessing no appearance of civilisation, stocked with rabbits and covered with furze, bracken and irregular patches of long, tough grass'. From the mid-century onwards he had the one landmark of Sir Francis Dashwood's lighthouse, Dunston Pillar, 'cheering the heart of many a way-faring traveller who trod with devious steps the wide and pathless heath'. The turnpiking of the road later in the century rendered the light redundant, and it was replaced, at George III's Jubilee in 1810, by a statue of the monarch. George in turn fell a victim to progress when he was removed during the last war as a hazard to aircraft from the nearby RAF station; he remained for many years in a dismembered state until his head and bust were rescued a few years ago and re-erected in Lincoln Castle.

Dunston Pillar, bereft of light and monarch, still stands, as do traces of the 'neat square court with a little dwelling house at each corner', the large plantation of firs (all described in the *Gentleman's Magazine* in 1774) and the farmhouse into which a large room, built by Sir John King Dashwood for the accommodation of fashionable society intent on Thursday afternoon tea and cards, was later converted. Also standing, though it ceased long ago to be an inn, is the 'Green Man', once the only haven of safety and rest in many miles. Once it provided refreshment to the traveller and a centre for local events such as the annual Statue Hiring Sessions for farm servants. Attached to it was a club room built about 1740 for the local gentry, where 'the symposiasts held their periodical sittings and according to

the custom of the period seldom parted sober'. The room survives, but the busts of the members and their coats of arms,
which adorned it, are now gone.

On a grim, grey day on the Heath it is still possible to get some
idea of the former desolation of the scene. An almost flat
tableland is varied by shallow valleys and knolls; few signs of
human habitation are to be seen. But the picture really gives
little idea of what the Heath once was, for everything that we
see is man-made and little more than two hundred years old.
Enclosure brought the field shapes, the dry stone walls, the
hawthorn hedges (some straggling now, some proudly trim-
med), the fine network of straight minor roads with their wide
verges. Enclosure later brought the hedgerow and roadside
timber and the plantations, the isolated farms with their com-
fortable-looking houses and fine ranges of buildings, where
nineteenth-century stone mingles with Dutch barns of the
1930s and 40s and modern silos, grain-driers and all-purpose
hangars. Cattle are few; sheep, in spite of their former plenty,
are fewer; wheat and barley, beet and potatoes now rule the
Heath, their monotony relieved in spring and early summer by
occasional bright yellow fields of rape.

Visitors in the late eighteenth and early nineteenth centuries
saw the taming of the Heath in progress. In his *View of the
Agriculture of Lincolnshire*, Arthur Young says, 'The vast
benefit of enclosing can, upon inferior soils, be rarely seen in a
more advantageous light than upon Lincoln Heath ... a very
extensive country studded with new farm-houses, barns, offices
and every appearance of thriving industry .... Progress in
twenty years is so great that little remains to do.' Even in
Young's day, however, rabbit warrens, once a staple industry,
were still a feature of the area; Charles Chaplin let three to four
thousand acres at Blankney as warren. Rabbits were in fact at
this time an integral part of a complex system of husbandry
which involved ploughing up fifty or sixty acres of warren,
surrounding them with stone walls, paring and burning the turf
to provide fertilizer for turnips, then following the turnips with
barley. Both turnips and barley were then repeated, after which
the land was laid down again to warren. The rabbits were fed in
winter on ash boughs, gorse, oat straw, sainfoin grass and
clover. A warren of one thousand acres would, it was estimated,

produce about £100 profit each year from a crop of about two thousand couples.

The boundaries of the Heath are clearly defined to the north by the Lincoln Gap and to the west by the sharp escarpment where the road from Lincoln to Grantham follows a line of stone-built villages. On the east the limestone of the Heath sinks almost imperceptibly into a belt of clay and sand which in turn gives way to the fenland of the Witham valley. Here is an alternative route between Lincoln and Sleaford, the 'way of the towns', much preferred to the direct route by the mendicants and hawkers of former days because of the richer pickings offered by its numerous villages.

There is one more, much older, route which crosses the Heath, the Roman Ermine Street which runs south from Lincoln to Ancaster and beyond. In parts it is metalled for modern traffic; elsewhere it is a splendid broad green lane, impressive rather than pretty, edged with hawthorn, elder and wild rose bushes as it presses on across a landscape completely open but for the occasional post-enclosure plantation or belt of trees. Views to the east across the Heath are extensive; westward the slightly higher edge of the escarpment cuts off the view, except for very occasional glimpses over the edge to the low fields and the Vale of Trent beyond.

A little to the west of Ermine Street and about ten miles south of Lincoln is Temple Bruer, in its site, though not in its surviving architecture, one of the most impressive medieval monuments in the county. A preceptory of the Knights Templar was founded here late in the reign of Henry II, which passed to the Knights Hospitaller on the suppression of the Templars in 1308. The lords of Temple Bruer were among the greatest of local feudal magnates, and the rents of their tenants and the profits of their farms went to swell the general revenues of the order. Relations with their neighbours were not always amicable, hostility sometimes flaring up into violence; this, combined with the hostility of the natural environment, necessitated a settlement capable of both self-defence and self-sufficiency. Of the medieval buildings only a late twelfth-century tower and a few fragments survive, although the foundations of the round church of the Templars were excavated in the present century. The whole complex, however, of medieval tower, seventeenth-century house, later cottages and splendid farm buildings, produces a fine impression of a pioneering settlement in an unfriendly landscape.

The line of villages which follow the steep western scarp of the Heath and which are linked by the road from Grantham to Lincoln are among the handsomest in the county. All are stone built; several of them have exceedingly fine churches, and all have a good array of farmhouses and cottages which range in date from the seventeenth to the nineteenth century. There are rarely more than one or two seventeenth-century examples in any one village, but over all enough survive, in this as in many other parts of the county, to show that at this period (probably more than in the Elizabethan age) substantial yeomen were investing their wealth in new houses, or new additions to old houses. The evidence of probate inventories bears out the architectural evidence and suggests also that they were at the same time investing much more than their ancestors did in the luxury of the furnishings of their homes. To cite one random example, in 1623 William Bundworth, a modestly well-off farmer of Barkston, had a 'new parlor' furnished with a table, carpet, livery cupboard, chair, ten stools (four of them 'imbrodered') and cushions.

For much of its length between Grantham and Lincoln a lower level of marlstone protrudes westward beyond the limestone scarp. This produces a stepped effect in the slope up to the Heath. This is particularly pronounced at Leadenham, where heavy traffic on the A17 grinds slowly up one steep hill to the village only to be faced with an even steeper one beyond.

The lower layer produces ironstone whose greeny-gold mingles charmingly with lighter-coloured limestone in Caythorpe, where a number of houses, and even the church, are built in bands of the two contrasting stones. Fulbeck has some splendid houses set among magnificent trees, including the eighteenth-century hall of the Fanes. In the church are memorials to the family and also to Thomas Ball who died in 1673, '50 years a faithfull servant to Sir Francis Fane'. The monument tells of his travels with his master into Holland, Denmark, Germany, Lorraine and other European countries 'where he considered the courts and camps of most of the European Princes, their splendor & mutabilitie, concluding with the preacher, there was nothing new under the sun and that all was vanity'.

This row of villages is dotted with the eighteenth-century houses of the gentry, built in positions where they command extensive views over the lowlands to the west. Their parklands sweep down the slope to mingle the green of trees and grass with the gold of the corn. At Wellingore the layers of marlstone and limestone merge into one, and from the south the village appears to be pushing out westward on a promontory. Navenby has a fine street of mingled brick and stone; there is no great house here but a whole succession of buildings on a modest and comfortable scale. Northwards to Lincoln the village delights continue, easily missed because they usually lie just off the main road. At Waddington, for instance, a village dominated by its enormous RAF station, the nicest houses lie in a maze of streets to the west of the A607.

The villages which line the eastern flank of the Heath all take their share of both the limestone soils and the fen lands of the River Witham. This produces parish shapes which form elongated rectangles; east to west they can stretch up to ten miles but are rarely more than a mile from north to south. Both landscape and villages are on the whole less prettified than the western row, though there are extensive plantations both on the Heath and along the sandy belt at the fen edge, and the countryside is, or was, 'enlivened by several noblemen's and gentlemen's seats'. At Nocton the hall built for the Earl of Ripon in 1841 is now a hospital, but the church rebuilt to Sir George Gilbert Scott's design in 1862 as a memorial to the Earl is one of the county's most interesting pieces of Victorian ecclesiastical architecture. Nearer to the centre of the Heath, away from the main village line, are the ruins of Bloxholm Hall, the seat of Robert Adam Christopher, the county's Tory MP in the nineteenth century, and Ashby de la Launde, where the plantations of the park surround an Elizabethan hall, much altered and now a country club.

Returning to the main row of villages, of Blankney Hall, the home of the Chaplins, only a fragment is standing, but the whole landscape is a memorial to their planting and agricultural improvements, and the village is perhaps Lincolnshire's best example of Victorian Tudor estate building. Every cottage it

Stamford from the south, *c*.1800

The monument to John, first Earl of Exeter (d.1700), and Anne, his wife, in St Martin's Church, Stamford

Stained glass
in Browne's
Hospital,
Stamford

Grantham

Kesteven inns: 'The Angel', Grantham, *c.*1830

'The Greyhound', Folkingham

Grimsthorpe, *c*.1800

Harlaxton: the stonework of its gardens is as grandiose
as the house itself

Kesteven villages: Swinstead

Belton, an estate village rebuilt by the Earls Brownlow
in the nineteenth century

Stragglethorpe church

The Car Dyke at Martin-by-Timberland

Sleaford market-place, *c*.1800

Crowland's triangular bridge: an early eighteenth-century view
before it was bereft of water

seems is a *cottage orné*, adorned with chimneys of fantastic variety. The family, with fifteen thousand acres on their Kesteven estates, as well as seven thousand on the wolds, was among the three or four largest landowners in the county. Charles Chaplin (1786-1859) was responsible for most of the planting and improvements on the estate; later in the century Henry Chaplin was one of those larger-than-life figures that the Victorians loved, a friend and mentor of the Prince of Wales, prominent in hunting and horse-racing.

Just south of Blankney a stream descends from the Heath and flows beside the main street of the village of Scopwick. Road, water and grass divide two rows of fine stone houses. Here in 1838 the Reverend George Oliver in *Scopwickiana* wrote a description of the village and the life of its inhabitants at a time when Charles Chaplin's improvements on his estate were in progress but still far from complete. Most of the farmhouses had been rebuilt, and preparations were in progress to replace some of the labourers' cottages, 'placed on the borders of the stream . . . a prolific source of ague and rheumatism'. Through chinks in the stone and thatch the wind visited the inmates somewhat roughly in cold weather. Until recent improvements the stream had invariably overflowed in wet weather to such an extent that one could only progress down the village street by means of stepping-stones.

At harvest time the labourers and their families rose at three in the morning to work in the fields, the men reaping, the children making bands for the sheaves and the women binding. After sixteen hours of this back-breaking work they returned home, 'tired it is true but not out of temper, their honest countenances . . . beaming with benevolence and good humour; and passing harmless jokes on every one they meet'. The wages for their labours were eked out by the fruits of gleaning after harvest and by the products of the allotments which all of them had, producing sufficient vegetables for the year's supply and enough potatoes to feed a pig. Bacon and potato pie was a favourite item of diet, eaten with an appetite 'for which the epicure would exchange his soups and ices'.

To us, conditioned by sub-Marxist historians to look for crypto-revolutionaries under every smock, Mr Oliver's account of the bucolic pleasures of a life of almost unremitting toil may seem bland and naïve. He was, after all, writing within a few years of the 'Captain Swing' riots when for a time it had looked as if the whole of the rural labouring population might rise and when a number of anonymous threatening letters had been received by Lincolnshire farmers. But, in this county at least, the landowners and farmers suffered little more than a good scare, and elaborate arrangements for calling out the militia and raising a force of special constables proved in the end unnecessary. By 1838 Scopwick suffered from no disorders more serious than an over-addiction to the comforts of tobacco among the women and an understandable rebellion against Sunday School among their offspring. The clergyman's worst worry, 'a dark shade in the religion of this otherwise quiet parish', was the village youths' habit of gambling at 'chuck-hole' in the street on Sundays. Even the ale-house was no problem; its formidable landlady allowed neither drunkenness nor late carousing and after two or three pints sent the men home to their wives.

The Northern Kesteven Fenland

On its southward course from Lincoln the River Witham is
bordered on the Kesteven bank by a broadening strip of fen up to
three or four miles wide, whose boundary with the higher lands
is marked by the still surviving Roman canal, the Car Dyke.
Between Sleaford and Tattershall the merging of the main river
with the Slea and other water-courses produced what must once
have at times resembled an inland sea and is now a broad arc of
flat lands which join up at their southern end with the belt of fen
along South Kesteven's eastern margin. The Saxon invaders
settled on the ridges and islands of sands and gravels which rose
shallowly above the surrounding marshes. One such ridge runs
down from near Blankney, through Martin, Timberland and
Walcot to Billinghay, 'the island of the Billings'. To both east
and west it commands enormous views across a fenland almost
bare of trees, with the Heath rising gently in one direction and
Tattershall Castle prominent in the eastern middle distance.
Mud and moisture were the main features of these villages
before the drainage of their fens, and abominable roads. At
Walcot in about 1800 they were 'extreme bad', while Thorpe
Tilney's 'neat pleasant mansion house with suitable offices' was
in such a bad country for roads that it was hard to find a suitable
tenant.

At about this time, however, improvements were already in
progress. In 1799 a traveller looked north from Tattershall
Bridge and saw hardly anything but water and the corn all lost,
but farther west, where the fens of Anwick, Kyme and Billinghay were already banked, the land was dry and the crops safe.
Within a decade or so the whole countryside was transformed,
and greater profits from the land brought about corresponding
investments in the buildings. Many of the farmhouses date from
this expansive period after the enclosure and drainage works
were completed. There are, for instance, several nearly identical

ones built by the landowner on the Milnes estate at Martin and Timberland.

The Kymes, North and South, lie on another ridge of slightly rising ground above a wide expanse of fen. South Kyme has in its parish church a small survival of a priory of Augustinian canons and nearby the lofty tower-house built by Sir Gilbert de Umfraville in the mid fourteenth century. Other traces of what must once have been a stately ensemble of priory, mansion and park are now gone. John Byng was attracted here to sketch the venerable-looking church in 1791; he found the roof falling in and the interior in a state of filth and ruin that beggared description. To make matters worse, he was 'driven off in much nervous disorder by a herd of bullocks'. Kyme was plagued with undisciplined cattle in the twentieth century, too; one of them got stuck up the tower in 1946.

Four miles south-west of Kyme, across a landscape of drainage dykes and enormous fields, the magnificent spire of Heckington church marks the beginning of a row of fen-edge villages which stretches southward to the Northamptonshire border at Market Deeping. Helpringham, Great Hale and Swaton all have fine churches, the former of them looking (outside at least) rather the worse for wear on a recent visit. But all the churches in this area must give pride of place to Heckington, one of the most outstanding in a county where fine churches abound. It was built all of a piece during the flowering of the Decorated style of architecture in the early fourteenth century. Richard de Potesgrave, King Edward II's chaplain, whose tomb is in the chancel, was almost certainly responsible for much if not all the building.

It is a large church, 164 feet long and with a spire about 180 feet high. One could spend hours admiring the exuberant decoration of the exterior, where monsters, demons and men stand out over the niches where saints formerly stood, poke their heads out from foliage encrusted pinnacles and parade in rows above the varied tracery of the windows. The interior is lofty, light and spacious, a little bare in appearance at first after the decorative fantasies outside. In the chancel, however, piscina, sedilia, Easter Sepulchre and founder's tomb are masses of figures and foliage, angels in differing attitudes and saints. Heckington has other attractions also: it is a large village with some good seventeenth- and eighteenth-century brickwork in its streets and a magnificent eight-sailed windmill – alas! a whited sepulchre; it no longer works.

3

Holland

It is all too easy in writing about the Parts of Holland to concentrate on two facts to the exclusion of all others: first that it is flat, second that it is full of magnificent churches. To our ancestors Drayton's description of its 'foggy fens', 'foul woosy marsh' and 'vast and queachy soil with hosts of wallowing waves' provided in one snappy word-picture all that they needed to know of the vast county of Lincoln. Later, when the woosy marshes had been drained, the admiration of such men as William Cobbett for fenland agriculture and fenland churches tended to perpetuate the myth that Lincolnshire was all fens: 'The whole country as level as a table . . . . The horizon like the sea in a dead calm . . . . The land covered with beautiful grass, with sheep lying about upon it as fat as hogs stretched out in a stye . . . . Everything grows well here; earth without a stone as big as a pin's head; grass as thick as it can grow in the ground; immense bowling-greens separated by ditches.' The rich grazing lands have mostly given way now to market gardening and the growing of potatoes and vegetables and bulbs, but even now the fame of these fenland activities and of Spalding's tulip parades, and the uniqueness of the fenland landscape, spread the picture of this area as typical of the whole of the county.

The pattern of ancient settlement in Holland follows a low ridge of silt, so low that no contour lines betray its existence on the Ordnance Survey map. On the seaward side lie the marshes which have been reclaimed from the sea; on the internal side are the peat fens. The belt of silt is narrow in South Holland, marked by a single row of parishes running from the borders of Norfolk and Cambridgeshire through Holbeach to Spalding. North of the River Welland the belt is broader, and settlements fan out from Spalding north-eastwards to Boston and northwards towards Sleaford. Beyond Boston a narrow strip again carries a single line of parishes lying between the sea and the Witham fens. The 'town-lands', as they were called, are marked on the map by the dense maze of roads and lanes which surround the villages and contrast with the straight and regular layout of roads in the interior fens and the sparser, though still winding, network on the outer marshes. These town-lands provided ground, though far from a plentiful supply of it, for the growing of crops, and from them the inhabitants gradually branched out on either side to colonize fen and marsh. The lines of long-stranded sea banks are testimony to this process throughout the area. So are the extraordinarily elongated shapes of the parishes, especially the South Holland parishes which reach out from the original settlement half-a-dozen miles or more towards the sea and as far again on the landward side.

There is a considerable amount of evidence that great areas of the fenland were already colonized in Roman times. Air photography has revealed a number of settlement sites which consist of clusters of houses with fields and ditched roads leading out to open areas of grazing land. The decay of the Roman Empire, however, must have brought about the break-up of the organization needed to keep this land under agricultural production, and later settlers had all to do again. The eleventh and twelfth centuries were a particularly active period of land reclamation in the region, when secondary settlements served by parochial chapels sprang up at the limit of seaward and landward expansion in many parishes. Further extension followed in the thirteenth and fourteenth centuries, when chapels were built in places like Sutton St Edmund, Gedney Hill and Cowbit to serve some even remoter nuclei of population.

The system of husbandry followed in Holland until comparatively modern times was designed, above all, to exploit the extensive grazing lands provided by the reclaimed fens and marshes. Every village had unstinted grazing; hence the enormous numbers of cattle and sheep; hence also the large size of most of the villages in an area whose great commons would support the livestock of an almost unlimited number of inhabitants. Arable farming on the narrow belt of town-lands played a subsidiary, though important, role. Thomas Aubine, for instance, a Sutterton husbandman of modest means who died in 1616, had the lease of three grass closes and 2½ acres of 'summer eaten ground' as well as the common pastures for the support of his two cows and eighty sheep. The only evidence of

arable farming in his inventory is a small crop of hemp, barley
and beans. He lived in some style in a house with a hall and two
parlours, made cheese and butter and ate from pewter plates. He
had not succumbed to the new-fangled habit of venturing upstairs to sleep; the only room on the chamber-floor was used for
the storage of linen-wheels, old barrels and other such trash.

Substantial houses of the seventeenth and eighteenth centuries, built of dark, richly coloured brick, are to be seen in many of
the fenland villages. From the evidence of surviving documents
their inhabitants appear to have lived in considerable comfort,
amply fed by the agricultural wealth of the area. And after their
death they were given a good send-off. At Sutterton again, the
funeral feast of Miles Sivers was furnished with eighteen dozen
loaves of white bread, ten dozen cakes, twenty-five pounds of
butter, three stone of cheese and ten gallons of ale. The parson
received 10s. for a funeral sermon and Thomas Johnson 4d. 'for
bidding the neighbours to the funeral'. A few days later the
valuing of the deceased's goods called for a quarter and a leg of
mutton, thirty-three loaves, fruit, spices and another barrel of
beer.

The deeper fens provided a plentiful supply of wildfowl and
fish; some of the inhabitants were employed full time as fishers
and fowlers. In 1617 Thomas Browne of Moulton left two boats
on the river valued at £1.3s.4d. fishing and fowling tackle worth
£1.13s.4d. and fish in the pond valued at £1.6s.8d. Daniel Defoe
speaks of the fenland trade of sending live fish to London 'by
carrying great butts filled with water in wagons'.

The process of reclamation from both sea and fen was a long
and costly one, subject to frequent setbacks when the elements
claimed their own again. In 1607 the people of Gedney claimed
that they were unable to give any exact measurement of their
marsh land. A large area which at one time was clear could
within three hours be covered with six feet of water. The very
existence of the region depends on the maintenance of a complex
system of banks and drainage channels, the responsibility now
of public authorities but formerly of the inhabitants as a whole.
Their livelihood, their safety even, was preserved by a whole
range of dues and duties – labouring work, heavy drainage
rates, administrative chores, or perhaps all three, which all had
to perform. These laid a heavy burden upon rural communities

and demanded an intimate knowledge of their land, of the purpose and state of every dyke, which we can scarcely imagine when we gaze at this flat and somewhat anonymous expanse.

In its essentials the law relating to the upkeep of the fenland drainage system changed very little between 1427 and 1930. At the heart of the system were the Commissioners of Sewers, empowered to oversee, raise rates, carry out work, make laws and punish owners and tenants who failed to carry out their responsibilities. To them the sewers' jury reported in enormous detail on the state of the drainage and upon the person responsible for any defects. At parochial level the dyke-reeves were responsible for levying the rates demanded by the commissioners and for the organization of drainage works within their parishes.

Arrangements for the performance of the necessary works upon the banks, bridges and sewers show a bewildering variety of methods which could change from place to place, even from yard to yard. Some was carried out by 'menwork', every inhabitant owing one day or more each year, 'with the cartes of all them that have & occupie cartes & the rest with spades & barrowes'. On occasions this system broke down because of the unwillingness of the inhabitants to carry out their duties and the dyke-reeves had to pay labourers to carry out the work. The drainage of some areas, particularly newly drained lands, was financed by a rate per acre, while many stretches of bank were the responsibility of individual landholders, a method known as 'joycement' from the 'joyce books' in which these lengths of bank and the landholders charged with them was set down.

The success of all these works of drainage depended, as it still does, on the ability of the four main fenland rivers, the Nene, the Welland, the Glen and the Witham in the northern part of Holland, to carry the inland waters away to the sea. This calls for both an efficient system of drainage channels and pumping stations (once wind-driven, then steam, now oil-powered) to collect the waters of the fens and also an unimpeded outfall for the rivers into the Wash. The former works were more or less concluded in the late eighteenth and early nineteenth centuries and the last sections of deep fen drained at that time. That these works had only a limited effect was due to the fact that the rivers had an almost literally uphill task to get the waters away to the sea. It was only with the perfection of their outfalls, late in the nineteenth century, that the full effects of earlier drainage schemes could be experienced.

Some understanding of the drainage system is needed to make sense of a region which otherwise is liable to seem full of water-courses ranging from the minute to the mighty, proceeding in no obvious direction with no certain purpose.

Most of the western margin of Holland, together with its northern regions up to the Witham, an area known as the Black Sluice level, drains through the South Forty Foot Drain which runs northwards near to the Kesteven boundary, then swings east to join the Witham near Boston. This also picks up the waters of the adjoining Kesteven fens and of the streams coming down from the upland areas. East and south of this the waters from the 'town-lands' of Kirton Wapentake, between Boston and Spalding, all flow through a number of drains, such as Kirton Drain, Five Towns Drain and Risegate Eau, into the Welland beyond its junction with the River Glen. Deeping Fen, the vast area of fenland between the Rivers Glen and Welland, drains through Vernatt's Drain into the Welland. Finally in South Holland a number of ancient water-courses running from the fen through the town-lands and marsh directly into the Wash were found to have an inadequate fall to carry off the inland waters and the South Holland Main Drain, cut under the powers of an Act of Parliament of 1792 now carries water from the interior fens to the River Nene near Sutton Bridge.

South Holland

The stone of Market Deeping and Deeping St James at the extreme south-eastern tip of Kesteven soon gives way to brick as one follows the A16 towards Spalding through the Adventurers' Lands of Deeping Fen. These are the lands given, in return for their outlay, to the company of 'Deeping Fen Adventurers' who carried out a partial drainage of the area in the late seventeenth century. It is a countryside of scattered cottages and farms, an enormous hedgeless plain of corn stretching out to far horizons lined with a few dwarfed trees. At Deeping St Nicholas in the heart of the fen a minor road branches southwards to Crowland. The only perceptible rise in the ground is the high bank which has been raised to keep the River Welland within its bounds. The little town of Crowland stands among trees near the county boundary, a total contrast to the bare landscape which surrounds it.

For centuries Crowland was surrounded by water for much of the year; drainage and enclosure changed its surroundings out of all recognition in the late eighteenth and early nineteenth centuries. It was an island entirely when, in about the year 699, a young Mercian nobleman named Guthlac, disillusioned in turn by a military career and by the comparative comfort of a regular monastic rule, came here by boat to seek God in the solitary life of a hermit. Here he lived on barley bread and muddy water in a hut, resisting alike the promptings of despair, the blandishments of the Evil One and the assaults of a motley band of demons. The saint's biographer describes them vividly: their ferocious eyes, foul mouths vomiting flames, horses' teeth, long necks, scabby legs, knobbly knees and raucous shouts. ('A great many stories are told of the devils of Crowland, and what conversation they had with the monks, which tales are more out of date now than they were formerly,' says Defoe with all the scepticism of the Age of Reason.)

Tales of Guthlac's saintly life began to circulate, and visitors sought him out in his inaccessible cell, among them Aethelbald, who was to become King of Mercia in 716 shortly after the saint's death. The King enriched the shrine which was built to house Guthlac's body and was certainly instrumental in encouraging the cult of the saint. There is no definite contemporary evidence, however, of any monastic foundation upon the spot for another three centuries, though Crowland Abbey was in existence before the Norman Conquest. It was almost certainly after the conquest that the need for solid evidence to support the abbey's title to its possessions resulted in the codification of a series of traditions about its early history into a whole series of forged charters and even a forged chronicle, which endowed it with an exalted history and extensive royal benefactions in the Anglo-Saxon period.

'Nothing can be more noble, more Gothic, or more elegantly carved than the front (now tottering) of Croyland Abbey; a beauty of the richest workmanship; my eyes gloried in the beholding, whilst my heart sickened in the destruction.' So wrote John Byng in 1790; he was equally upset by the vile tea, rank butter and bad bread provided at the inn. Even today, the surviving portions of the abbey buildings convey an extraordinary sense of grandeur, of pride in craftsmanship and of a great legacy of devotion. The principal remains are the north aisle, now the parish church, surmounted by a mighty tower ending in a rather squat spire, and portions of the ruined nave. The west wall of the nave survives to a sufficient extent to reveal something of its former greatness. It is thirteenth-century work, the doorway surmounted by a tympanum showing scenes from the life of St Guthlac. Above it the outline remains of a large and elegant window, spreading outwards toward the top and surrounded by saints in niches. Much of the former abbey site is covered by the graveyard which surrounds the church, a sea of urns and cherubs in light-coloured stone.

The abbey ruins must have provided the town with an excellent quarry for centuries; a good deal of stone can be seen mingled with a pleasant, dark, multi-shaded brick. Crowland has several good streets of eighteenth- and nineteenth-century houses; rows of trees here and there add shade and variety. At the centre is an extraordinary fourteenth-century, triangular – or, to be more exact, three-legged-bridge. It is stranded high above the surrounding roadway, long bereft of the three streams which once met beneath it. Upon it is a large seated figure, perhaps of Christ, and perhaps brought here from a position on the west front of the abbey.

The road from Crowland to Spalding follows the Welland bank, a lofty elevation which allows wide views in all directions over a landscape still mainly of cornfields and bare of trees apart from an occasional windbrake. Along this stretch the bank was built at some distance from the river to allow it room to flood; Cowbit Wash, the area between the two, was long the Mecca of fenland skating. Cowbit, sheltering on the landward side of the bank, grew up as an outlying hamlet of Spalding; a parochial chapel was licensed for the inhabitants in 1363, and the present church, brick with stone tower and chancel, seems to be almost entirely fifteenth-century work.

The town of Spalding grew up around a rich and important Benedictine priory, all trace of whose buildings has now gone. The original town site was on a triangle of land bounded by the priory to the south-west, the River Welland to the east and an ancient drainage channel named the Westlode to the north. Evidence of medieval extension beyond the Welland survives in the parish church and the adjoining Ayscoughfee Hall. By the early eighteenth century there had been further expansion beyond the original site, especially along the river north of the church where there was already a continuous line of merchants' houses and warehouses. For the river and its trade were Spalding's main support; it stood at the lowest point at which the Welland was bridged before the nineteenth century and at the highest point of navigation by seagoing vessels. Here coal for Stamford was trans-shipped to smaller boats, together with grocery goods from London, timber, pitch, tar and other goods for the inland areas. Down the river came corn, flour and malt from Stamford, lime and limestone, and all the produce of the fens.

Spalding is full of good Georgian buildings; the houses and warehouses along the tree-lined banks of the river are among the most pleasant features. Nearby, the enormous parish church of mainly fourteenth- and fifteenth-century work and Ayscoughfee Hall form a much earlier enclave, interrupted by the modern District Council offices. Ayscoughfee Hall, where John Byng in 1790 found 'all in disorder and decay – like the owner', is a fifteenth-century brick house with various later alterations which include a severe Tudorization of the 1840s. West of the Welland Georgian continues, mingled with Victorian buildings, through the market-place and into Sheepmarket, with the towered and battlemented Sessions House of 1842, and Broadgate where the museum of the Spalding Gentlemen's Society is situated. The origins of the museum, though not the building which houses it, go back to 1727, when a room, 'wainscotted and pressed round', was prepared to hold the collections of the society, itself by this time some fifteen years old. The members were dedicated to 'improvement in the liberal sciences and polite learning', taking it in turns to read papers on antiquarian, literary and scientific subjects. They met each Monday at four, with a Latin dictionary and a Greek lexicon always to hand, their physical needs supplied by tea and coffee, twelve clean pipes and an ounce of tobacco, a chamber-pot and a good fire which was under the immediate supervision of the president, sitting on the right side of the chimney.

The main road through South Holland from King's Lynn, the A17, crosses the Welland at Fosdyke, some seven or eight miles on the seaward side of Spalding. In the late eighteenth-century this route was passable at low tide with care and usually with a guide who charged 3d per horse. Byng crossed over in 1790 on horseback and the following year in a curricle; the guide, he thought, was about as useful as one from Hyde Park Corner to Kensington. Fosdyke was at this time at the height of its fame as a bathing resort, and an inn had been built for the accommodation of the bathers. Its sands disappeared, however, following the erection of an embankment and bridge to carry the road across the washes at all states of the tide. The bridge was opened in 1815, built of oak and standing on piers which consisted of rows of complete trunks driven twenty feet or more into the bed of the river. It stood until it was replaced by an iron bridge early in the present century.

To drive the whole length of the silt ridge which carries South Holland's town-lands and the row of magnificent churches for which the area is famous, one should cross the Welland at Spalding and take the A151 to its junction with the A17 at Fleet, then follow the latter road to Long Sutton, branching off there to Tydd St Mary and the Cambridgeshire boundary. Every major architectural style is represented in the churches, sometimes in a single building. Each one demands a visit: all cannot be described, and to pick out one or two is almost impossible as it does grave injustice to the others. Fleet is unusual with its lofty detached spire; Long Sutton has a magnificent Norman nave and a very early spire. Gedney is spectacular, enormous and unsurrounded, with an immensely tall tower and an interior made light by a clerestory which seems designed to consist of as little stone and as much glass as could possibly be achieved. The light illuminates the browns and dull reds of an early Tudor roof supported by alternating arch-braces and tie-beams. Rather squashed in by the organ are monuments to the Welby family, including the memorial erected in 1605 to Adlard and Cassandra. They are depicted kneeling at a *prie-dieu*, sober in black with large ruffs, surrounded by roses and coats of arms and foliage.

All the villages in South Holland have large nuclei and have also a wide and sometimes thick scattering of cottages, smallholdings, farms and outlying hamlets in the surrounding marshes and fens. The two small towns, Holbeach and Long Sutton, both grew up as markets and centres of commerce and business on a strictly local scale. Cobbett was 'delighted with Holbeach, a neat little town, a most beautiful church ... gardens very pretty; fruit trees in abundance ... the land dark in colour and as fine in substance as flour'. A good deal of attractive Georgian building can be seen throughout the town and also along the enormously long main street which gives Long Sutton its name. At Sutton Bridge the A17 crosses the River Nene and soon reaches Norfolk. Here, as at Fosdyke, the passage up to the early nineteenth century was a dangerous route, passable only at low tide, and even then the wise traveller accepted the services of a guide. The bridge and the embanked approach roads completed in 1831 were an enormous engineering undertaking which employed about 1,500 men for two years on the bridge and 900 men and 260 horses about 3½ years on the road. 'Of course this bridge when completed will become a great public accommodation ... and will no doubt have the effect of infusing into the resuscitated market of Long Sutton renewed life and vigour.' This hopeful forecast in 1826 appears to have been well founded, for the population nearly doubled between 1821 and 1851, by which time a 'pleasant and well-built suburb of good houses' had sprung up at Sutton Bridge together with warehouses and wharfs for timber, coal, corn and other goods.

The main road through the towns gives only one picture of the fenland landscape; to see the whole, the traveller should venture both inland to the fens and seaward through the marshes. The following description of one random route typifies any number which could be followed over the vast network of minor roads in the area. At Cowbit one leaves the A1073 from Spalding to Crowland to drive through corn and sugar-beet and potato fields to Moulton Chapel, one of a string of settlements which probably have their origin in eleventh- and twelfth-century reclamations of the fen. It now forms a sizeable village with a good deal of modern building grouped round the extraordinary brick church of 1722, whose octagonal construction is somewhat obscured by the late nineteenth-century square addition. Down through Moulton Fen and into Great Postland one is rarely far from a house; cottages of red-brown or stock brick; the large farmhouses surrounded by wind-brakes of poplar often seem to date from the Regency or perhaps early Victorian period. In Great Postland, once an enormous tract of fen belonging to Crowland, occasional bits of pasture with grazing sheep appear among the predominantly arable fields. Here the B1166 runs eastward past Whaplode Drove and Holbeach Drove to Gedney Hill; there are many houses scattered along the roads around here, with small fields, varied crops and other signs of small-holder farming.

At Gedney Hill the hill has to be taken on trust. This is another sizeable settlement with a late-medieval church; the earliest of its houses cannot be later than the early eighteenth century. Bumping along the badly founded roads through the long stretch of fen towards Gedney itself, the modern traveller can sympathize with the bald statement of one of his predecessors: 'The roads to Gedney Hill in winter are not passable but to those who have no fear & are used to such dangers.' At the fen edge the change in landscape to the long-established closes is marked. Fine eighteenth-century farmhouses of a lovely mottled brick mingle with cottages, some of them tiny with apparently only one room on each floor. Above them rises the splendid slender tower of the church, its ridiculous spirelet looking like a pair of spider's legs propped together. Seaward of the village is another long road to the coast. Gedney Dyke, where a notice announces 'Main Street Rebuilt 1826', is dominated by the derelict tower of what was a large milling complex. There is still no sign of the nearness of the sea, except for the unmistakable light in the sky. The road undulates very slightly over sandhills down to Gedney Drove End, already a hamlet of some size in 1830. It shelters behind a high bank from which the sea is visible beyond the vast salt-marshes of the Wash.

Through the reclaimed marshland of Gedney and Holbeach a number of routes can be followed back to the A17 near Fosdyke Bridge. The roads sometimes wind along the tops of what are obviously former sea banks. Piecemeal reclamation has continued since, but the last great push to reclaim these lands was in the late eighteenth century. After that came the settlement of the area, the building of the opulent-looking farmhouses, Regency or early Victorian most of them, and the formation of the settlements such as Dawsmere, Holbeach St Matthew and Holbeach St Marks, each provided later with its Victorian brick church and vicarage. Exposure to strong winds led to the planting of trees in all the hamlets and around many of the large farmhouses. These are now mature, and the avenues of beech, elm and sycamore give shade to the roads and put shades of green into a landscape otherwise devoid of it except when the corn is growing. Away from the trees the vistas are enormous; at harvest groups of yellow combines move in echelon over a vast expanse of golden corn; at ploughing time the whole ground turns sandy-pink as the soil is turned.

The Welland to the Witham

The pattern of landscape and settlement which is to be found in South Holland continues beyond the Welland and throughout the ancient Wapentake of Kirton. Here, however, we find rather narrower belts of coastal marsh and inland fen and the town-lands spread out to carry lines of villages northwards from Spalding to Donington and Swineshead as well as north-eastwards to Boston.

A little to the west of Spalding the modern pumping station at Pode Hole stands at an impressive confluence of water-courses which here empty the waters of Deeping Fen into Vernatt's Drain. The A151 to Bourne crosses the River Glen at Pinchbeck West, passing on the way through a varied patchwork of crops in the small fields: corn, vegetables, bulbs and little pasture closes. The road then follows the river to the Kesteven boundary at Guthram Gowt, 'a very solitary place where the fens were open'. Here the South Forty Foot Drain reaches but does not join the river, and goods were once trans-shipped between boats on the two.

Northwards from Spalding the built-up area reaches almost uninterrupted to Pinchbeck, the first village along the A16, with an enormous church whose exterior appears to be all fourteenth- and fifteenth-century work, but the interior takes the architectural story back to at least the thirteenth. The village has a good deal of new building in it but has always been large. The population was over three thousand in 1851 and over three hundred families by the early eighteenth century. By 1604 it was an important enough centre to support a mercer, John Subbury, who was able to supply the inhabitants with frankincense, quicksilver, Damask prunes, barberry conserve, points and laces, Spanish needles, shoe buckles and arrow-heads. Also in his shop were whale bones and needle cases, coloured silk, lace, leather buttons, sweet soap and black soap, whipcord and bowstrings.

At Cowhurn in Surfleet was once a ferry over the Welland, out of use by about 1800, but 'great numbers of Scotch beasts used formerly to pass this way into Norfolk'. The tower and spire of Surfleet church lean alarmingly towards the main road; inside, the fourteenth-century effigy of a knight could be that of Sir John de Cressey who died in 1383 or of Sir Hugh de Cressey who died in 1346. Both left instructions that they should be buried in Surfleet church, the former with the proviso 'if I die in England'. At Gosberton the A16 swings eastwards, towards Boston; the A152 continues northwards through the village, which has another of Holland's memorable churches (this one cruciform, fourteenth and fifteenth century throughout) to the small market town of Donington. There is plenty of Georgian brickwork to be seen in its streets and market-place, such as the grammar school founded under the munificent charity of Thomas Cowley in the early eighteenth century. He left such large estates to charitable uses that, according to Arthur Young, it actually worked to the disadvantage of the town; the poor rates were high, 'arising from the lower class of persons gaining settlements in the parish by every means in their power, merely through the expectation of benefiting by the said charity'. In the church is a monument to Matthew Flinders, the explorer, who was born here, showing a ship in full sail, together with memorials to his father and grandfather, who were surgeons in the town.

Like so many of the Holland churches, Donington's church is a testimony to the wealth of the area being thrown into a great wave of beautification, enlargement and rebuilding in the fourteenth and fifteenth centuries. At Bicker the greatest effort was earlier, for here we can see a magnificent and impressive Norman nave and thirteenth-century chancel. The sea once came almost up to the village here, at Bicker Haven. The flat alluvial fields are full of many varieties of vegetable and are a great hive of activity at planting, hoeing and harvesting times. Swineshead is a large village, once a market town, but by 1826 its market was 'now nearly deserted, and little business done at it except in the evening when the principal farmers assemble at the Griffin Inn'. Their purpose was perhaps more social than businesslike; however, even if the market was moribund at this date, the large fair on 2nd October for the sale of cheese, onions and other goods was said to flourish still. At Swineshead there is another vast fourteenth- and fifteenth-century church, the exterior alive with gargoyles, heads human and half-human and a laughing pig. Inside is a fragment of what must have been a magnificent monument to Sir John Lockton. The surviving panel shows his children, standing or kneeling in respect or lying in hooded cradles; eight of the eleven carry skulls to show that they have predeceased their father. The Locktons' house stood on the site of the Cistercian abbey where King John fell ill of his last sickness after his unfortunate experiences at the crossing of the Wash. He struggled on from here to Sleaford along roads where up to the eighteenth century travellers soon needed guides in the wet season, then on to Newark to die. All trace of the monastic buildings has now gone and had already gone in 1791 when John Byng had the misfortune to choose Swineshead's village idiot when he was enquiring for them. The question, 'Are there any ruins?' brought the reply, 'I know of no brewings,' and his considerable confusion before he was directed to the farmhouse on the site and the fat old farmer who confessed to youthful target-practice with a pistol that had carried off the nose of the one remaining medieval figure.

From Gosberton the A16 approaches Boston through another string of ancient settlements. Sutterton and Algarkirk lie close together, the latter sat among a maze of twisting, narrow lanes by deep dykes. Among the small fields near the village are a few pasture closes to serve as a reminder that this area was once famous for some of the finest grazing land in England. The cruciform church shows a mixture of periods, the latest of them a costly and enthusiastic restoration in the 1850s. The interior is lightened and the exterior made striking by a fine row of clerestory windows. The Beridge family provided rectors in this parish for some 250 years from the mid seventeenth to late nineteenth centuries, and for much of this time they were patrons of the living and major landowners as well. Among their many memorials in the church one prays modestly 'that (if so may be) their bones may rest undisturbed until the Resurrection Day'.

Kirton-in-Holland is another of the small market towns of the area, full of a magnificent dark brick of the seventeenth and eighteenth centuries. By the early nineteenth century it had lost its market and had been reduced to village status. At the same time its ancient grammar school, founded in 1624, had become more or less the private property of absentee masters who put in incompetent deputies, one of whom was reduced first to parochial relief as a pauper and then to confinement in a lunatic asylum. Early in the same century its parish church, still large but once larger, had its transepts and crossing de-molished and the crossing tower rebuilt at the west end. Perhaps surprisingly, it remains a most impressive building.

Between Kirton and Boston, where the parkland of Wyberton Hall and Frampton Hall spread across the A52, for once the utilitarian air of the Holland landscape breaks out into planta-tions and pleasantness. It seems almost an intrusion in an area where one sometimes feels that nothing taller than Brussels sprouts can grow. Single trees, clumps and avenues of them reach back from the main road for about a mile to the village of Frampton, where the house built for Coney Tunnard in 1725 looks across the park to the massive and beautiful church. There is a lot of Norman and Early English work in it and, on the outside wall of the south transept, a little head of a toothy man with an inscription saying that he is stuck up there because he forswore Christ. Inside is a striking, many-branched chand-elier, the gift of Coney Tunnard in 1722, 'for an example to all pretenders of love to the church which by their acts don't show it'. To this exhortatory inscription he adds a pun on his Christ-ian name in the shape of a little rabbit sitting on the top.

Boston and Northwards

The entrance to Boston on the A16 from Spalding, where the
Victorian country villas which the merchants built towards
Wyberton give way to the sometimes sadly decayed Georgian
town houses nearer to the river, which had been their houses in
earlier days, is a reminder of the town's *raison d'être* as a trading
port. So are the warehouses which still survive along the banks
of the river. For it was the River Witham and the access by the
river, from Lincoln and the hinterland beyond, of the wool and
other exports of a vast area which made Boston a medieval boom
town. At the time of the Domesday Book it did not exist; by 1205,
according to the evidence of a tax raised upon the goods of
merchants, it was a port second only to London in importance.
From the early thirteenth century its great annual fair was a
magnet for traders from the whole of England and from the
Continent as well. In 1336 the King issued letters of protection
to large numbers of German merchants and fourteen ships
travelling to the fair of St Botolph. During the fourteenth
century the German merchants of the Hanseatic League established permanent quarters in the town.

With the rise of the town the religious orders appeared on the
scene; friars of the Augustinian, Dominican, Franciscan and
Carmelite orders all had houses here. Boston's religious gilds
also were numerous, richly endowed with lands and other goods
and exceedingly popular. They provided religious ceremony,
fellowship, prayers after death and if necessary support during
life for their members. St Mary's Gild paid the stipend of a
grammar-school master as well as of the array of priests, choristers, dapifers and others associated with the services and cere-
monies. Nor was charity forgotten: a thousand loaves of
wheaten bread and a thousand herrings were to be distributed
annually to the poor at the feast of the Purification. The wealth
of the gild appears in an inventory of its goods made in 1534; it
included rich vestments and altar furnishings, cross, chalices,
candlesticks and other silver items amounting to over a

thousand ounces, and relics such as St Anne's finger and a piece of stone from the Holy Sepulchre.

In Foxe's *Book of Martyrs* is the story of how the members of the gild of St Mary obtained from Pope Julius II an extensive indulgence which among its terms allowed them to eat flesh in Lent and gave to attendance in their chapel at the major feasts the same spiritual potency as a pilgrimage to Rome itself. They enlisted the young Thomas Cromwell to obtain the papal ear for them, which he did by means of an English song which attracted the Pope's attention on his return from hunting and the present of 'certain fine dishes of gelly after the best fashion' of English make, which were unknown in Italy. 'The Pope's holy tooth greatly delighted in new fangled strange delicates and dainty dishes', and, after cautiously persuading a cardinal to make the first trial, he happily granted the indulgence in return for the recipe.

By 1571 the corporation of the borough was claiming that Boston was so destitute of ships and trade of shipping, that it was liable to fall into utter ruin and decay. In 1607 they petitioned Parliament that its name should be placed on a list of decayed towns. But things are never quite as bad as a corporation likes to tell the government that they are, and the port books of the early seventeenth century show that it continued to have a steady trade, though sadly less no doubt than in its heyday. Ships like the *Fortune* of Amsterdam, Abraham Israel master, were frequently in the port with cargoes of spices, Brazil wood, French and Spanish wine and Norway deals. Outwards they took hempseed and linseed, glue, uncast lead, coarse woollen stockings, leather and sheepskins. Ships from Scotland brought salt. Ships from Boston itself, like the *Rose Anne*, brought wine, vinegar and prunes from Bordeaux or sailed to Calais laden with butter and goose quills. Eighteenth-century and nineteenth-century improvements both to the inland waterways and to the outfall through the Wash brought a further revival and a thriving trade in corn, coal and other goods. Its importance as a local market and administrative centre in an area where trade and population increased markedly following drainage and enclosure, together with the establishment of manufacturing industries in the town in the early nineteenth-century, contributed to a steady rise in the number of inhabitants from about 3,000 in the early eighteenth century to 6,000 in 1801, to 15,000 in 1851 and 25,000 in 1961.

Apart from the glory of its parish church there are few architectural reminders of Boston's medieval importance. The shell of the Dominican friary survives and has now been restored for use as a theatre. The fine hall of the gild of St Mary was used for a long time as the town hall. It has undergone many alterations but retains its fifteenth-century roof. It now houses a museum. But the church of St Botolph alone, one of the country's largest parish churches, is in itself evidence enough from the period of the town's greatness. Its tower, the world-famous Boston Stump, culminating in a marvellous window-filled octagon supported by flying buttresses, is of course the best known and most unusual feature. Work on it started in 1309, and the whole church is a product of the fourteenth and fifteenth centuries.

A perambulation of the town is full of surprises, delights and some horrors. The Gild Hall and Fydell House, built on a grand scale for William Fydell in 1726, stand in close proximity to a particularly nasty cinema. Georgian is the predominant accent among the older buildings, and there are plenty of places like the market-place and Wide Bargate where there is room to stand back and admire. As well as the grander houses there are many Georgian and early Victorian terraces to be seen stretching out from the town centre in all directions along waterways as well as roads.

North of Boston the villages lie on a narrow strip of land between the coastal marsh and the East Fen. To follow the whole line, one should leave the town not along Spilsby Road, replete with late nineteenth-century villas, but through the timber-yards and terraces of Skirbeck Road to Fishtoft. Here the Norman church lies among modern housing development and the houses where in about 1800 many graziers lived 'on their own freeholds like gentlemen'. Winding lanes lead to the sea bank at Freiston Shore, where the amazingly palatial Georgian inn is a relic of the time when this was a thriving summer resort for 'invalids and persons who wish to enjoy the salubrious exercise of sea-bathing'. By the late nineteenth century its popularity was over; the place is a lonely one now, the sands long since overgrown and the sea a long walk away across the marshes. Freiston village lies two miles inland; a seventeenth-century farmhouse stands on the site of the priory founded in 1114. The priory church survived to serve the parish, its Norman nave encapsulated in fifteenth-century tower and clerestory and brick north aisle.

Near Freiston our route northwards along the line of settlements joins up with the A52, the main road from Boston to Skegness. All these villages are large, with cottages and farmhouses spilling outwards from the nucleus down winding lanes towards the fen and the marsh. Like almost every parish in Holland, all have magnificent churches, with a great deal of evidence of lavish expenditure in the fourteenth and fifteenth centuries to beautify and enlarge existing buildings. Leverton has a particularly sumptuous chancel, rich in decoration of leaves, flowers and grotesques. The tower leans away from the nave, then its upper stage leans back to the perpendicular, a rather odd effect. Inside, the fifteenth-century screen has survived and the stairs up to the rood which once surmounted it. After being painted over and obscured in the Protestant days of Edward VI, this was restored to its full glory under Mary only to be taken down altogether in 1562 when the religious pendulum swung back once more in Elizabeth's reign. The churchwardens' task was a difficult one in this time of Reformation and Counter-Reformation turmoil, and the cost to a parish not inconsiderable. The fate of the rood loft was shared by ornaments, vestments and other furnishings, thrown out, replaced and at last thrown out again. The churchwardens' accounts survive for the whole period to tell a story which must have been duplicated in almost every parish in the land.

From Leverton it is only a few miles to the northern boundary of Holland, through Leake and Wrangle, whose cottagers Arthur Young found to be 'rather a lawless set'. They took in bits of the waste, with no legal title to them at all, and grew potatoes. A more friendly observer described them as peaceful and contented, 'rejoicing in their independence and confidently maintaining that none but the idle and dissolute need fear to become paupers, work upon the roads or find shelter in the workhouse'. Their life had much in common with that of the southern Lindsey parishes which shared the adjoining fenland with those of northern Holland.

4

Southern Lindsey and the Witham Fens

Holland's northern boundary, with Lindsey, follows an erratic course. From Wrangle, the most northerly of its seaward line of village, it plunges south again to a point only two miles north of Boston at Cowbridge, only to turn once more, following the Witham to Chapel Hill near Tattershall. This boundary reflects the final division, after drainage and enclosure, of an area of fen over which the adjoining Holland and Lindsey parishes all had rights of common. This vast area, subdivided into the East, West and Wildmore Fens, together with Holland Fen (alias 'Eight Hundred' or 'Haut Huntre' Fen), which lies to the south and west of the Witham, can well be considered as a unity. All were formed by the immense struggle of the Witham to empty its waters into the Wash.

The landscape as we now see it is that produced by the straightening of the course of the river in the 1760s and the drainage of the fens in a series of undertakings carried out between the seventeenth and early nineteenth centuries. The result of these enterprises is an enormous level plain criss-crossed with wide, straight drainage channels and narrower subsidiary dykes and the long, straight roads which follow them. The roads run along banks raised above the surrounding countryside, and from them one looks out over vast fields of corn, or sometimes of potatoes, peas, onions and brassicas, inter-spersed here and there with pastures where sheep and cattle graze. Sometimes the view is almost treeless, it is often hedge-less; other places, Carrington for instance, are positive oases of mature timber. Many of the farmsteads are protected by trees; others, together with many of the abundant scattered cottages, are now seeking shelter with windbrakes of poplar or Leyland cypress. In all this vast plain one is rarely far from a house; few of the buildings are earlier than the 1820s, most of them are later, constructed for farmers, smallholders and cottagers who colonized the fens in the nineteenth century when the land was finally brought under the plough or the spade.

Before the final and effectual drainage of the late eighteenth and early nineteenth centuries, the whole of the area varied, according to place and season, between rough pasture, morass and water. Hollar's map of 1661 in Dugdale's *History of Imbankment and Drayning* shows the fens as they must have been for centuries, apart from the lines showing Sir Anthony Thomas's recent drains. Between the East Fen and the West Fen there juts down from the wolds a ridge, or rather a series of islands, reflected in the names given to them by their Anglo-Saxon settlers: Stickford, Stickney and Sibsey (two islands and a ford). These parishes have always formed a southern promontory of the county of Lindsey, and their communication with Boston was cut off by the fen, although the A16, Boston's main communication with the north of Lincolnshire, now passes through them. West of the ridge lies the West Fen, where Hollar's map clearly shows one or two small centres of permanent, ancient settlement, such as Medlam and Moorhouses. Further west still lies Wildmore Fen, and this also had a few small settlements such as Newham, Hundlehouses and the aptly named Frog Hall, 'an ancient little stud and mud alehouse'.

Holland Fen also, not shown on Hollar's map, had an ancient settlement in Brothertoft and scattered farms like Rooms Hall, 'a large house by the river Witham . . . when Holland Fen was open it is said the occupier had near 20,000 sheep; next year intended to complete that number and have 20 shepherds with every one a silver hook, but he died too soon'.

The fenland landscape in the eighteenth century was described by a number of observers. The earlier drainage works had been more successful in Wildmore and West Fens than in the deeper East Fen, though many even of the drier areas were liable to winter flooding. Nowhere was entirely safe as winter pasture; 'some keep sheep in winter there, and suffer accordingly,' Young darkly comments. Where flooding did occur, the pastures were covered with coarse grass; unlike the East Fen there were comparatively few reed beds in Wildmore and West Fens. The grass itself was tough enough

And that she calls her grass so blady is and harsh
As cuts the cattel's mouths, constrain'd thereon to feed

says Michael Drayton; but there was even rougher pasture in parts of Wildmore: Arthur Young rode through whole acres covered with thistles and nettles four feet high and more; the thistles were 'in such enormous quantity, that a common complaint (among the sheep) is sore noses, with such a prevention of feeding that numbers die'.

It was in the East Fen that most of the genuine morasses were to be found; two thousand acres were permanently under water, and a great deal more consisted of reed beds, while the whole fen was covered with water in the winter season. The large pools, or 'deeps', which had names like 'Rogger', 'Arch Booze', 'Domine', 'Goup Hole' and 'Gass Water', were connected by water-courses called 'rows' or 'havens'. 'It was a pleasant excursion in summer time to row from pool to pool. The centre of each was quite free from weeds . . . from three to four feet in depth of singularly pellucid water . . . so clear and shallow was the water that a person in a boat could, with a hay-fork, spear the large bream that were passing.'

The fens provided a good and comparatively easy living for many of the inhabitants of the surrounding parishes. Twenty-nine parishes in North Holland and the Soke of Bolingbroke had unlimited common rights in East, West and Wildmore Fens, the whole system being governed by rules laid down in 1548 and little amended over the next 250 years. The rules covered the stocking of the fens, the marking of the stock (each parish had its own brand), fowling, fishing, reed-gathering and mowing.

The total area of the East, West and Wildmore Fens was about sixty thousand acres. It was the *unstinted* nature of the common which was important to the surrounding commoners. The tenant of the smallest cottage had unlimited rights and could gradually make his fortune by building up enormous herds of sheep, cattle or geese. In summer the area was full of stock: 'Upon driving the West Fen in 1784,' according to Arthur Young, 'there were found, 16th and 17th September, 3936 head of horned cattle. In dry years it is perfectly white with sheep.' He estimated a possible five sheep to an acre, which if accurate would produce an incredible total of over a quarter of a million.

Like Texas, Lincolnshire is a Big Country, and it abounds in tall stories, especially, no doubt, for agricultural correspondents.

Apart from lethal thistles, the stock had to survive a variety of ills; among them was sheep rot, caused by the frequent wetness of the ground – forty thousand lost in 1793, Young was informed; 'nor is this the only evil for the number stole is incredible; they are taken off by whole flocks'. Great commons, he observed, nurtured a mischievous race of people, and thus 'the morals and eternal welfare of many are ruined for want of an enclosure'. Gangs of villains from neighbouring parishes like Coningsby committed numerous outrages, laming, killing, cutting off tails and wounding a variety of cattle, hogs and sheep. In winter the horses often got onto the ice and were split when their legs went in all directions. These were the celebrated 'Wildmore Tits', a breed of small, generally grey horse of allegedly Arabian descent, which were much in demand. The 'Pepper Gang' of Mareham-le-Fen dealt extensively, and not always fairly, in this breed; their victims were said to have been 'peppered'.

Some places in or beside the fen, such as Frithbank and Brothertoft, specialized in the breeding of geese, on the whole for feathers rather than food. Some flocks were enormous, 'a frontager named Green, living at Moorhouses, having had at one time a stock of two thousand old brood geese'. The down was plucked five times a year, the feathers twice, from the live birds; it was claimed that this caused no discomfort if done at the right time when the feathers were loose. In spring young birds were sold off and marched away towards London. In April 1812, when John Cragg was valuing the West Fen for enclosure, knowing that this would mark the end of the goose industry, 'out of curiosity sake, as well as a memorandum for future when such a thing might either be forgotten or disbelieved', he noted down 'at the mouth of a little boy gosserd ten years of age' the details not only of the care but also the names of some ninety brood geese. Some of the names reflected the appearance of the bird, like 'Grey Toppin', 'Old Painted Lady', 'Blade Nab' and possibly 'Small Beer Bod'; while 'Mrs Wright', 'Mrs Pacy', 'Jem Huckbar' and 'Dick Waltham' may have possessed for an imaginative ten-year-old certain fleeting facial resemblances to local residents. Each goose was taken down to the water for a few minutes each day, then returned to its nest in the goose-house, an oblong building of mud and stud with a thatched roof. The nests were ranged on the walls as in a cote for outsize doves and in front of each nest was 'a long greensward sod with a hole made in it to put oats for their feed'. As Cragg foresaw, the geese did not long survive enclosure; foreign down and foreign quills replaced the Lincolnshire product in the featherbeds and inkwells of London.

The wildfowl and fish of the area also provided a fruitful source of food and income for the commons. In his *History of Boston*, Pishey Thompson includes a drawing (reproduced in many later books about the Fens) which shows two fen 'Slodgers' as they would have appeared returning from a fowling excursion in the East Fen in about 1780. They are wearing broad-brimmed hats and short, rough cloaks and carry long, hooked poles over their shoulders. Slung about them as they tramp between the ponds and reed clumps under a bird-filled sky are the fruits of their sport, which look like wild geese. The fens north of Boston were as prolific in wild life as were those of South Holland. A speciality of the East and West Fens was the gathering of sticklebacks. Arthur Young tells of a man who earned 4s a day by selling them at a halfpenny a bushel: 'They are the most powerful of all Manures.' This area was also one of a number in Lincolnshire which specialized in the capture and sale of wild geese by means of duck decoys, particularly in the East Fen in and near Friskney parish. The main supply of ducks, widgeon and teal for the London market came from this small area.

Friskney still has its 'Decoy Farm', and the rounded clumps of trees of former decoys can be seen here and there (three can be seen along the road which leads from the village through the fen towards New Leake and Stickney), but the enclosure saw the end of most of them. In Oldfield's *History of Wainfleet* one of the decoys is described. It consisted of a pond in the centre of a clump of trees; at the corners of the pond, channels, or 'pipes', led off, covered with netting, which after gradually narrowing culminated in a funnel net. The decoymen kept a number of tame 'decoy-ducks', conditioned to follow a trail of food up the pipes, thus encouraging the wild birds to follow and be captured. If they were too full or too drowsy to follow, the decoymen sometimes made use of a small dog. 'This attracts the attention of the wild fowl who, not choosing to be interrupted, advance towards the small and contemptible animal that they may drive him away.' Lured himself by small quantities of cheese, the dog lured the birds far enough down the pipes for the decoymen to appear behind them and frighten them forwards into the net.

The same small area of the East Fen near Friskney and Wainfleet also included a large area where cranberries grew wild and in abundance. The commoners picked them in vast quantities, receiving about 5s a peck from traders who sold them on, mainly in Cambridgeshire, Lancashire and Yorkshire, for making cranberry tarts. Cranberries were the speciality of a small area; the fens as a whole before drainage and enclosure provided most of the materials for constructing the houses of the surrounding inhabitants, which were usually built of stud and mud and thatched. They provided peat turves for their fires, slow to light but of a heat so intense that 'it is said that men often tied the leg-bone of a horse before their skins to prevent them from being scorched'. They provided winter fodder for their cattle, gathered from midsummer onwards according to strict and ancient rules.

> Every person having a right of common ... had the privilege of employing two labourers, and with them he would go down into the Fen on the evening before Midsummer day, and lie down until they heard the report of a gun which was fired exactly at ... midnight; then each party would arise and set to work. By common agreement all the fodder they could mow a path round became the frontager's own property. After completing one circle, each party hastened to find fresh ground ... as long as any remained unclaimed, after which they completed at leisure the mowing of those parts they had surrounded. When the reaping was over, the fodder was ... boated away ... to the fenside.

We have already heard Arthur Young's opinion of the character of many of the fenland commoners; other observers were equally distressed by the effect of 'great commons' and an easy, or at least an irregular, livelihood on the moral welfare of the inhabitants. John Cragg for instance found Chapel Hill a 'sad, blackguard place'. The description of the pre-enclosure inhabitants of Brothertoft in Marrat's *History of Lincolnshire* is well-known:

> They had hitherto lived a kind of predatory life, kept a few geese, and some of the more opulent a few sheep, and perhaps a cow, or a mare

which once a year brought them a foal . . . but they had had freedom
to range over a large track of land . . . . A life of laziness is generally
preferred; and fishing and shooting and catching wild fowl may be
called amusement rather than labour. Hence, like the Aborigines of
North America, they lived a kind of lawless life, almost in a state of
nature, and their ideas, wild as their native fens, were not very easily
subjected to reason or control.

This insubordination to reason and control was at its strongest
when attempts were made to drain the fens in the seventeenth
and eighteenth centuries. In the reign of Charles I both Holland
Fen, by Sir William Killigrew, and the East, West and Wildmore Fens, by Sir Anthony Thomas, were subject to drainage
operations which were, technically, by no means unsuccessful.
Both contractors, however, encountered the almost universal
opposition of the commoners, who claimed that their livelihood would be ruined and that the contractors were, in any case,
receiving far too large allotments of land in reward for their
services. Everywhere the story was the same: there were riots,
fences were pulled down, sluices were destroyed – especially
during the uncertain times of the Civil War; then the richer
among commoners fought them through the courts during the
Commonwealth, when the climate was by no means favourable
to contractors who owed their title to recent Crown grants. At
last they either died or retired from the scene impoverished and
exhausted, and the commoners remained triumphant and the
fens only partially drained for over a century.

In the winter of 1763 the fens suffered the greatest flood in
living memory. Not one of the 22,000 acres in Holland Fen
remained dry. This served as a spur for further improvements,
and an Act passed through Parliament in 1767 for the draining
and enclosure of Holland Fen. The actual progress of the work
was hampered over the next five years by riots, murders and at
one time a threat of open warfare. A mob of about a thousand
was prevented from setting fire to Boston only by the presence
there of the Scots Greys. Stacks were burned, sheep hamstrung,
'John Woods of Swineshead North End was shot dead as he was
sitting by his own fire.' Captain Wilks was shot in the face, and
'A person of the name of Hammond crept under the bed to hide
himself, at the same time believing and crying out that he was

Holland churches: Crowland – the north aisle of the abbey church, now the parish church, and the few surviving fragments of the nave

Algarkirk

Boston, *c.*1800

'Fen Slodgers': a nineteenth-century impression of the fenmen of an earlier period

Louth

Walesby church

shot also, which was afterwards found not to be the case.' In spite of all obstacles, however, the works went ahead, and we are told that 'Many who had used every effort to oppose it, lived afterwards to see their own folly.' Examples are given of a man who gained a scanty and not particularly honest living mainly by fishing and fowling who after enclosure rented land and accumulated a large fortune and great respectability.

The far larger project for the final drainage and enclosure of East, West and Wildmore Fens commenced in 1802 and was carried out over the next ten years. It was an immense undertaking but entirely free from the violent reaction which had hampered earlier works.

After drainage the alteration in the landscape and in the occupations and, if we are to believe contemporary report, in the character of the inhabitants was swift. 'The population has grown in numbers, in health, and in comfort . . . dreary swamps are supplanted by pleasant pastures, and the haunts of pike and wild fowl have become the habitation of industrious farmers and husbandmen.' Brothertoft, that haunt of the sturdy fen-savage became, of all things, for a brief period an industrial hamlet. One of Lincolnshire's many improving landowners, John Cartwright, whose radical politics earned him the title of 'The Father of Reform' and the political dislike of most of his neighbours, built Brothertoft Hall, cultivated woad on a large scale and set up a processing plant on the North Forty Foot Drain, accompanied by a long row of cottages for the labourers. The settlement was given the name Isatica after the Latin name of the plant. It did not survive for long, however, although woad growing continued at various places in the fens until well into the present century.

The landscape of the area as we now see it owes almost everything to the engineers who drained it and the settlers who put up their usually business-like and unprettified red-brick houses and brought the ground under cultivation. Apart from one or two small, ancient settlements and the three villages of Stickford, Stickney, and Sibsey, the main nucleated settlement was in the seven new villages of Eastville, Midville, Frithville, Carrington, Westville, Thornton-le-Fen and Langrickville. These were erected on land sold to pay for the costs of drainage, enclosure and the erection of parochial chapels for the spiritual welfare of the inhabitants of the newly reclaimed land. Apart from the main settlements there are innumerable scattered farms and cottages.

Most of the drainage channels which can now be seen are the products of the 1770s drainage of Holland Fen and the later East, West and Wildmore project. Sir Anthony Thomas has left his mark on the landscape in the Newham Drain which runs down approximately along the boundary of the West Fen and Wildmore to join the Witham at Anton's Gowt ('Anthony's Sluice'), where his name is preserved on the modern map. But it is to Rennie, who was the engineer of the later scheme, that most of the channels owe their being: the wide, straight main drains for fenland water like the Hobhole Drain which runs through the East Fen to the Witham Bank on the seaward side of Boston and the catch-water drains which follow the northern fen edge to channel highland water away from that of the fens themselves and carry it down right through the centre in its own segregated course. Cowbridge, just north of Boston on the B1183 is a good place to get an idea of the complexity of the whole undertaking. It is a sort of aquatic Spaghetti Junction where the main West Fen Drain converges with Stone Bridge Drain which carries the highland water. By an ingenious arrangement of levels and sluices, the West Fen water can be allowed to pass under that in the catchwater and flow along Cowbridge Drain to join that of the East Fen in Hobhole Drain. The whole is made even more ingenious by the provision of a 'side cut . . . in which there is a lock to allow the passage of boats from the West Fen to Hobhole Drain'.

An exploration of this fenland could have no better start than the road out of Boston to Cowbridge, along the banks of the Maud Foster Drain, past the fine early nineteenth-century five-sailed Maud Foster mill. Many of the houses here are of about the same period or a little later, and there is a liberal sprinkling of public houses to cater perhaps for its flourishing water-borne trade between the town and the fens. Beyond Cowbridge the road continues through the heart of the fens to Revesby at their northern margin. It passes through Frithville and Carrington two of the post-enclosure new parishes with their very similar Church of England chapels of red brick of 1821 and 1817 respectively. The landscape of the two parishes is a total contrast: Frithville has little greenery to protect it, while Carrington is almost lost to view among avenues of mature ash, elm and copper beech. Medlam, a little further north and on slightly higher land, is an ancient settlement of pasture closes neatly hedged with hawthorn. Farther north still, with the line of the wolds rising clearly ahead, lies New Bolingbroke, founded in 1823 by John Parkinson, a man of whom it was said that he had three ambitions: to sink a coal mine, to plant a forest and to found a city. The mine and forest will re-appear when we visit Woodhall Spa; New Bolingbroke was to be his city or at least his industrial town, 'built in such a situation that it might have a water communication with Boston, and nearly all parts of the surrounding fens, by means of navigable drains'. In spite of optimistic forecasts from time to time that it was 'improving', New Bolingbroke obstinately refused to improve to any marked degree, although by the 1850s it had a population of 650 and a church built in 1854 on a much grander scale than the fen chapels of Frithville and Carrington. Parkinson's hand can still be seen in one or two terraces and a crescent of brick cottages which he built for the workmen in his crêpe and bombazine factory; but his vision never really bore fruit, and he himself was soon bankrupt.

The main A16 from Boston to Spilsby is another good road from which to view the fens. Since it follows the ridge of slightly higher ground on which the earliest settlements of Sibsey, Stickney and Stickford were placed, it provides enormous views on both sides. Like all the houses of the fen, these villages are brick-built, and the comparatively modern appearance of most of the building which seems to be little earlier than about the 1820s) is explained by the fact that here too the most popular building material at an earlier date was mud and stud. At Stickney Fen Side a side road branches off to the left; one can follow this to Hagnaby Lock and then follow the West Fen Catchwater Drain to Revesby Bridge. The landscape to the north is now no longer fenland but fen edge; hedges and hedge-row timber begin to appear in ever-increasing quantities until one emerges from the fen among the plantations of Revesby's parkland.

In 1714 under an Act of Parliament for the sale of the estate of Henry Bowes Howard, Earl of Berkshire, 'the Manor of Revesby, and the scite of the late dissolved Monastery of Revesby . . . and the Capital Messuage or Mansion House called Revesby Mansion House', together with sundry farms and woodlands in Revesby, Kirkby or Bain, Tumby and Wilksby, came onto the market. The purchaser, at a price of £14,000 was Joseph Banks, a Sheffield attorney. His recently married son, a second Joseph, entered into immediate possession and proceeded to furnish and improve the house and estate, always under his father's watchful eye. The wood had to be protected against the 'daily filching' of the people of Mareham and other villages; improvements to the house were carried out under the direction of Mr Sherlock, who referred to the elder Joseph such questions as the amount of wainscot in the best chamber and whether extensions should have the same hipped roof as on the original house. Son consulted father also on the furnishings and what to do about the 'most base villanous' action of Mr Nash of Fleet Ditch in sending a bed which was 'the most scurvy thing that ever was imposed on anybody'. His wife was worried that her father-in-law's designs would lead to the main hall being used as a 'pashaage' between the dairy and kitchen, making it quite useless to dine in 'or the jentlemen to take a bottell in the afternoon in'. There were problems about the quality of the bricks; the Billinghay men were a pack of rogues; a man from Spilsby was mentioned; finally John Broadley of Hatfield in Yorkshire contracted to make a hundred thousand bricks in the close at Revesby where bricks had already been made, at 6s per thousand of merchantable, well-burnt bricks, Mr Banks to find wood for fencing the brickyard, wood and coal for burning the bricks and fen thatch for covering. The wood for the building came from Tumby woods, cut and shaped by John Harrison, who came from Saxilby to do the job at half a crown a hundred foot.

By the time of old Joseph's death in 1727, work on the house seems to have been completed, but it was left to his son to carry out his father's design of rebuilding the parish church (it was once more rebuilt in 1890), and he also carried out his father's other intention of building almshouses for ten 'poor decayed Farmers who are come to poverty by loss of Cattle or other Inevitable accidents and not by Idleness, Drunkenness or other Extravagance'.

The second Joseph died in 1741 and was succeeded by his son

William, who died in 1761. It was William's son, another Joseph, who brought fame to Revesby and to the family name. Sir Joseph Banks (1743-1820) bestrode the Lincolnshire of his day like a colossus, as indeed he bestrode the world of natural history, agriculture and exploration. President of the Royal Society, moving spirit behind Cook's voyages and his companion on the first, arguably the founder of modern Australia, correspondent of every scientist in Europe – his influence can be found everywhere. Similarly in his native county there was scarcely a project, whether it was a fen-drainage, an enclosure, a canal or even the removal of Lincoln Minster's spires, in which he did not expect to be consulted. His autumn visits to Revesby were almost like the progresses of a monarch. For most of the rest of the year he was in London at his house in Soho Square, keeping in touch with every detail of estate affairs through his agents at Revesby. He was a formidable and very human man, reported by reliable authority to have been addressed as 'Cousin Joe' by the lower classes in the neighbourhood, though perhaps only around the time of Revesby Fair in October when his profuse hospitality to all and sundry was based on the principle that overmuch subsequent sobriety meant that his ale had not been brewed strong enough.

Banks did not lack detractors; nor did Revesby. John Byng looked on both with a scornful eye: 'The park is flat, dismal and unimproved; the house mean and uncomfortable; with an horse pond in front; with no gardens or comforts, but when a man sets himself up as an eccentric character and (having a great estate and the comforts of England at command) can voyage to Otaheite and can reside in a corner house in Soho Square, of course his country seat will be a filthy neglected spot.' We cannot gauge the fairness of this criticism because ironically the man who left such a mark on history has left comparatively little which is now visible in and around Revesby itself.

This is because the Banks tradition of care for their estates was continued with equal enthusiasm by their successors when Sir Joseph's property was divided at his death between Sir Henry Hawley, who received Tumby, and a son of the Earl Stanhope. Revesby Abbey, which now stands empty, is not the house of the Banks family but a later one designed for the Stanhopes in 1843 by William Burn. Most of the estate architecture also dates from their period, when farms and cottages, church and almshouses were all rebuilt.

Timber is as much a feature of the area now as it was when the first Joseph bought Revesby or when large quantities were sold in the period of peak demand during the Napoleonic Wars. This is partly because of the importance attached to the growing of timber by successive owners, but due partly also to the nature of the soil. Where the ground rises slowly out of the fens and the Witham valley towards the wolds, there is a belt of 'moorish' ground, formerly wild heaths and the hunting parks of the lords of Tattershall and Scrivelsby and the abbots of Kirkstead. Much of it was poor land for agricultural purposes, like that described in about 1810 as 'soil a sharp poor sand and much annoyed by vipers to such a degree as to kill horned cattle by their venemous bite'. In many such areas timber could be the most profitable crop.

West of Revesby, after emerging from Tumby woods, the road passes through Coningsby and Tattershall towards the River Witham. The small market town of Tattershall and the large village of Coningsby have expanded to accommodate a large RAF station, whose Ministry of Defence neo-Georgian mingles somewhat uneasily with the genuine article.

The glory of Tattershall and one of the sights of England is its castle, a piece of medieval brickwork almost unique in its grandeur and scale. Centuries of decay, before the building was rescued by Lord Curzon in 1912, have cleared away many of the subsidiary buildings which originally surrounded the great tower, thus accentuating its dominance. All that remains, apart from this, are the foundations of two of the towers of a thirteenth-century castle and foundations of the kitchens. These are surrounded by an inner moat, lined in parts with the original fifteenth-century brickwork. Beyond this, but within an outer moat, are fragments of stables and a gatehouse which now houses the ticket-office and a small museum.

The first impression given by Tattershall tower is one of monumental strength; it looks as impregnable to assault as any Norman keep. Architectural historians are agreed, however, that defence was not its principal *raison d'être*. The walls may be of enormous thickness; there may be machicolations around the battlements through which arrows and boiling oil could be poured on would-be attackers; but the walls are pierced not by arrow slits but by windows of considerable size. The main purpose of this building was as the private residence of its owner, Ralph, Lord Cromwell, Lord Treasurer of England, and doubtless also as the administrative centre of his Lincolnshire estate.

The Cromwells were a Nottinghamshire family from the village of that name who, in the mid-fourteenth century, obtained possession by marriage of the lands of the de Tateshales. Ralph was born in about 1403, served in the French wars in his youth and became Lord Treasurer in 1433. At about this time he started work at Tattershall. His inspiration was almost certainly continental; perhaps from France, perhaps from as far afield as the castles of the knights of the Teutonic Order in East Prussia. He was certainly an innovator in the imaginative use of brickwork in this country. His brickmaker and brickman, and probably the man in overall charge of the works, was Baldwin Docheman, probably a German. Baldwin made enormous quantities of bricks at Edlington Moor, half a dozen miles north of Tattershall – as many as half a million a year in several years covered by the fragmentary surviving accounts. Vast amounts of wood were needed to fire the brick clamps: fifteen thousand fagots were cut in my lord's wood at Stixwould in 1434-5, as well as timber trees bought of the abbot of Bardney by the acre, and seventy-four cartloads of fuel brought from Tattershall Chase to fire the limekilns. Ancaster limestone was used for the stone facings and wold sandstone from Salmonby for the foundations, used there because it is highly impervious to the waters of the moat.

Cromwell's castle passed to the Earls of Lincoln in the sixteenth century and was one of their residences for about 150 years. It then passed to absentee owners, the Earls Fortescue. Brickwork is not such an attractive quarry as the stone monuments of antiquity; so, although in some decay, the tower survived more or less intact until 1910, when Earl Fortescue sold it. There followed a frenzied period of purchase by a Nottingham speculator, who in turn was compelled to sell by his bank. The building was in danger of ruin; its magnificent fireplaces were ripped out for export to America. A national campaign to save it succeeded in interesting Lord Curzon, who bought it himself in 1911 and then, with financial assistance from various sources, bought back the fireplaces in the following year. (They cost a good deal more than the whole of the rest.) The castle was restored, mainly at Lord Curzon's expense, and bequeathed by him to the National Trust in 1925.

The layout of the great tower is a simple one: a single large room at each level, each communicating with a number of smaller ones in the angle towers. There are a few surprises, however, for the visitor. The first is that, of the three doors facing him as he approaches the tower, one leads to a basement, the other to a ground-floor room, neither of which communicates directly with each other or with the upper floors. It is only through the smaller doorway in the south-east tower that he finds the spiral staircase to the rest of the building. All these doorways in fact once led not into the open air but into a complex of kitchens, passages and the original great hall of the castle, fragments of which survived in 1726 when Samuel Buck's engraving was published. The basement of the tower may have been a servants' hall, the ground floor perhaps a parlour; the three upper rooms were almost certainly the private suite of the Lord Treasurer, connecting with but somewhat withdrawn from the main public rooms of the castle.

This private suite consists of three great rooms of equal splendour; their individual functions are a matter of guesswork. Presumably the upper room was the bedchamber: only the very great went upstairs to bed before a much later period, but Lord Cromwell was one of the very great. The first-floor room was perhaps his great hall (as opposed to the communal great hall of the castle). The room between is approached by a splendidly brick-vaulted passage in the thickness of the wall, which might have been used as a waiting-room, and could therefore have been his chamber of audience for transacting business, holding court and receiving suitors. Whatever their purpose, they are splendid rooms, and the elaborately carved stone fireplaces are of great interest. They are covered with shields of arms, subjects such as knights slaying lions and, constantly recurring, the motif of the Treasurer's purse (either in pride of office or in thanksgiving for the profits which fell upon its holder). In the upper room the purse combines with the name of its owner in the shape of the plant Gromwell.

Up one more flight of the spiral staircase are the battlements, which provide marvellous views over wolds and fens and the valley of the Witham. Closer at hand the view to the west is over enormous water-filled gravel pits and to the east over Tattershall and Coningsby themselves, with, at the tower's foot, the church and seventeenth-century almshouses. Small enough at ground level, from the top of the tower the almshouses look like desirable residences for the Seven Dwarfs. Be warned, however, that the winds blow furiously and only the hardiest are likely to want to spend long admiring the view on any but the warmest of days.

Tattershall Castle, and his other houses at South Wingfield in Derbyshire (still surviving) and at Colleyweston in Northamptonshire (now gone), provided for the comfort of Ralph Cromwell's body. His arrangements for the future well-being of his soul were equally thorough and on the same lavish scale. At his death, probably early in 1456, he left money for three thousand Masses and directed that he should be buried in Tattershall church, which he was in the process of having rebuilt. The chancel seems to have been completed by this time but not the nave, for he requests that he should be buried in the choir and transferred to the body of the church when it is completed. Modestly he desires that his memorial should in no way interfere with the priests performing divine service. These priests would be the members of the college of secular canons which he had founded to serve the large church.

The church is as fine a monument to Cromwell as is the castle. Here the material is Ancaster stone. The founder's brass and that of his wife are still to be seen, in a somewhat mutilated condition, as is that of his niece (all this mighty building programme was carried out by a childless man) and those of several of the canons of the college. They lie in a church full of space and height and light. It would not, of course, be so full of light, but for the loss of most of its medieval glass, of which only a small amount remains. Surprisingly its loss is not through puritanical fervour but owing to a purely business transaction: in 1757 Lord Fortescue sold all the glass from the chancel to the Earl of Exeter. Much of it is now, as we have seen, in St Martin's, Stamford, and some at Burghley House.

William Banks of Revesby superintended the operation on

behalf of Lord Exeter and soon began to regret his involvement. The original agreement was for the purchaser to have the stained glass in return for reglazing the windows in plain glass and making good all damage. Lord Fortescue's steward persuaded Banks to agree instead to a single money payment to himself. At this point the townspeople rioted, assaulted the glaziers who were removing the glass and threatened them with death if they carried on with their work, and secured the solidarity of the boatmen (both as useful potential rioters and as being capable of hindering the transport of the glass). They expressed total disbelief in the steward's intention ever to reglaze the windows and feared for their lives, condemned as they would be to worship in a church open to the elements. At this Mr Hartford, the steward, huffed that he would advise Lord Fortescue never to do any more repairs to the chancel; the chancel, he said, correctly enough, was no concern of the parishioners. Somehow the *impasse* was resolved; Lord Exeter received the glass at a total cost of £33.13s.8d, including £24.2s.6d to Mr Hartford for the glass and £3.13s.5d to the unfortunate glazier, Charles Kirkham, for all his troubles. The parishioners, as they had feared, were left to shiver; in 1791 John Byng found the nave shut off from the chancel by a deal door to keep out the wind: 'every pane of its wonderful glass has been pillaged – and not replaced by any other'.

North of Tattershall between the Rivers Bain and Witham is an area of sparse settlement and poor soil. The main road to Horncastle follows the old River Bain and the Horncastle Canal. A minor road leads due northward to the small town of Woodhall Spa, passing near to the remains of the Cistercian abbey of Kirkstead. Woodhall seems almost out of place in Lincolnshire; its desirable residences among the trees give it something of a Surrey appearance. No house predates the Victorian period, for the town sprang up from nothing during the nineteenth century.

The story of Woodhall's rise and development as a health resort is an odd one. John Parkinson, whose attempt to found an industrial town at New Bolingbroke has already been mentioned, was convinced that he would find coal in this area. In 1811 he commenced a bore-hole and persevered until he had reached a thousand feet, spurred on, it is said, by some of the

workmen who occasionally took pieces of coal down the shaft
and produced them as if newly discovered. No coal was discovered, and Parkinson's money ran out; the shaft gradually
filled with water and overflowed. The water was discovered to be
saline, and various people experimented with it as a purgative,
a remedy for sick horses and a cure for rheumatism. The squire,
Mr Hotchkin, discovered that it was good for his gout. In about
1830 a horse-driven windlass was installed to draw up the
water; in 1834 a bath house was built, then the Victoria Hotel. A
resident doctor was appointed. The spa was now well equipped
to cope with the valetudinary multitudes who flocked to such
establishments. All that was needed was some reasonably convenient means by which they could actually get to the place. J.
Conway Walter, the historian of the area, recalls the roads of his
youth as 'so bad that the writer recalls going there for the first
time, when the ruts were so deep that the pony-carriage broke in
the middle and had to be abandoned'. The road from Horncastle
passed through a 'veritable Sahara'; westward a carrier's cart
'struggled through the sand once a day' to connect with the
Witham steam packet at Kirkstead. As with so many industrial
towns, Lincolnshire's health town had to wait upon the railway
for its expansion. The opening of the Boston to Lincoln line
through Kirkstead in 1848 and the construction of a branch line
through Woodhall to Horncastle seven years later were the
making of the spa, and the second half of the century was a
period of expansion; a church, a large hydropathic establishment, more hotels and, 'streets of lodging-houses, semi-
detached or detached, or single villas, and handsome residences'
had appeared by the end of the century. So had a hospital and a
home for gentlewomen in reduced circumstances in need of the
treatment. The surgeon-major at the hospital, Mr R. Cuffe
MRCS, opened his own sanatorium for the reception of high-
class patients, whilst the hospital itself was much frequented by
the suffering poor from all over the country. Some came hob-
bling on crutches, we are told, who before they went 'ran in the
foot-races at the village sports' and left their crutches nailed to
the walls of the bath house as mementoes.

At the turn of the century visitors waxed lyrical about its
beauties. One described Woodhall: 'as unlike the usual run of
fashionable watering places as one can well imagine . . . there

are wild moors purple with heather and aglow with golden gorse; a land of health and the air deliciously bracing'. It was a place where 'the faded spirit, the enfeebled frame' might draw fresh energy from the air and the peace of the surroundings as much as from its saline bromo-iodine waters, described by Bradshaw's *Dictionary of Bathing Places* as useful for everything from rheumatism to skin complaints, from women's diseases to congestion of the liver.

In an age when one takes the tablets rather than the waters, Woodhall is no longer a place to come for the cure. But it is still a popular place to live and, with its Victorian and Edwardian houses, its wooded setting and miles of woodland walks, and its lack of too much heavy traffic, it is a good place for a quiet holiday. Many of Lincolnshire's places of interest are within easy reach – easy that is if you have a car; needless to say, the railway no longer exists.

It is the woodlands that give Woodhall Spa its character. John Parkinson had a hand in this also; his third ambition was to plant a forest, and here he actually succeeded, but cruel injustice has led to the wood now being known not by the name of the planter but as 'Ostler's Plantation', after his mortgagee and succeeding owner. It now consists mainly of Forestry Commission conifers. Another of the many patches of woodland in the neighbourhood is Waterloo Wood, and a monument records that it was raised from acorns planted to celebrate Wellington's victory. The victor's bust still stands on a column with a celebratory plaque in a field by the road from Woodhall to Old Woodhall. Much of this area is comparatively recent plantation, but we are on the verge of what was, after South Kesteven, the most extensively forested part of Lincolnshire at the time of Domesday Book. The claylands to the north were heavily wooded; this was where Lord Cromwell felled his underwood at Stixwould and bought timber from the Abbot of Bardney for his works at Tattershall; and the forest had originally extended onto the sandier soils between Woodhall and Tattershall. Scrub and gorse alternated with timber on land practically useless for anything but the chase, and the neighbouring magnates squabbled over hunting rights. In 1259 the Abbot of Kirkstead and Robert of Tattershall settled such a dispute by agreeing that Robert could enter certain of the Abbot's enclosed woods to hunt,

provided that he entered by the gates, but certain other woods
he should not enter, not even to bring out his dogs if they had
gone in there, but 'shall call the dogs back by mouth and horn
and wait for them outside the woods'. After the Reformation the
lords of Tattershall, now the Earls of Lincoln, continued to feud
with their neighbours over hunting rights. In the nineteenth-
century the feuds had subsided, but the woodlands were the
scene of poaching on a grand scale; it was once even reported
that a gang of Yorkshire poachers had hired a special train to
visit the area.

In 1837 Richard Ellison, the owner of Kirkstead Abbey, had
his poem *Kirkstead, or the Pleasures of Shooting* published for
the benefit of a Fancy Fair organized by the Ladies Patronesses
in aid of Lincoln County Hospital. He sings of its natural
beauties:

> Who loves the woodlands Kirkstead must love thee
> Who worships Nature thine admirer be.

hymns its former grandeur:

> There tow'ring lofty 'gainst the clear blue sky
> Its once fam'd Abbey's ruins meets the eye
> Within whose Close, by Moat encircled round
> The wrecks of olden grandeur strew the ground

and of course its sport:

> The Pheasant's brief but brilliant day is o'er
> The death-fraught tube, its muzzle pointed high,
> Obeys the steady hand and practised eye.

By 1837 the author must have been employing considerable
poetic licence to suggest any extensive 'wrecks of olden grandeur' at Kirkstead. All that remains today of the abbey itself is
one small but extraordinarily lofty fragment of the church. At
some distance, however, along the rough track lies what was
presumably a chapel before the abbey gates. It is small, exquisite, all of a period (mid thirteenth century) even to the
extent of having contemporary woodwork in the screen and
door, and is described by Pevsner as 'up to Cathedral standard'
as an example of the architecture of its period. It has had a
chequered career, being a 'donative' (i.e. a church which is more
or less the personal property of a private owner). Since the
owner was at one time a Dissenter, it served for a while as a

Nonconformist chapel, later falling into considerable decay, and was only finally rescued and restored early in the present century.

Kirkstead was one of several religious houses in or near the valley of the Witham between Lincoln and Tattershall. In close succession northwards from Kirkstead lie Stixwould, Tupholme, Bardney, Stainfield and Barlings. Of these Barlings and Tupholme belonged to the Premonstratensian order; Bardney and Stainfield were Benedictine, the latter a nunnery; and Stixwould was a house of Cistercian nuns. The Cistercians and Premonstratensians are known for their settlement on sites on marginal lands, such as woodlands and fenny grounds, and their activity in reclaiming such grounds and in pioneering farming techniques such as intensive sheep farming. The woodlands of the Witham Valley provided an area of sparse settlement ideal for their foundations. The older Benedictine order is not normally famed for agricultural innovation and the pioneering spirit, but the enormous possibilities presented by Lincolnshire's waste lands must have been an encouragement even to them.

John Byng rode that way on his 1791 tour, lured by the many monastic sites shown on his map. His disappointment gave astringency to his prose: at Barlings what remained 'must soon come to the ground, for they are daily casting away the stones', at the 'mean village' of Bardney there was nothing to see; at Kirkstead the 'miserable common, with some miserable cottages' showed the 'lofty relic to the greatest advantage'.

Still less now remains above the ground on any of these sites: nothing at all at Bardney, Stainfield or Stixwould, a bit of wall at Barlings, and a fragment of the refectory incorporated in the wall of a farmhouse at Tupholme. Walter in his *Records of Woodhall Spa* comments that its incorporation in the farmhouse wall is all that has kept the fragments standing, 'otherwise they are so worn away at the lower part with cattle rubbing against them that they would be in danger of falling'. Unfortunately the farmhouse itself is now empty and derelict and will perhaps not be a reliable prop for many more years. He also records the story of the ghost of a headless lady there, an obvious feminist who so terrified a farm labourer in the act of beating his wife that 'he never belaboured her again'.

This whole triangle between Woodhall, Horncastle, Wragby and Lincoln mounts gradually from the Witham fens across the clay vale to the wold foothills. No major roads pass through it; instead it is traversed by a network of minor roads which amble without apparent purpose round bend after bend. They are hopeless roads for anyone in a hurry, especially in the late autumn when they are mud-covered and full of slow-moving caravans of lorries labouring towards Bardney to discharge the annual tribute to its sugar-beet factory. The villages are mostly small, brick-built, scattered on the whole rather than nucleated – typical settlement for an area reclaimed in the past from heavy woodland. The churches are small and on the whole undistinguished; many were more or less completely rebuilt in the last century following earlier neglect. A number of very fine scattered farmsteads are to be seen sometimes, with houses of considerable age, often on medieval moated sites. In some cases these are the 'halls' of the small-scale gentry who abounded in the sixteenth and seventeenth centuries. Poolham Hall and Halstead Hall are two such houses within a mile or two of Woodhall, the former on the site of a sixteenth-century manor house of a branch of the Thimblebys of Irnham, the latter probably one wing of a sixteenth-century house of considerable size, built perhaps by the Welbys who held and lived at Halstead in the late fifteenth and early sixteenth centuries.

The whole area varies from fenland to hedgeless prairies of corn, to ancient-looking closes or to thick woodland. A road from Woodhall to Bardney twists beside dykes lined with oaks and ash trees through a flat countryside. Bardney's sugar-beet factory becomes the dominating feature of the landscape, dwarfing Lincoln Cathedral's distant towers. Bardney itself is much the largest village for a considerable distance around. It grew up around the ancient abbey but owes its present size to the importance of the Witham river trade and more recently to sugar beet and canning. The present appearance is more work-manlike than beautiful, but there is plenty of Georgian and earlier brickwork to be seen among the Victorian and later houses, as well as one of the larger and more interesting parish churches in the area and the site of the abbey.

At Bardney one can either cross the Witham into North Kesteven or follow the road through the fens to the north of the river towards Lincoln. To the north lies a well-wooded area of small scattered villages: Stainfield, Gautby and Goltho. Each of these parishes possesses a small, brick-built church, each of them the site of a now disappeared great house. At the former the Tyrwhitts had their home, pulled down and replaced by something much smaller in the nineteenth century. Gautby was the seat of the Vyners, wealthy London merchants who built up a great estate in Lincolnshire for many years before they deserted it for their Yorkshire seat at Newby. At Goltho the Granthams were already going very much to seed in the early eighteenth century, and accumulating debts forced the last of the family to sell out to the Mainwarings. There is now only a small scattering of cottages among the trees near the farm on the site of their mansion house, but half a mile away, alone in the middle of an enormous field of sugar beet, is the small brick church, splendid in itself and in its interest as being a building almost entirely of the mid seventeenth century, hardly the most prolific period for church-building. A clump of lofty sycamore and dead elms surrounds it and threatens to take over the whole of the churchyard. The church has been redundant for years and was falling into severe decay but is now being restored.

From Gautby's decayed Great Park towards Bardney the landscape could be northern French: a great plain, part corn, part sheep-pasture, is edged by forest. Islands, capes and headlands of wood gradually enclose and become a solid mass. The Forestry Commission had given the title 'Bardney Forest' to much of the woodland in this area, far beyond the bounds of Bardney Abbey's original woods. East of Gautby and Minting, another scattered village with much pasture land, the country-side takes on a totally different appearance: we enter a gently rolling prairie where for what looks like miles every hedge has been grubbed up to produce a single, enormous arable field. An occasional derelict farmhouse stands forlorn. Recently planted roadside saplings will, if they survive, some day re-introduce some green. Meanwhile rows of enormous rolled bales provide windbrakes in the more exposed places; one farm bungalow shelters inside a complete square of them as if stockaded against Indian attack.

Towards Horncastle the ground rises to the first foothills of the Wolds at Thornton and Langton and Thimbleby, a place which arouses a sudden pleasure with its vista of white thatched houses along the main street. Thatch is in fact far from uncommon in this part of Lincolnshire. There is more to be seen in the valley of the River Bain as it flows southwards from Horncastle to Tattershall, at Haltham for instance. The Bain was canalized in the 1790s between Horncastle and the Witham and 'found to be a very beneficial convenience for the whole vicinity of country'. The canal proprietors fought a fierce war of squibs and placards to keep the railway out of Horncastle in the 1850s, but lost. The canal decayed, and in due course the railway was axed. The long-disused canal is now a peaceful stream, its banks yellow with ragwort.

5

The Lindsey Coastal Marsh

From Wainfleet and Skegness northwards to the mouth of the Humber stretches the coastline of the ancient county of Lindsey,

> Whose shore like to the back of a well-bended bow
> The ocean beareth out.

For its whole length of some forty miles runs a coastal plain, never more than ten miles wide, sometimes less than five. This is the Marsh, described by an observer in 1827 as, 'An immense plain, bounded on one side by the sea banks, on the other by the wolds, almost hidden in the foggy exhalations which arise from the intervening fen . . . unbroken . . . save here and there by a church, a cottage or a farm, and occasionally enlivened by the herds of cattle and flocks of sheep which form the riches of the country. There are no villages to be seen as such, no assemblies of houses.' A stranger, he continues, must think that this area is the abode of poverty and want, but he will be wrong. 'A marsh farmer . . . appears a favourite of Fortune and Felicity . . . he lives in the midst of plenty blest with all that can make life desirable. Labourers, too, appear to be strangers to poverty and want.' As early as 1629 another commentator had remarked that 'in the marishes beyond Wainfleet it is hard to find a poore man'.

These comments on the wealth of the area must be taken with some caution, as must the remark that there were no nucleated villages. The Marsh had, and has, plenty of villages, and these villages did not lack their poor at most periods of history. If many parishes in the area were comparatively free from poverty, the reason lay in the large and in many cases increasing areas of pasture, gained from a receding sea. This was the likely encouragement for an increase in population during the Middle Ages which made the Marsh one of Lincolnshire's most densely settled areas by the mid sixteenth century. But the sea was not everywhere giving; some parishes gained land, others lost it, in a constant see-saw battle which continues even now.

The pastures were the glory of the Marsh and encouraged an economy which specialized in meat-production. The region was famous in particular for the fattening of cattle, and agricultural observers judged with critical and discerning eyes the quality of its grassland, which varied from parish to parish. Arthur Young, for instance, runs through the northern Marsh villages dividing their pastures into those which were good for 'feeding' and fattening and those which were good enough for 'breeding' only, where cattle and sheep could breed and hold their weight but not increase it. Rich and succulent grass was needed to put on the thick layer of fat demanded by the taste of the period and necessary also to support the beasts on their long journeys to the markets of London, the Midlands and Yorkshire.

From the seventeenth century, at latest, to the nineteenth, marshland graziers made healthy profits by buying cattle from distant parts of Lincolnshire and beyond, and fattening them for sale. Increasingly, however, more and more of the land came into the hands not merely of absentee landlords but even of absentee tenants. As early as 1630 a farmer from Minting, near Lincoln, had a holding thirty or more miles away at Ingoldmells, and by the early eighteenth-century wold farmers who bred sheep or cattle 'were under a sort of necessity of takeing a quantity of Marshlands to feed 'em with before they sold 'em (for their own lands were too poor to fatt 'em)'. This invasion of 'foreigners' reached its greatest extent in the late eighteenth and early nineteenth centuries. 'By degrees the wold farmers have gradually been getting the whole, except some few small occupations,' said Arthur Young in 1813. At about the same time John Cragg found at Sutton-in-the-Marsh a 'level rich country much in grass, very thinly inhabited, the Wold farmers being chiefly the occupiers'.

It was perhaps this concentration on pasture farming which led to a corresponding neglect of arable improvement. Enclosure came late, not until the 1830s and 1840s in many places, and the open arable fields betrayed the problems encountered in dealing with a strong clay soil and also, according to Arthur Young, the lack of initiative of landlords, farmers and stewards, 'all five centuries behind in every idea relative to strong land'. He travelled in September from Tetney to Covenham through open fields 'covered with thistles, past their blossom, high enough to hide a jackass'. Edmund Oldfield, who described the southern portion of the Marsh in his *Account of Wainfleet and the Wapen-take of Candleshoe* published in 1829, agreed that, 'in no part of England has there been less improvement of the mode of cultivation'. He ascribed this charitably to the natural fertility of the soil, 'Where nature has been the most bountiful of her gifts, the exertions of man . . . are generally the least conspicuous'.

The lack of resident landlords (by the eighteen century few gentry were actually seated on their Marsh estates) may help to account for agricultural backwardness. It certainly helps to explain the treelessness of much of the landscape, and, combined with the clay soil, it was a major cause of that nondescript appearance which most early travellers found in the Marsh villages. They saw straggling settlements where only the principal farmhouses aspired to brick and tile. Smaller farmhouses were built of 'mud and stud' (rows of upright stakes or beams, or 'studs', were in-filled with osiers, reeds or even straw, which was daubed with clay, or sometimes plaster or mortar, to make the walls) as were all the labourers' cottages. In 1848 the vicar of Willoughby complained of a cluster of such 'mud huts' opposite his gates where eleven people slept in one unventilated room and where the whole group was served by one privy with no door, no roof and no sides. Such accommodation was a challenge for the improving landlord, and gradually during the nineteenth-century brick and tile replaced mud and stud. Much of Willoughby was on the Ancaster estates, where Lord Willoughby de Eresby's tenants were encouraged to improve their holdings by the supply of free bricks and tiles from estate brickyards if they found the labour. Improvement, however, was a long process, and Lord Willoughby's agent grew to approve of mud and stud as a building material: 'For £20 a good sized cottage may be built to last 80 years, which is better than a high-rented one for a labourer.' He feared the hasty changes which might be produced by too-frequent visits of the landowner himself to this outlying estate.

The comparatively few older brick houses of the Marsh are of a rich red-brown colour, flecked with specks of blue and black, a delight to the eye, especially when they are set off by the varying greens of the pasture closes and mature trees which surround many of the older farmsteads. Most of these bricks were produced to order by itinerant brick-makers who set up their clamps on any suitable neighbouring bed of clay. The more modern, more even, red brick in which the greater part of most villages is constructed dates from much later, from the mid nineteenth century onwards, when brickyards appeared ever more thickly over the Marsh to provide the wherewithal for the great rebuilding. By 1876 there were over twenty-five in the area. One reason why this was impossible earlier, apart from the great urge for 'improvement' in all its forms which was a feature of the Victorian age, was transport. Without good roads, heavy loads can only be carried with ease from and to places which are easily accessible by water. Before at earliest and the 1820s travellers were universal in their condemnation of the roads in the Marsh. The clay was as impervious to improvements in transport as it was to improvements in cultivation. In about 1800 a traveller found Tetney to be 'eleven miles N.E. of Louth by the sea in a cold clay country, cursed roads'. Grainthorpe was 'in a low cold wett part of the country, terrible bad roads'. At Burgh-le-Marsh the roads were, of late years, very much improved, where before travellers had been forced during the winter to leave their horses at Spilsby and walk. In 1829, according to Oldfield, the main roads were now very good at all seasons. 'The bye-roads . . . are on the contrary very bad for at least six months in the year,' and their condition was a fair specimen of what even the main roads had been like a few years before. 'To the credit of the inhabitants of this district, however, it deserves to be recorded, that at an immense expense they have procurred materials from a considerable distance and have put their principal roads into excellent repair, without calling in the aid of a Turnpike Act.'

Even today many of the roads of the Marsh wind and twist in a most trying fashion for the motorist as they follow the courses laid down by the drier ground of earlier centuries. In some cases it is sea banks long since redundant or the wild eccentric line of ancient settlement which mark out the line of the roads. This is particularly clear between Grimsby and Mablethorpe, where a minor road runs south from Tetney through a series of villages at what was probably the safe seaward limit for Anglo-Saxon settlement. Further east runs the A1031 which follows a line of later settlements, often along what was once the sea bank ('Seadyke Way' in Marshchapel). Most of the villages along this road were originally secondary settlements from the inland parishes; the place-names suggest it: 'Marshchapel', a chapelry in the marshes belonging to Fulstow; 'Somercotes', a collection of huts or sheepcotes used when the stock was feeding in summertime in the coastal marshes. Several of them are so recent (in terms of the age of most Lincolnshire villages) that they first appear in the records not in Domesday Book itself but at various dates in the following two centuries.

Through the marshland run the streams, canalized and embanked for many centuries, which carry the upland water down to the sea, Waithe Beck, the Long Eau, the Great Eau, Willoughby High Drain, the Steeping River. 'Eau' or 'Ea' is a common Lincolnshire word for a water-course; it comes from a root common to both Romance and Teutonic languages, in this case probably an Anglo-Saxon word for 'river', rather than from the French 'eau', as one would at first assume. The outfall of many of these streams is through small 'havens', breaks in the coastal sandbanks formerly used as harbours. Tetney Haven is one, given a new lease of life in the eighteenth and nineteenth centuries by the opening of a canal from Louth. Saltfleet Haven, the outfall of the combined Long Eau and Great Eau, was a port of considerable importance in the Middle Ages. Wainfleet Haven, where the Steeping River runs into the sea, was probably of even greater importance.

As in the fens the upkeep of the drains and sea banks was a matter of the utmost importance. Each Wapentake had its Commissioners of Sewers who met regularly to receive petitions, to make orders and to act on the verdicts of the jurors, whose business it was to look into the state of the whole drainage of the area and to report upon it. A single year's proceedings of the Court of Sewers for the area, 1665 for instance, shows both the complexity of the network of rights and responsibilities and the importance attached to them. Individuals who defaulted in scouring the dykes for which they were responsible were liable to be fined the large sum of 40s, the threat of which was usually enough to bring them to heel. Sometimes a whole community defaulted and was fined, though this was often merely one stage in a complex dispute over who was responsible for what. The Commissioners had to decide on such problems as whether Skegness and Winthorpe, which drained to the sea partly through Burgh Drain, should contribute to its upkeep; or whether the parish of Tetford had the right to obstruct the passage of waters from South Ormsby. The people of Welton complained that the Orby people had placed a 'shittle' (a sluice) at such a point that it drew off the water from Welton's pastures in summer, but it was closed up in winter so that their grounds were 'surrounded and overflown'. No doubt drainage squabbles exacerbated jealousies between neighbour and neighbour, between village and village, but the system of collective responsibility may also have given to all a sense of the interaction of their various parts in the whole mechanism by which these works 'of great consequence and concernment to the country' was performed.

Just to the south of Wainfleet on the west side of the A52 from Boston is a pasture field covered with extraordinary ranks of small, rounded mounds. These are 'saltcotes' or 'salt-hills', examples of which survive throughout the Marsh and the fens around the Wash. They are the visible evidence of an industry which flourished in the area from the Iron Age to the seventeenth century, the evaporation of salt from sea water. The mounds when excavated prove to contain salterns, low, round hearths made of hand bricks (lumps of clay squeezed into shape by hand) covered with the debris of fires and of the earthenware vessels in which the brine was evaporated. A coastline of scrubby country with a clay soil cut by tidal creeks was ideal in providing the raw materials for this industry. In the Iron Age, and more especially in Roman times, the evidence is even more plentiful from around the Wash than it is from the Marsh. The Roman or pre-Roman Salter's Way, which runs from the fens past Donington in Holland and south of Grantham to join the Fosse Way in Leicestershire, was almost certainly a route by which this most important commodity was exported to other parts of the country. By the early Middle Ages the main centres of salt-making may have moved northward. The documentary as well as the visual evidence is plentiful: thirteen salterns in the Domesday description of Tetney, for instance. Manorial rents were often paid in salt. In the sixteenth century the

Fulstow salters were travelling as far afield as Gainsborough market to sell their goods. The industry, however, seems to have collapsed rather suddenly by the middle of the next century. Holinshed's *Chronicle* mentions the disaster of the great tide of 1571 when 'all the salt-cotes where the chief and finest salt was made were utterly destroyed to the utter undoing of many a man and greate lamentation of old and young'. But one natural disaster could scarcely cause the total collapse of an industry which did not rely on heavy capital investment; no doubt the salterns were repaired. The construction of defensive banks on the seaward side of the saltcotes in the early seventeenth century may have contributed to their decay; or other centres of the industry may have taken over the Lincolnshire salters' markets; or their supply of easily available brushwood for fuel may have run out. Possibly they found that the production of meat was now more profitable than the manufacture of its preservative; at Tetney in 1627 the salt floors were decayed and turned into good pasture for sheep.

Lincolnshire's medieval and later coastline, then, was an area of small harbours in inlets of the sea, saltcotes, rough pasture and scrubby sandhills. Many areas were gaining land, but some, Skegness for instance and Trusthorpe, were losing it, and the whole was subject to occasional disastrous floods like the one of 1571, the inspiration probably of Jean Ingelow's famous poem, 'High Tide on the Coast of Lincolnshire'. Away from the havens after the decay of the salt industry only a few shepherds and warreners would be found actually on the coast. In 1709 the parishioners of Skegness reported at the bishop's visitation that they had no chest for alms 'nor would it be of use in our very small parish'. In the 1720s Burrell Massingberd of South Ormsby, lord of the manor of Ingoldmells, employed a general factotum on his Skegness property to act as shepherd, to 'constantly fish and fowl and come up with crabs, shrimps and cockles . . . as often as he has anything worth bringing'. At the very least he should bring fish up to Ormsby at every spring tide, to be accompanied always by not less than two couple of Skegness rabbits, together with fowl whenever possible. He was to receive his share of the fish and game which he could sell and also to receive a percentage of the value of waifs, strays, royal fishes and wrecks. These were all the perquisites of the lords of the coastal manors. Cash received from the sale of wrecks appears in medieval accounts of the manor of Ingoldmells, and as late as 1829 one of Burrell Massingberd's descendants was receiving reports of cases of champagne, mirrors and books, 'washed on shore from some foring ship in these last heavy gales'.

The Lincolnshire coast was exceedingly dangerous and unsheltered for shipping. In the early nineteenth century, led by Charles Burrell Massingberd and other landowners, an attempt was made to set up rescue stations. A Lincolnshire Coast Association was formed in 1826 and received its first lifeboat from the national association which was placed at Gibraltar Point near Skegness. A contemporary report of the founding of the association bears witness to the unenviable reputation of the marsh-men:

> Perhaps no race of men possess so little of the milk of human kindness as the inhabitants of Saltfleet, and some other of the marsh towns and villages, and better had a vessel be stranded on the coast of Africa than on the shores of Lincolnshire. . . . These Christian savages on their sand-hills patiently 'Abide the pelting of the pitiless storm,' and when they see a vessel driving on the beach, clap their hands and shout exaltingly. THANK GOD A WRECK. . . . [It is] the practice of these inhabitants to run up scores at the ale-houses . . . to be paid off at the next GODSEND.

Other inhabitants, however, were more interested in rescue than wrecks, and the words of one of them should be allowed to redress the balance. Writing to Massingberd in 1827, John Booth confesses to overpowering excitement 'at the recollection of the transactions of that memorable night when the eleven poor Swedes were saved – never did Fox-Hunter feel more ardour . . . than when hand joined in hand on that memorable occasion'.

The first hardy sea-bathers seem to have made their appearance on this uninviting coastline in the early eighteenth century. By the early years of the nineteenth century inns were ready for their reception all down the coast from Cleethorpes to Skegness (as well as at Freiston and Fosdyke in Holland). In 1826 Sutton was 'an improved bathing place' where the sands were remarkably fine, broad and firm. By the turn of the century Skegness possessed 'an excellent Hotel for the accommodation of sea-bathers and a good sandy shoar'. John Byng was less complimentary; his description of the vile, shabby inn, its harridan of a hostess ('all filth, shelling peas and making tarts'), its lack of amenities ('no gardens, no walk, no billiard-room, nor anything for comfort or temptation') and its abominable food ('some miserable smelts and some raw, rank, cold beef') is one of the most entertaining sections of the most entertaining of travel-journals. To make matters worse, it was full, and 'from all these miseries and a kitchen stinking of strong mutton and a roasting hog' he had perforce to hurry away.

The bathers could be fickle in their likes and dislikes, transferring their allegiance from Cleethorpes to Mablethorpe to Skegness to Freiston Shore. Not all coastal developments were a success: the inn at Saltfleet failed. Byng described Saltfleet as a 'poor place under a sea-bank, with a wretched inn bathing-house', but he was by now thoroughly jaundiced against the Lincolnshire coast. There are, however, clues to the mixed success of some resorts in his description of his ride to Saltfleet along the sands, 'the widest I ever rode upon . . . with a North wind full against us'. On the Lincolnshire coast it was, and is, sometimes a long trek from the resort to the sea, and the climate was and is often exceedingly 'bracing'.

The development of this stretch of exposed and inhospitable coast from the resort of the intrepid and comparatively moneyed few to the playground of millions was the product of the second half of the nineteenth century. By 1903 the author of Murray's *Handbook for Lincolnshire* could say: 'The sea-coast places, which are practically only four, Cleethorpes, Skegness, Mablethorpe and Sutton-on-Sea, are the great summer playground of the working classes in Nottinghamshire, Derbyshire and Leicestershire, besides drawing in many from Yorkshire, and even Lancashire, who are conveyed by the spirited northern railways in express excursion trains every day through the summer at fares for which, south of London, one could hardly get to the suburbs.' Cleethorpes got off to a flying start. The arrival of the railway at nearby Grimsby in 1848, and an easy omnibus connection from there, opened up the Lincolnshire seaside to easy and quick access from the manufacturing districts for the first time. The other resorts had to wait till later in the century. Once the link was opened, and especially when the cheap fares were available the visitors came in flocks. At the turn of the century Skegness had a quarter of a million, by 1913 it had 750,000, in the summer season.

There was, of course, more to this development than merely the provision of transport. Landlords, railway companies, local authorities, landladies and tradesmen combined in producing a whole infrastructure of piers, promenades, bowling-greens, cricket pitches, amusement arcades, bathing machines, board-ing-houses and pleasure gardens for the entertainment of the visitors.

The developments of the railway age were limited to the three easily accessible areas of Cleethorpes, Mablethorpe and Sutton, and Skegness. Between the wars the rise of the car opened up almost the whole of Lindsey's coastline to the threat of random development, stemmed somewhat by the compulsory purchase of large stretches by Lindsey County Council in the 1930s under the Sandhills Act. The post-war years have brought the ad-ditional delights of holiday camps and caravan sites in great abundance.

The resultant *mélange* in a stretch of seaside which caters for every taste from the most gregarious to the most misanthropic. It is still possible to find stretches of sand, even at the height of summer, where your nearest neighbour is scarcely within hail-ing distance and where there is hardly a building to be seen, except perhaps the ruin of some wartime concrete defence-post crumbling away among dunes covered with sea-buckthorn. Several stretches of the Marsh and dunes are now protected as nature reserves. At one, Gibraltar Point near Skegness, apart from the interest of the abundant bird-life, one can see both on the ground and in the explanatory display at the visitors' centre the gradual development of the marshland as the sea retreats.

The southern entry to the Lindsey Marsh is at Wainfleet, a town which can be summed up in the words of an early nineteenth-century commentator: 'It still retains thus much of its former grandeur that it is the neatest and most compact town thereabouts.' By that time the importance of its haven as a port was long gone, and it was navigable only to small vessels. The final blow to the haven was probably the drainage of the East

Fen, by means of which all the fen waters were made to flow south to join the Witham. Wainfleet is still, however, a town rather than a village; some of the terraces of houses would look quite at home in a London square. The nineteenth-century red-brick buildings around the market-place are all on a similar scale and give a pleasant unity. The most interesting building in the town is the school, founded in 1484 by William Waynflete, Bishop of Winchester, as an act of pious benevolence towards the place of his birth. It stands now splendid and somewhat marooned among prefabricated school buildings of the present century. This is another of Lincolnshire's fine pieces of medieval brickwork and has an interesting connection with the finest of them all, Tattershall. William Waynflete was one of Ralph, Lord Cromwell's executors and responsible for the completion of Cromwell's college there. He must have been familiar with Tattershall Castle, and the circumstantial evidence is strong that his interest in brick as a building material may stem from there. A contract survives which shows that Henry Alsbroke of Tattershall was involved in the construction of Wainfleet School, though apparently as a carpenter rather than a brick-mason.

North of Wainfleet the A52 soon reaches Skegness, Lincolnshire's greatest contribution to the amusement of millions. From here the area of coastal development takes in Ingoldmells and to a lesser extent Chapel St Leonards. Then there is a partial reprieve, where a minor road follows the old sea bank, while lanes lead to parking places under the modern one, before another long strip of built-up seaside between Sutton-on-Sea and Mablethorpe.

Inland the Marsh roads twist along dykesides through a landscape which is flat, hedgeless, often almost treeless, much of it still pasture, through villages which contain a superb series of churches, second only to those of Holland. Many of them are very large; the fifteenth century is often the predominant period in their construction. Addlethorpe and Burgh-le-Marsh near Skegness are examples of this period, the former full of fine medieval woodwork, which is perhaps more plentiful in this area than anywhere else in the county. There is more at Burgh, where the church of the small market town is rivalled in size and splendour by the great tower of the windmill, and at nearby

Croft which may be a little earlier than the other two churches.

The first slight upward slopes from the Marsh towards the wolds are marked from Burgh up to Alford by a much more wooded countryside. The major landowners of the area chose this stretch of land to build their seats and to surround them with parklands and plantations. Gunby Hall and Well Vale were the centres of large estates; Boothby Hall the seat of the Walls family in the parish of Welton-le-Marsh of a lesser one, but one of great historical interest to Arthur Young. 'I was on a sort of classic ground, for here was first reared that breed of true Lincoln sheep which afterwards became so famous in the county.'

Gunby was the seat of the Massingberds; Sir William started work on the construction of the hall around 1690. Most of the bricks were locally produced; some were Dutch, imported through Hull. In 1698 one of the ships bringing them was captured by a Dunkirk privateer and had to be ransomed. Stone for the facings came from Ketton in Rutland, carried by boat down the Welland and then round to Skegness. On Whit Monday 1701 the shell must have been complete, for on that day Erington the carpenter received a 2s.6d tip when he began to nail the floors. Work on the ceilings was going on in 1702, and the whole house was finished probably in 1706, when the baronet totted up his expenditure and worked out that the whole job had cost him £2,134.9s.3½d. Spread out over more than a decade, using as far as possible both materials and workmen from the estate, the new house was not the drain upon the family fortune that a building more speedily and lavishly put up could easily have been. The hall in its magnificent park now belongs to the National Trust.

Westward from Gunby the upland landscape of the wolds takes over almost immediately; a little to the south, however, the Marsh extends rather more inland along the valley of the River Lymn, or Steeping River as its eastern canalized portion is called, which reaches the sea at Wainfleet Haven. There is still an enormous amount of marshland pasture in this area, around Thorpe St Peter and Irby and Bratoft, where a moated site shows the whereabouts of the Massingberds' earlier seat, before they moved to Gunby.

At Halton Holegate just to the east of Spilsby the Marsh has given way to gently rising ground. The large greenstone church with its splendid clerestory is almost entirely a fifteenth-century building, restored in 1846. Inside, the woodwork is its principal feature; the restorers found a nineteenth-century craftsman equal in skill and humour to his medieval predecessors. The poppyheads of the bench ends are delightful: women with varying hair-styles, some of them bearded, pelicans, a king, another pot-bellied king and a pair of beautiful owls are probably medieval. The nave roof of dark oak has golden angels and painted bosses; one or two very odd-looking heads actually seem to be wrapped round the main beams. The ochre-coloured ceiling of the chancel must belong to the 1846 restoration. The man responsible for this restoration, the Reverend T. H. Rawnsley, incumbent from 1825 to 1861, can be seen looking beetle-browed and fierce among a fine array of vicars' photographs. Glass with lacy, grey, geometric patterns commemorates him in a number of windows. He was a great figure in the area, whose absences from his living, with minimal provision for the performance of the services, produced the local riddle: 'Why is Rawnsley like England? Because he expects every man to do his duty.'

Spilsby, 'a small, but thriving and well-built market town', in 1856 also earned some importance as the administrative centre and meeting-place of the Court of Quarter Sessions for southern Lindsey. The imposing Doric portico of its now-disused Sessions House greets the traveller from the west. The hub of the town is its market square with a market hall of 1764, whose original open arcades are now filled in with a garage, and the comfortable shape of the White Hart Inn, with a lifelike statue of a hart crowning a projecting bay. Brick and stucco of varying tints are almost the sole building materials. Virtually the only stone to be seen is in the church, with a tower of rough greenstone and a body of all too smoothed and scraped Ancaster stone. It was heavily restored and enlarged in the 1870s.

It is the Willoughby tombs which are the feature of greatest interest of both the church and the town. The area around Spilsby, together with lands somewhat further north, near Alford, were the heartlands of the estates of the medieval Barons Willoughby de Eresby. They took their distinguishing title from Eresby, on the outskirts of Spilsby, and kept and occasionally occupied a great house there until it was destroyed by fire, 'with the boiling over of a plummer's pot when the roof was repairing', in 1769. Later generations are buried at Edenham in South Kesteven, but for Peregrine, the 'Bold Lord Willoughby', as well as for his father and mother, the pull of the resting-place of their ancestors was greater than their loyalty to the parish church of their principal residence, Grimsthorpe.

The earlier generations represented here are the first three Lords Willoughby, who died in 1348, 1372 and 1396. The second Lord rests his mail-clad feet on a dog of almost human features, which looks up somewhat reproachfully at this treatment. Round the tomb is a frieze of tiny monastic figures. The third Lord lies beside Elizabeth, his fourth wife; Margaret Zouche, her predecessor, has a separate memorial brass. The fifth Lord Willoughby, who died in 1410, and his wife are also commemorated by a brass. The side chapel in which they all lie was the original chancel of the church. When the first Lord endowed a chantry of the Holy Trinity in 1348, it was placed here and a new chancel built. By 1384 the chantry was served by a master and twelve chaplains.

There are no tombs between 1410 and that of the Duchess of Suffolk and Richard Bertie erected after his death in 1582. This is the most imposing of them all, filling the whole of the original chancel arch. Its back, facing the body of the church, is adorned with suitable texts; the front has busts of Bertie and his Duchess, supported by large figures of a monk, a benevolent-looking wild man and a Saracen king who seems to be wearing some kind of surgical support. Their son, Peregrine, the tenth Lord, reclines in a statesmanlike attitude on his wall monument, which he shares with his daughter, who leans rather nonchalantly on her elbow. At his death in 1601 Peregrine was Governor of Berwick, a hot spot during periods of strained relations between England and Scotland. His body travelled by ship to Grimsby, where his coach met it to carry it to Spilsby. The cortège travelled overnight and arrived at an empty, locked Eresby House at six in the morning. Ten servants were left attendant upon the dead lord in the gatehouse while Mr Guevara, who was in charge of proceedings, went in search of keys and credit for their victuals.

The 'neat market town' of Alford is about ten miles north of

Spilsby. Here, as in most of the small towns of Lindsey, the predominant feature is nineteenth-century brick and tile, symptomatic of the modest expansion of its markets and fairs and local commercial importance brought about by the arrival of the railway. A canal to the sea had also been projected but was never built. The thatched seventeenth-century manor house and a number of cottages roofed in the same material stand out now, but in the late eighteenth century thatch was almost universal in the town. Possibly there would have been more such survivals but for an accident in which many of the houses round the market-place were burnt down 'from a cartridge from one of the cavalry on exercise'. On the slopes above the town the splendid parkscape of Well Vale surrounds house and church, which both date from the first half of the eighteenth century.

Two or three miles north-east of Alford is the tiny thatched church of Markby, with box pews and a two-decker pulpit. About as far south is the large village of Willoughby, which gave its name to the family. There are no monuments of the medieval lords in its fine early Perpendicular church; these are to be found at Alford. By the early nineteenth century Willoughby seems to have become one of the problem parishes of the Willoughby d'Eresby estate. The farms all had their lands scattered and intermingled over a wide area, and most of the farmhouses and buildings were far from their fields, lying in the centre of the village 'in among public houses and beershops; it is the destruction of many farmers and engenders bad habits among their men'. Much of the housing for the poor was shocking; the group of mud huts which was the sight greeting the Reverend Thomas Dupré whenever he went out through the rectory gates in 1848 has already been mentioned. His was a jaundiced view, in any case; he criticized the farmers and fell out with the agents of the estate; only their permission to shoot over the Willoughby lands could possibly reconcile him to the gloom of barbarity of the place, and that permission he could not get. Much rebuilding was, in fact, going on in the area at about this time; in 1856 the county *Directory* could describe Willoughby as 'a neat village'.

North of Alford the villages fall into two well-defined lines. Nearer the coast the row of settlements are strung out on or near the A1031; the Theddlethorpes, the Saltfleetbys, North and South Somercotes. At this point the road and the line of villages swing inland; from them narrow lanes go down to the vast expanses of marsh and sand at the mouth of the Humber. Marshchapel has another good Perpendicular church, as has Tetney. We are now getting into the catchment area of Grimsby, and many of the villages at the northern end of the Marsh have expanded considerably to satisfy its housing needs. In some cases this may give a compact and nucleated appearance to settlements which were once very scattered indeed, as further south the Saltfleetbys and Theddlethorpes still are.

The earlier inner line of villages runs south from Tetney, through Fulstow, the Covenhams and the Cockeringtons to Manby. The minor road which connects them is a winding one even by the standards of the Marsh, but the traveller who follows it is rewarded by villages of dark brickwork set among trees and pasture fields, distant views of the wolds to the west (and the apparently equally elevated banks of Covenham reservoir to the east) and, of course, more good churches. At Yarburgh the doorway is carved with a representation of the Fall; Adam and Eve fall prey to the serpent while moles look out from the roots and a bird nests in the branches of the Tree of Knowledge. At Alvingham a path over a stream past a watermill and farmyard leads to a churchyard beside the Louth canal where two parish churches stand side by side, those of Alvingham and North Cockerington.

6

The Southern Wolds

At Spilsby one is on the threshold of the Lincolnshire Wolds. Northwards and westwards the roads cross them; even the road south to Boston skirts them for a while; only back towards the coast are they avoided. This area of chalk upland, about forty miles long from south to north and perhaps fifteen miles in width, is the one region of Lincolnshire of any size upon which connoisseurs of the picturesque have habitually bestowed their seal of approval. Admittedly these wolds, with a maximum height of about 550 feet, are not exactly Alpine in the majesty of their proportions, but nature's undulations and acclivities and the plantations of the improving hand of man combine to provide a landscape which has given delight to generations of travellers. Chalk is the basis of the landscape, and almost everywhere it is brought to the surface at every ploughing. A universal feature of the land at many times of the year is the scattered chalk lying over the brown soil like a mist. On the western slopes, sometimes over quite considerable areas, an underlying bed of sandstone comes to the surface, sometimes red but more often the distinctive green sandstone which is so commonly seen as a building material among the wolds and in the surrounding areas.

Viewed from the adjoining lowlands of either marsh or fen, the rising ground of the wolds always dominates our horizon. To William Cobbett's daughter, accompanying her father on one of his rural rides, the effect of the first sight of the wolds after a lengthy tour in the Fens was like the first sight of land after a voyage across the Atlantic. The beauty of Lincolnshire's uplands to the eye of the picturesque tourist was equalled by their attraction for the early settlers in search of a home. They provided sheltered valleys with easily workable soil eagerly sought by the Saxon and especially by the Danish invaders. In the southern wolds in particular the settlements are very thickly scattered, and a large proportion of them have the Danish ending 'by'. The thickness of the primary settlements left little room for later infilling, so that the 'thorpes', usually associated with secondary, subsidiary settlements, are few and far between. Paradoxically, although the closeness of the settlements one to another suggests heavy colonization at an early period, the area is now one of comparatively sparse population. Most of the parishes are small, and few villages have grown to any great size. The amount of arable land in the valley bottoms available to each parish was limited, and the slopes of the hills provided only warrens for rabbits or pasture for the fine-wooled sheep whose fleeces, with those from the Kesteven uplands, were among the most valuable in medieval England. Before the late eighteenth century farmers had neither the techniques nor the capital to produce worthwhile arable crops from the hungry chalk land of the wolds. Small acreages, limited arable land, demanded few labourers. The typical south wold village is therefore small, and only small churches were needed to accommodate small populations. Some settlements did not survive; there are a number of 'lost' villages in the area, particularly around Louth, and a number which have shrunk to little more than a single farm and a tiny church or no church at all.

Few of these churches now have a resident vicar or rector; they are combined into large groups under, usually, a single incumbent. Thus the contracted Church of England in the late twentieth century is forced to ape the less official arrangements of former years when the smallness of the parishes and their often exiguous endowments produced a not dissimilar situation. 'It is not unusual in many parishes to have divine services performed but once in three weeks or a month,' says Arthur Young. The absence of public worship would, he feared, drive the farm-labourer to depravity, licentiousness and alehouses. Fortunately perhaps for their morals, even alehouses were often few and far between.

Arthur Young reminds us in his comments on wold farming how much this landscape, like most of Lincolnshire, owes to the hand of man. Before high corn prices during the Napoleonic Wars encouraged the massive expenditure of money and effort needed to bring such marginal lands into cultivation, much of the upland area was fit for nothing but a very thin scattering of sheep or for rabbit warrens, which were an important part of the agricultural economy of the region. 'Forty years ago', says Young, 'it was all warren from Spilsby to beyond Caistor.' At Withcall near Louth, for instance, when the whole parish was held in one enormous farm of 2,700 acres, the tenant had 1,000 acres of warren. Farther north at Thoresway an even larger holding of 3,000 acres included 1,700 acres under rabbits. They were bred chiefly for their skins, which furnished the hat-trade of London and the industrial North, the wolds apparently specializing in silver-skin, while the Lincoln Heath, another area suited to this branch of agriculture, bred more for the common grey.

The attraction of warren-farming of these poor soils was a good return on a small capital outlay. Rents were cheap, perhaps 5 to 7s an acre at about 1800, and the outlay was small. Several hundred acres of warren could be managed by one warrener, who received about £20 a year plus two cows for his wages. Extra helpers at killing time, which lasted from the second week in November till Christmas, when the skins were in prime condition, were paid 8 or 9s a week and their keep. At Thoresway Mr Holdgate spent about £85 a year on three warreners and helpers, £42.10s.0d on fencing and the same on food for the rabbits; his total expenses were about £870 and his profits on the sale of ten thousand couples came to £300. 'Take this how you will, it explains the reason for so many of these nuisances remaining. The investment of a small capital yields a return that nothing else will.'

The warrens were efficiently fenced, if the neighbours were lucky, with sod walls capped with bundles of furze. These did not last for many years, but the warrens themselves were most productive when frequently moved. After a few years in the same place the rabbits bred with growing reluctance, though, since one of Arthur Young's informants told him that a single buck would serve a hundred does, there were perhaps reasons other than the need for a move for exhaustion to set in. It seems to have been normal around 1800 for stretches of old warren to be ploughed up for one crop of corn, followed by a crop of turnips, followed by a sowing of seeds ('artificial' grasses such as clover) which was grazed by sheep in its first year then turned over again to rabbits. Thus rabbit husbandry fitted in with the general course of agriculture of the region. To writers such as Young, however, it was an anachronism, producing little wealth, employing little labour and relying on low rents from unimproved land. The enormous Thoresway farm he found 'as well managed as the warren allows it to be; but it is to the eye a melancholy scene, more of desolation than culture'. And, by the time he was writing, many of the rabbit farmers themselves were deciding that corn and sheep would now be a better investment. Mr Ansell of North Ormsby, whose warren was considered one of the best managed, was of this opinion. The price of 10d or 11d for a top-quality skin was considerably lower than it had been a few years earlier, and the carcases only fetched about 4d a couple after costs of killing, drying and carrying to markets up to sixty miles away were taken into account. The cost of protecting them against the various types of vermin which preyed upon them was heavy, notably, that of protection against those 'infinitely worse vermin, the poachers'.

Sheep were not prospering on the wolds during most of the eighteenth century. The fleeces of the small, fine-wooled, short-stapled descendants of those animals which had once been one of Lincolnshire's great sources of wealth went out of demand through growing imports of cotton and fine merino wool from abroad. And the heavy, ungainly, long-wooled marsh and fen-land sheep were liable to lose weight rather than gain it in the struggle to find subsistence on the rough upland pasture. The wolds were subservient to the lowlands; sheep were bred here to go for fattening on the richer pickings below. The gradual introduction of fodder crops from about the 1770s onwards was ultimately to change the agriculture and the landscape of the area.

The process of bringing rough pasture into a more intensive farming system began with 'paring and burning'. The gorse was uprooted, the ant-hills chopped up, the turf peeled up, then heaped up and burned when it was dry enough. The ashes were then spread before the land was given its first ploughing. The resulting crops of turnips and seeds could support, it was claimed, up to twenty sheep an acre, where only one could live before. Furthermore the sheep in their turn manured the land for the growing of grain crops, opening up enormous areas to the production of corn where such husbandry could not previously have been considered. Tennyson was a woldsman, and no doubt his Northern Farmer is referring to the wolds when he says:

> Dobbut look at the waste: theer warn't nor feead for a cow
> Nowt at all but bracken and fuzz, and look at it now
> Warnt worth nowt a haacre, and now there's lots of feead
> Fourscorr yows upon it and some of it down i' seead.

There are still plenty of sheep to be seen in parts of the wolds, but artificial fertilizers make it possible now for large stretches to consist of almost uninterrupted arable. Whole areas are a universal brown at ploughing time, or green with growing corn, or golden in high summer, or perhaps lined with a geometric pattern of flames and overhung with great palls of smoke as the stubble is burnt. Those who abhor the latter phenomenon can perhaps take comfort from the thought that something similar has been going on for centuries. Apart from paring and burning, Arthur Young found on the wolds, 'the most singular practice that I ever met with in manuring; it is that of spreading dry straw on the land and burning it'.

All the main roads which cross the southern wolds give splendid views, but perhaps the best general impression of the area can be gained from the Bluestone Heath Road which runs south-eastward along the line of a prehistoric track over the high lands from the A157 near Welton-le-Wold to the A16 just north of Ulceby Cross above Alford. In fifteen miles there is no village on the road, scarcely even a house, but a constant succession of views, changing totally every four hundred yards it seems, show the wold landscape in all its variety of broad plateaux, solitary rounded hills, valleys broad and narrow, and tree-filled combes.

Horncastle to Spilsby

The Romans chose a site for a town at the confluence of the small River Bain and the minute River Waring in a broad valley between the wolds and their last foothills. Cobbett damned Horncastle with rather faint praise, as 'not remarkable for anything of particular value or beauty, a purely agricultural town; well-built and not mean in any way'. George Weir, the author of a history of the town published in 1820, is in agreement: 'The rebuilding of many houses in a handsome manner, within the last twenty years, has given the town an air of respectability; but the effect . . . is materially diminished by the narrowness and irregularity of the streets.' The reason for this great rebuilding was that common one in the county, the almost universal use of mud and stud in earlier centuries. Time has lent enchantment, however, to the many late Georgian buildings, predominantly of red brick, which would have been modern to him; and the later additions harmonize well with them. It is a pleasant town to potter around and small enough to wander through all the main streets in a couple of hours without undue exertion. The greenstone church, mainly Early English and Perpendicular, lies close to the small market-place, and near to the church is the old grammar school, presided over from 1671 to 1684 by Francis Bonner, who fell foul of the governors for 'the severe beatinge and iniuringe and illuseinge of his schollers'. Close by, near the junction of the rivers, lies the basin of Horncastle Navigation, the canal which linked the town with the Witham. This was built under an Act of Parliament of 1792, and contemporary reports stress its importance as a spur to the trade, building and population of the town; between 1801 and 1811 the population increased by six hundred. This growth was the product of trade rather than industry; there had been a number of tanneries in the town in earlier days, but it was as a centre for the movement of corn and wool, and as a market for the numerous villages in the neighbourhood, that Horncastle thrived in the nineteenth century. The canal was the town's main trade route until the 1850s when the railway arrived, though not before a brisk war of broadsides and placards between the railway promoters and the canal lobby who, masquerading under pseudonyms such as 'Fairplay' and 'Behind the scene', tried to preserve their monopoly of communications by holding out to local tradesmen the prospect of a mass exodus of customers to the superior shopping centres of Lincoln and Boston.

The name of Horncastle was famous throughout the land for its annual horse fair, one of the greatest in England, Europe or the world, according to the euphoria of a number of descriptions. For one week in August horse-dealers flocked here from all over the country, accompanied by a motley throng of entertainers, card-sharpers, prostitutes and pickpockets. Stories of the fair abound, like that of the unfortunate clergyman who sold his horse for £25 and bought another for £40, only to find that he had bought back his own with a docked tail, clipped mane and the star on its forehead concealed with dye. Some of the dealers used rough methods to drive a bargain, as when a gang of half a dozen cornered an old man to try to force him to sell for £4 a horse which he had paid £14 for; another, according to legend, pursued the vicar into church and settled a price with him at the foot of the pulpit as he came down from delivering his sermon.

The rip-roaring frontier atmosphere of the horse fair must have presented almost insuperable problems to the forces of law and order, and indeed the records show that in the early Victorian period even a small town like Horncastle was a place where drunkenness, prostitution and petty crime abounded. In 1838 the town appointed its first paid police force, of two, later three, constables supplemented when necessary by supernumeraries. The 30s a week needed for a trained officer from London or Hull was considered excessive, and local men were employed for half that wage, one of the first of whom lost his job on being strongly suspected of pandering for one of the town's numerous houses of ill fame. The low-life of a small country town is portrayed vividly in the surviving notebooks of the constables. Innumerable inns and beer-houses, open to all hours, generated drunken brawls: 'tremendous row in Dog Kennel Yard, 2 women fighting, several men of bad character and 5 prostitutes . . . such a row was never heard in Horncastle before'. Apprentices and labourers were tempted to gamble their money away at skittles, cards, 'Puff and Dart, The Devil among the Tailors, Ringing the Bull' and other such games. The extraordinary name of a local tailor produces the startling information that 'Saint Paul was in the streets beastly drunk' when people were on their way to church.

South and east of Horncastle between the Bain and the wolds the land slowly rises from the flat grounds of the valley through a series of gentle undulations towards the steeper slopes beyond. It is one of many parts of Lincolnshire where the proximity of busy main roads fails to make any impression on a general air of remoteness and tranquillity. Tiny villages, often with minute churches, and scattered houses are joined by a network of narrow roads, many of them, however, with those broad verges which are a feature of the parliamentary enclosure landscape. Rising from the broad, low and rather bare valley of the Bain, the western edge is dominated by the parkscapes of Revesby and Scrivelsby, which almost merge into one. The views in this gently undulating landscape are sometimes wide, sometimes cut off by plantations or rising ground.

At Scrivelsby, 'Home of the Champions', the ancient home of the Dymokes has gone, and the greenstone church, standing apparently inaccessible in a field by a plantation, is almost entirely a Victorian restoration, but it does retain some earlier features, including tombs of the Dymokes and one medieval effigy of a knight and his lady which is probably a monument to members of the Marmion family. The layout of the splendid park, where sheep and cattle graze beneath mature trees, perhaps reflects the design of Humphrey Repton, who was at work here in the late eighteenth century. At the entrance the 'Lion Gate' is surmounted by a beast of benevolent aspect. The royal beast denotes a royal function, for the Dymokes, since the reign of Richard II, and the Marmions before that, have been hereditary champions to the monarchs of England.

North and east of Scrivelsby the land rises steadily towards the Horncastle to Spilsby road. Mareham-on-the-Hill lies on the lower slopes, a typical wold mixture of buildings, mainly brick, with a small whitewashed church and thatched cottage; its title is justified by the enormous views to the south and west. Above it the land rises again to Scrafield, a village which by 1800 had lost its church and shrunk to a single farm of 'wold land for sheep'. It remains a single farm of Dutch barns, stumpy grain silos and a mid-nineteenth-century house approached by a road lined with ash and beech.

Further south between Scrivelsby and Revesby the upward eastward slope is at first a very gentle one. A narrow road through fields and occasional plantations leads from Haltham-on-Bain, through Wood Enderby, past the solitary small and chapel-like church of Wilksby, through the gated pastures of Claxby Pluckacre, to Miningsby, a rise of less than a hundred feet in four or five miles. This was a far from productive land for its early inhabitants: the rather obscure 'Pluckacre' appended to Claxby may imply heavy or clogging land or, more fancifully, a soil so poor that each ear of corn was plucked singly. In about 1810 the villages tended to be dismissed by commentators with phrases such as 'a mean village . . . stud, mud and thatch in chiefly cold clay'. This was Wood Enderby; Miningsby was also 'a poor, mean village' of 'not very bad' land. Beyond Miningsby the wolds begin in earnest. A road lined with beech and syca-mores leads up past Miningsby reservoir, constructed in 1850 to supply Boston with water, to Hareby and Asgarby, 'a wold lordship of useful old enclosed land', much of it once sheep walks. There are still stretches of pasture on the steeper slopes, but much of the area consists of broad sweeps of arable. The views from these fine, high wolds southwards over the fenland are enormous.

From Asgarby or from Miningsby reservoir roads descend towards Old Bolingbroke, into a bowl of land, flat-bottomed, full of crops, with a few trees dotted inconsequentially here and there, lying between sandstone hills, 'like a bay with an opening to the south'. This once flourishing market town still had a small trade in earthenware in the early nineteenth century, but its significance was never a commercial one but rather that of the stronghold and administrative centre of the considerable Duchy of Lancaster estates in Lincolnshire. John of Gaunt succeeded to these estates by marriage, and in 1366 his Duchess, Blanche gave birth to Henry of Bolingbroke, the future King Henry IV. Little more than mounds remain of Bolingbroke Castle, though excavations are gradually revealing the first few re-maining courses of masonry. The village, rather larger than most of those in the area, lies pleasantly on a slope, all brick with a number of good Georgian houses. The church, restored and reduced in size in 1890, was probably built by John of Gaunt in the 1360s as an addition to an earlier building.

The wold parishes near Spilsby have occasionally been given the jesting title of 'Spilsbyshire'. This was once an area of small resident squires, few of them with estates of more than five hundred to a thousand acres. Their buildings and plantations add interest to a landscape already rendered attractive by the alternating hills and valleys of the River Lymn and its tributary streams.

'One of the finest parts of Lincolnshire I have seen, and it would be reckoned fine in any county, is from the hill above Dalby to Spilsby; from that hill the view of rich enclosures, spreading over a varied vale, and the opposite hill, with Partney church and village . . . altogether form a very pleasing scenery.' Thus Arthur Young enthuses, and a number of travellers followed him to pick out this particular prospect, which is indeed a very fine one, but only one among the many beauties of the area. The view from Candlesby Hill at the south-eastern corner of the high land is enormous, over the Marsh to the east and the fens to the south, and equally diversified. Between Dalby and Candlesby lies Skendleby in a typical steep-sided valley, a small village of brick, with some thatch and one or two chalk-built houses. Above Skendleby the road to Dalby follows the valley side, and one looks eastward across to cornfields with clumps of timber, to the mini-parkscape and Regency house of Skendleby Lodge, and to the prehistoric long barrow known as Giant's Hills. A little farther north the site of the deserted medieval village of Fordington is clearly visible in the pastures in front of another large farmstead. To the west of a ridge where the road now climbs, towards Dalby, is a deep, sheep-filled hollow of land.

A little to the west of Dalby in a small, steep, wooded valley is Langton. A tiny school, a small, round thatched *cottage orné* and a few other houses lie near to the church which stands on a tump over a small stream. Its exterior, bare brick with overhanging eaves, gives it the appearance of a minor monument of the Industrial Revolution, an effect accentuated by the spirelet which has lost its cap and looks rather like a funnel. Inside, however, all is grace and Classicism. All the woodwork is of identical style and period (early eighteenth century). The fluted columns of the reredos are balanced by those of the western gallery. The box pews, each with their candlesticks, are laid out down each side of the church, as if in a college chapel, and among them stands the three-decker pulpit. Langton was the home of Doctor Johnson's loved and much respected friend Bennet Langton, and the great doctor seems to have visited the village on at least one occasion. It is recorded, though not by Boswell, that here he was so impressed by the steep sides of the valley that he determined to roll down it. Attempts to dissuade him were put aside with the reply that he had not had a roll for a long time. Therefore he removed keys, pencil, penknife and other impedimenta from his pocket, lay on his side and rolled to the bottom.

Below Langton the views broaden in the valley of the Lymn. The graceful white spire of Sausthorpe church is a prominent feature of the landscape, which, on closer inspection turns out to be of brick not of limestone, and nineteenth century not fifteenth. The church was totally rebuilt in the 1840s by Charles Kirk for the Reverend Francis Swan at a cost of £3,000. The Swans were parsons and chief landowners here for several generations, adding considerably to their already far from negligible wealth by building development on their Lincoln estates.

South of Sausthorpe, on the side of the valley, is Raithby, 'an earthly paradise' according to John Wesley, who visited his friend Langley Carr Brackenbury here on a number of occasions and preached in the little chapel, now Lincolnshire's oldest surviving Methodist chapel. It forms part of the outbuildings of the hall, and both were built by Brackenbury in about 1779.

Tennyson Country

The central section of this southern half of the wolds lies to the south of Bluestone Heath road and surrounds the large village of Tetford. The landscape can best be described as 'choppy': ridges and intervening steep valleys seem to point in all directions. This is the landscape celebrated, though in a tantalizing unspecific manner, in many of Tennyson's poems, and it is an area of pilgrimage for Tennyson lovers.

> Far to the North, where Lindsay props the skies,
> Embosomed in her mountains Tetford lies
> Whose rustic bowers present secure retreats
> From winter rigours and from summer heats.

The author of this is not Tennyson but a poet of rather lesser eminence, Langhorne Burton, who in 1772 wrote to celebrate a club which he and other neighbouring gentry attended monthly at the village inn in Tetford, to enjoy the innocent pastimes of skittles, bowls, 'the thoughtful pipe and wit-inspiring bowl'. Tetford's position in a narrow plain between the surrounding wolds lends some credence to the phrase 'embosomed in her mountains' and provides an attractive setting. The village itself, however, is not one of any particular attraction. No description can improve on that of White's *Directory* of 1856: 'a considerable and well-built village in a pleasant valley'.

The population increased from 301 in 1801 to 799 in 1851; quarrying for lime was a local industry and is still carried on, but no doubt Tetford's population, like that of a number of the larger wold villages, was also a reservoir of labour for the farms of the more sparsely peopled neighbouring parishes. It was parishes like this, also, which became particular strongholds of Methodism in Lincolnshire and where the battle between Anglicanism and Dissent was waged often with ferocity for much of the nineteenth century. In the 1851 religious census Methodist congregations outnumbered Anglican by four to one. In the 1870s the two parties were engaged in controversy over the setting up of a Board school in rivalry with the Church's National school, a dispute which ended in compromise. A few years later, in the miserably wet harvest of 1879 the Rector, the Reverend A. B. Skipworth, offended many of his parishioners by urging the farmers to take advantage of a sunny Sunday to load their corn. He even set an example by going, with his sexton and his labourer, to load a wagon. Incensed villagers gathered round to hiss and no doubt saw the judgement of Heaven when the rector's wagon stuck fast in a muddy gateway and could only be extricated after several hours hard work.

At precisely the same time the Methodists in the neighbouring parish of Bag Enderby were suffering at the hands of a descendant and namesake of the bard of the Tetford Club. Langhorne Burton of Somersby possessed an estate of eleven thousand acres, a shortage of tenants because of the agricultural depression, an increasing lack of cash (as appeared later when he went bankrupt) and a rather old-fashioned idea of his position as squire which led him to threaten eviction to a cottager in Bag Enderby whose house was used for Methodist meetings. The squire was obviously a staunch Church of England man – not staunch enough, however, to overcome aversion or inability to pay his tithes. The rector in turn was therefore impoverished and unable to pay his parish rates. In 1879 Bag Enderby consisted of a church, three farms and a few scattered cottages; there was no school, no chapel, no reading room, 'while one will look in vain for a house licensed to sell intoxicants'.

The church of Bag Enderby and that of the neighbouring parish of Harrington are among the most interesting in the southern wolds. Enderby church can be dated approximately by the memorial inscription to Albinius de Enderby, 'who caused this church and tower to be built and who died on the vigil of St Matthew the Apostle 1407'. Harrington, like Enderby of the universal green sandstone, was almost completely rebuilt in 1855 but retains a fine array of earlier monuments to the Copledike and Amcotts families. The Copledikes held Harrington from about 1300 until the death of Thomas Copledike in 1658. 'Of ancient stock here lies the last and best,' his monument proclaims:

Who hath attained to his eternal rest,
This monument bespeaks not him alone,
It says the family with him is gone.

In 1673 the estate was purchased by Vincent Amcotts, who immediately set about improving the Elizabethan home which he found there. The result is one of Lincolnshire's most satisfying houses, mellow brick in a delightful small park.

Harrington, Bag Enderby and Somersby lie in a beautiful, gently undulating, well-wooded countryside of tree-lined roads and short horizons. The small cornfields, often of very sandy soil, are a total contrast to the chalky prairies of the higher wolds. Here and there by the roadside one sees an isolated long, low cottage, thatched and whitewashed, a descendant of the universal mud, stud and thatch of earlier days. The land slopes gently down to the River Lymn, joined at Somersby by an even smaller stream, Tennyson's brook.

George Clayton Tennyson, rector of Somersby and Bag Enderby, was the son of George Tennyson, a successful Market Rasen attorney. At Somersby 'the owd Doctor', as the inhabitants affectionately and inaccurately called him (he died in his early fifties), raised and educated a large family. Three of his sons were later to achieve fame as poets, and Alfred was to be one of the most famous men in England. His fame brought fame to Somersby, although, after Dr Tennyson's death in 1831, the family left the area never to return. By the later years of the century longevity in Somersby guaranteed the attentions and *douceurs* of tourists anxious to hear at first hand stories of the youth of the great man. And the oldest inhabitants willingly obliged, a little puzzled, it seems, at all this fuss about a family they had liked but had considered distinctly peculiar. 'I suppose he's a great man now, a lord and what not, and does a deal o' work for the Queen,' said one. Another spoke of Dr Tennyson's building operations; he had extended his rectory to cope with a growing family and was 'a reet clever old chap as a harchitect', but most of the actual building was carried out by the rector's man, Horlins, an addict who 'would have built for ivver' if permitted.

The rectory, with the 'owd doctor's' extensions still stands and next to it the castellated manor house built for the Burtons,

probably to a Vanbrugh design, in 1722. Opposite is the small
church, full of light from wide Perpendicular windows. A brass
has the kneeling figure of George Littlebury, who died in 1612
'being about the age of 73 years'. On the porch a sundial says
succinctly 'Time Passeth'. George Clayton Tennyson's plain
tomb is in the churchyard, as is also an almost perfectly preserved medieval cross.

West of Somersby are Salmonby, 'curiously situated among
great blocks of sandstone rock', and Ashby Puerorum, 'of the
boys', so called because it formed part of the endowments of the
choristers of Lincoln Cathedral. There are great stretches of
sheep pastures around here, backed by tumpy, sometimes tree-
topped, hills towards the higher wolds, and the enormous de-
pressions of former sandstone quarries. A number of porticoed
single-storey nineteenth-century estate cottages can be seen
near the grounds of Holbeck Manor. This 'multum in parvo or
conglomeration of rural beauties', as a nineteenth-century
newspaper described it, was built in the 1820s for the Fardell
family and consisted of a 'genteel residence, neat lodge, avenue
of elms, extensive ponds, picturesque rocks, and thriving
plantations'. Hoe Hill, once graphically described as 'a trun-
cated and somewhat obtuse cone', rises behind.

Two miles east of Tetford in a hollow beneath the Bluestone
Heath road is South Ormsby, one of the most delightful spots in
the wolds. The splendid church, very large for the area, stands
on a bluff at the edge of the well-timbered park of South Ormsby
Hall. It is a mixture of periods from the Norman doorway in the
south aisle (though this may have been removed from Calceby)
through to the Perpendicular of nave windows and tower. Mixed
up with the organ blower and church safes is the brass of Sir
William Skipworth, who died in 1482, and his lady. In a nearby
window are several roundels of sixteenth- or seventeenth-
century Continental glass: a smug-looking Paschal lamb, and a
lady reposing in bed while her servant baths the baby before the
fire.

In 1678 the South Ormsby estate was purchased from a
debt-ridden descendant of Sir William Skipworth by Drayner
Massingberd, a younger son of the Gunby family. Drayner was a
prominent Parliamentarian during the Civil Wars and remained unregenerately Whiggish enough to be imprisoned out

of harm's way during Monmouth's rebellion in 1688. Drayner's son Burrell Massingberd turned to Toryism and *belles lettres*. He was a patron of William Kent and, according to family tradition, an occasional contributor to the *Spectator*. Wryly he complained to friends of the *oves* and the *boves* (sheep and cattle), a nightgown that sticks like birdlime because of the damp, 'our vicar's sermons which grow spoile-puding long' and the entire absence of any subjects worth contemplating, all of which combine to 'reduce inventions naturally barren to the conditions of the hills about here, which produce nothing but moss and mushrooms'. In spite of his protests, however, he kept a keen eye on the *oves* and the *boves*, and his oversight of the estate was as careful and as well documented as his father's. Drayner's grandson, William Burrell Massingberd continued the family conversion from Whiggery to such an advanced Toryism that in 1745 he set off to join Bonnie Prince Charlie's rebellion at Derby (once more the story is a family tradition). Since the Prince was about to retreat back to Scotland, he sent his young recruit home with a miniature portrait as a memento, and the rest of Massingberd's long life was spent in less adventurous enterprises, such as the rebuilding of the family house in the 1750s.

The Louth Area

The Bluestone Heath road at one of its lowest points skirts Ormsby on the east, then climbs again, past the white skeleton of Calceby church to join the A16, the road which runs near the eastern edge of the wolds south from Louth to Ulceby Cross above Alford. Most of the valleys run west to east at the wold edge, carrying the streams down into the Marsh. Viewed from the lowlands, the slopes are often part covered by extensive stretches of woodland, and some of the villages, like South Thoresby and Belleau, are almost lost among trees. Belleau, approached by a narrow lane lined with willow-herb and convolvulus from the east, or by an avenue of beeches from the west, still shows among an array of enormous modern barns the dovecot and fishponds of the house sold by the irreproachably royalist Earl of Lindsey to one of the more extreme Parliamentarians, Sir Henry Vane, who enlivened his country Sundays by preaching to as many of his neighbours as would consent to listen. A little to the north the wold edge at Muckton and Burwell also retains in its woodlands traces of the influence left by the lost house of the Listers. Burwell lies in a dip on the main road: an inn, a hexagonal church hall and a few houses. Above it is the church, looking distinctly dilapidated.

The higher wolds west of Burwell become almost bare of trees and hedges, great rolling cornfields where combine-harvesters move in stately echelon. At the tiny settlement of Maidenwell the former school and a present telephone box stand in solitary splendour, bereft, it seems, of any possible custom. The landscape here, as in so many places, is deceptive, however: sudden green valleys appear magically, like that at Tathwell, where, as a nineteenth-century observer notes, 'while the present proprietor and previous occupiers have excelled in agricultural and ram-breeding pursuits as parts of the necessary business of life, they have displayed that fine taste and care in developing the works of nature, which is a sure index to the love of home and the possession of elegant and refined minds'. In the eighteenth century the wealthy Chaplin family was seated here and played a considerable part in the affairs of the county. This influence continued in the next century, but by this time their main seat was at Blankney in North Kesteven. George Chaplin was one of the great names in Lincolnshire agriculture at the turn of the century, champion of the Lincolnshire Longwool sheep against the New Leicester breed.

Withcall, in another narrow valley, was one of the places to which nineteenth-century agricultural correspondents went when they wanted to tell tall stories. Its rabbit warrens have already been mentioned. Richard Dawson the tenant of its 2,700 acres, who died in 1839, was wont to say that all Lincolnshire would make a couple of nice farms for him and his son and, looking over his enormous fields, to declare that he needed no other Heaven. In the 1880s a new owner, Nathaniel Clayton, the Lincoln agricultural machinery magnate, rebuilt the church, erected a school and put up cottages for farm labourers, many of whom had previously had to walk from Louth to their work. Throughout the nineteenth century the parish continued to be let as one farm until in 1887 the agricultural depression forced Clayton's tenant to give up and the farm was divided.

Louth is situated at the point where the central wolds join the Marsh. White's *Directory* of 1826 is picturesque and polysyllabic: 'It stands in a valley which is sheltered on the north and south by sloping hills of indurated chalk, covered with argillaceous soil, which command numerous and varied prospects.' Among these prospects none is more dramatic than the glimpses of the slender spire of one of England's most majestic parish churches which can be seen along several of the adjoining valleys. At closer quarters it soars majestically up for nearly three hundred feet and dominates the town, as it must have dominated the thoughts of the townsmen during the fourteen years in the early sixteenth century when it was being built. The construction of the spire was the culmination of a rebuilding of the whole church on a grand scale spread over a century or more. The first stone was laid on the top of an already grandiose tower in 1501. Stone was purchased from quarries at Wilsford in North Kesteven, transported by road and water to Dogdyke on the Witham and then carted some twenty miles to Louth, at a cost of 1s.6d upwards a load. John Oldman received 3d a day for winding the stone up the tower on a windlass made of timber from the abbot of Louth Park's wood (he gave one tree but charged 3s.4d for a second). The work was financed by gifts great and small: John Chapman, merchant, gave £20, John Wayth of Thornton gave 4d, by loans from Our Lady's Gild and the Holy Trinity Gild, even by pawning the church plate. At last, in September 1515, the weathercock was set upon the completed spire, and the church was consecrated by the parish priest and his brother priests singing *Te Deum Laudamus* with organ accompaniment (the organ, no doubt, being that bought by George Smyth, merchant, beyond the sea a few years earlier and sold to the church for £13.6s.8d), whereupon the churchwardens caused all the bells to be rung and gave bread and ale to all the people there, 'And all to the lofying of god, oure lady and all saynts'.

The rebuilding of Louth church had involved the whole local community. They loved their church, took pride in its beauty, its rich plate, vestments and ornaments; conservatives in religion, they were deeply attached to the festivities, pageantry and holidays of the medieval Church, however hazy some of them may have been as to its theological basis. They looked with deep disquiet upon Henry VIII's suppression of the monasteries and harboured dark suspicions as to his further intentions. Rumours circulated that all jewels and ornaments were to be removed from the churches, that there was to be only one parish church for each six or seven square miles and that they would lose all their holy days. Louth was one of the number of centres where in early October 1536 the Lincolnshire Rebellion broke out. On Sunday 1st October the churchwarden's account book records that no collection could be taken as there was no service because of the tumult of the people. Encouraged by their vicar, Thomas Kendall, and led by Nicholas Melton, *alias* Captain Cobbler, a shoemaker, the men of Louth joined the men of Horncastle, of Caistor and of many other parts of the county, especially the wolds, seized and imprisoned royal and episcopal officers, marched on Lincoln and sent a petition to the King demanding the restoration of the suppressed monasteries and the privileges of the church. Henry was frightened but furious at this presumption on the part of 'the rude commons of one shire, and that one of the most brute and beastly of the whole realm'. He ordered them to disperse, sending a hundred ringleaders with halters round their necks, or face an invading army which would destroy their goods, wives and children to the fearful example of all lewd subjects.

Faced with a royal army, the rebellion lost momentum and dispersed as quickly and as spontaneously as it had arisen. The rebels simply disappeared back to their homes, where they were allowed to remain unmolested apart from a few ringleaders who were executed. Louth and Horncastle, 'better stored of arrant traitors than any towns in England', were heavy sufferers in this lottery of blood. Among the Louth victims was Thomas Kendall, the vicar, in spite of the fact that, after sending the rebels on their way with his blessing, he seems to have taken flight, first to Oxford, then to Berkshire, finally to Coventry where he claimed to have been admitted to the Charterhouse. Ironically the Carthusians denied him, as he had denied his parishioners.

Constitutionally Louth was one of the country's more peculiar boroughs from its incorporation by Edward VI in 1551 until the Municipal Reform Act of 1835. In the charter of 1551 a Warden and six Assistants of the Town of Louth were appointed to govern both the town and the grammar school which was founded at the same time. The endowments of the now suppressed religious gilds were at the same time applied to the support of the school. Among its most distinguished pupils was Alfred Tennyson, who remembered his formidable headmaster with such lingering awe that years later he could not bear to walk down the lane past the school. Not for nothing did the common seal of the corporate body show 'a man exercising a birch upon the posteriors of a suppliant youth'.

Louth owed its growth mainly to its position as an important market at the junction of marsh and wolds. Some attempts were made, however, to introduce an industrial revolution here in the late eighteenth century. The corporation of the town acted wherever possible to encourage such developments. It produced a considerable share of the capital needed to construct a canal between Louth and the sea at Tetney, which was completed in 1770. It also contributed to the expense of road improvements in the area and other public works, so much so that in 1771 all corporation entertainments were discontinued for the time being as the town was in debt. In 1778 the corporation borrowed money to purchase materials and erect a building for a woollen factory and provided a site for the purpose at a nominal rent. In 1801 Adam Eve, a Louth draper, bought the corporation's interest in the project and ran it with some success until his death in 1831.

A visitor in the early years of the nineteenth century was impressed by the bustle of the canal basin, where a 'deal of business went on in coal and wool', by Mr Eve's wool and carpet manufactories and by a boatyard which built vessels up to the fifty tons burthen which the canal could take. But the town was too remote to have a bright industrial future, and even in their heyday the factories employed only a minute proportion of the population of the town. Far the greater proportion earned a living by serving the needs of the surrounding area. In 1856 there were thirty-five tailors, thirteen surgeons, thirty-six milliners and dressmakers, fourteen cabinet-makers and upholsterers and forty-two boot and shoemakers. Twelve private academics competed for custom with the grammar school, the rival Church and Nonconformist schools and a charity school. And in the bad old days before reforming nineteenth-century bishops forced their recalcitrant clergy into residence in the less attractive country parishes, towns such as Louth were positive rookeries of clerics, who cluttered the approach roads on Sundays with their gigs as they set off to take services.

Three main roads cross the high wolds to the west of Louth; they go to Market Rasen, to Lincoln and to Horncastle. All of them descend after eight or ten miles towards the valley of the River Bain. The descent of the Horncastle road at Scamblesby is the most dramatic, as are the views from the top of it, especially when one looks towards a winter sunset or when sometimes in late summer the light of the setting sun is diffused by the smoke of burning stubble.

The Bain valley, wide and rather bare near Horncastle, narrows to the north of the town and winds through some of Lincolnshire's most attractive scenery near Stenigot, Donington-on-Bain and Biscathorpe. On Red Hill at Stenigot a small area of ancient wold grassland has been preserved, full of a variety of wild flowers. The valley here is full of trees: in the grounds of Stenigot House, which run up to a tree-topped escarpment, along the roadsides, in the hedgerows of the sheep-pastures and in the plantations of poplars between Stenigot and Market Stainton. A little to the north the river, now a small stream, flows through the grounds of Biscathorpe House, stock brick of the 1840s, as is the tiny church with its ornate spire (a mere twenty-five to thirty feet high) and splendid grotesques. The roads are lined with oak and beech and the road through the pastures fords the minute river and an even smaller tributary before they broaden out into a lake.

Lost or shrunken settlements cluster thickly in this area. Biscathorpe itself is a lost village, and within two or three miles are four more: East and West Wykeham, South Cadeby and Calcethorpe.

The Western Edge

West of the Bain valley a Roman or pre-Roman road, the High Street, runs along the high wolds from Baumber near Horncastle to Caistor. Westward again, on the lower wold slopes and the beginning of the central claylands of Lindsey, the landscape owes much to planting and building on the three adjoining estates of the Turnors of Panton, the Heneages of Hainton and the Boucheretts of North Willingham. Of their seats, only Hainton survives, centre of by far the oldest of the three estates and of one of the oldest in the continuous ownership of one family in the county. John Heneage purchased much of the parish of Hainton in or about the year 1400 from the executors of Lord de la Ware. For over a century few additions were made to this nucleus, but extensive purchases in the reigns of Henry VIII and Elizabeth, mainly in Hainton itself and the immediately surrounding area, built up a large and compact estate. Hainton Hall was built in the 1630s, though there are extensive later additions and alterations. 'Capability' Brown landscaped the park in the 1760s. Many generations of Heneage monuments are to be found in the church.

The Turnors of Panton arrived on the scene much later, obtaining the estate by purchase in the 1770s. An early nineteenth-century guidebook found that 'the adjacent country has been much improved by ornamental plantations'. The house has gone, but many of the plantations remain. Although their Lindsey estates were more extensive, the Turnors, by the nineteenth century, preferred their Kesteven seat at Stoke Rochford and its closer contacts with civilization. As MP for South Lincolnshire in the 1840s, Christopher Turnor was naturally drawn in that direction, and his experiences on his Lindsey estates were not universally happy. In 1875 he committed the ultimate rural crime of shooting one of the Burton hounds (Venus by name) when the hunt intermingled with his shooting party. The holding of a splendid penitential meet at Panton Hall did not altogether dispel the consequent odium. He must also have incurred some unpopularity in many quarters as the patron who presented Thomas Wimberley Mossman to the livings of East and West Torrington. Mossman was a clergyman of wide tolerance, great holiness and advanced Ritualist persuasion. In the 1860s the citizens of Lincoln and Louth looked askance at his young men, the 'Mossman Monks' of the Order of the Holy Redeemer for preaching mission friars, when they paraded the streets 'in sacerdotal garb of an *outré* and outlandish character', singing Gregorian chant. Mossman died in 1885, just too soon for his resignation to join the Church of Rome to take effect. His successor opted at once for church restoration, for many Victorian clergy a much safer alternative to Ritualism.

Even church restoration, however, could arouse primitive passions. At the nearby village of Sixhills the Reverend W. A. Atkinson was at loggerheads with his patron, Edward Heneage, and the parish vestry over the fate of the church tower. In 1869 Heneage 'restored' the church, knocking down the tower, replacing it with a simple bell-turret at the gable end and (according to the vicar) using the stone for highway repair and his own garden walks. Divine wrath intervened when the bell-turret was destroyed by lightning. The vicar campaigned and collected for the restoration of the tower; Heneage and the members of the vestry were determined upon simply restoring the bell-turret. After years of argument and bad temper the vicar won his point in exchange for his resignation of the living (he retained the neighbouring one of South Willingham). The tower as it now stands is a monument to Mr Atkinson's obstinacy.

The western slopes of the wolds in this area are mostly gentle but still command enormous views over the Vale of Lindsey towards Lincoln or, as at Sixhills, north and north-west towards Willingham Forest and Market Rasen. Away from estate plantations the landscape can be bare of timber, with ash predominating the sparse hedgerow trees. The roads are narrow, sometimes winding lanes. The narrow verges of roads in early enclosed parishes contrast with those laid out under later Acts of Parliament. The Heneages, for instance, enclosed several of their parishes by early agreement with their tenants, and this is reflected in the layout of the roads.

At North Willingham the slope of the wold edge is a steep one, and Willingham Hill on the A631 is one of the steepest gradients on Lincolnshire's main roads. In 1815 it claimed the life of Ayscoghe Boucherett when the pole of his curricle broke and the horses bolted down the hill. The Boucheretts were in origin a French Huguenot family who acquired the Willingham estate in 1660.

7

The Northern Wolds and Humber Bank

The Market Rasen to Louth road provides a convenient line of division between the southern and northern halves of the wold area. There is little distinction in landscape features between the two halves except possibly for a greater amount of bare plateau in the northern section. The settlements are to be found mostly in the narrow valleys which cut, but not deeply, into the eastern edge and in folds of the steeper western edge. In the central area they are to be found chiefly in the valleys of the Waithe Beck, which rises near Kirmond-le-Mire and flows into the sea at Tetney Haven, and its tributaries.

Market Rasen is a good point of departure for the area. The main Grimsby road, the A46, skirts the base of the wolds as far as Caistor, the tops rising bare and green on the right. Another route cuts straight across the hills through Tealby and Binbrook. Tealby is delightfully situated at the wold foot on the River Rase, a small stream which brawls along its valley energetically enough to have driven a number of paper-mills in the past. The greenstone church stands on a bluff over the main road. But the pride of the village has now been destroyed. This was Bayons Manor, a Gothic baronial extravagance built to satisfy the romantic medievalism and claims to ancient nobility of Charles Tennyson, the poet's uncle.

George Tennyson, Alfred's grandfather, was a Market Rasen solicitor who throve on enclosure commissionerships and other legal business. His younger son Charles went in for the law, married well and pursued a career in politics. His strongly Liberal political ideas (he was Liberal member for Lambeth for twenty years and opponents castigated him as 'Charles Tennyson the Man of the People') fitted ill with the genealogical snobbery which delighted in the family's somewhat tenuous descent from the medieval barons d'Eyncourt. He adopted the additional surname to become Charles Tennyson d'Eyncourt and after his father's death in 1835, when Tealby was invaded by some two thousand mourners, rebuilt the house in magnificent style. A feast for friends and tenantry in the baronial hall is illustrated in his poem 'Eustace', written to commemorate a son who died in the West Indies and considered by at least one member of the family to be far superior to Alfred's rubbish.

The neighbouring village of Walesby also lies at the wold's foot, but for centuries the parishioners had to plod their weary way to church up to the top of a considerable eminence, until a twentieth-century rector took pity on them and raised the money for a new church, which was built in 1914. As a result the old church, one of the finest in the area, was in great danger of destruction. Fortunately it has been preserved with sturdy nave pillars of the period of transition from Norman to Early English, box pews and a seventeenth-century pulpit. The site is magnificent if windswept, with extensive views across the plain to Lincoln Cathedral and beyond. Normanby-le-Wold has another windswept church site, the church itself in the main of slightly later date than Walesby, as is nearby Claxby. Both have one or two large and flamboyant corbel-heads; a man on the chancel arch at Claxby and his twin at Normanby each has hand in mouth in a gesture which Sir Nikolaus Pevsner authoritatively informs us does *not* imply toothache.

In the early years of the nineteenth century, when the Reverend Richard Atkinson still collected tithes in kind, the church porch was the delivery point for tithe milk and was the scene of a battle royal between the rector's serving maid and tithing-man and a farmer and his daughter, intent on making their contribution to the already curdled contents of the receptacle. The maid, 'a smart dressy lass', suspected of performing very miscellaneous services for her employer, had her finery thoroughly drenched. Serving maids and tithe milk preserved Mr Atkinson to a green and slightly disingenuous old age. Considered moribund in about 1850, he sold the patronage of its living to his curate for £8,000, then proceeded to live for another twenty years in enjoyment of the curate's mortification at his bad bargain. The case, we are told, 'afforded a frequent theme for local gossip upon the uncertainties of life'. The whole Atkinson family, in fact, must have provided plenty of ammunition for local gossip: the rector's sister married a shady attorney, and his brother, a Caistor wine-merchant, achieved two bankruptcies and a spectacular failure to abduct a local heiress when he accidentally kidnapped her father instead.

At Nettleton is one of a group of late Saxon or very early post-Conquest towers which is to be found in the Caistor area. Travellers here in the 1690s marvelled at the moving bed of sand 'which had sprung out of the hill and encreas'd . . . and by that means undone several poore people'. It destroyed some of the dwellings and would have done more damage but for an intervening stream.

'The little town of Caistor has long since outlived ambition . . . to climb the face of the Wolds or spread over the plain below.' This nineteenth-century comment could almost serve for the present day. True, there has been some recent expansion in both directions, but on a very modest scale, and within a few hundred yards of the town centre the traffic thunders by up the hill on the A46 (or grinds to a halt in severe winter weather), scarcely noticing that a town is being bypassed. In 1695 it was 'but a little place yet mighty famous for its great markets and fairs' – the market 'abundantly supplied on Saturday in the season with fine cockle-shell fish', later information adds. Rebuilt once after a fire in 1681, the evidence of the small market square and the few main streets is of a later, early nineteenth-century rebuilding for the well-to-do merchants, tradesmen and professional men of the town.

As the name suggests, Caistor was a Roman fortified settlement, though there is little above ground at the present day to suggest this. Excavation has, however, given some idea of the extent of the Roman fortifications which enclosed an area stretching about three hundred yards westward from the market square by two hundred north to south. The church is somewhere near the centre. It seems likely that the town's Roman function was the one which it has retained ever since, that of a local commercial and administrative centre. Its distance from any major Roman line of communication, although a prehistoric trackway leading through Caistor from Horncastle to the Humber was no doubt in use, duplicates the reasons for its limited growth in more modern times, when those two spurs to expansion, the canal and the railway, did not approach nearer than three miles.

The church has another of the Saxon towers of the area and contains a curious relic in the Caistor gad-whip. White's *Directory* describes the ceremony enacted every Palm Sunday by the tenant of certain lands in Broughton-by-Brigg:

> He comes to the north porch about the commencement of the first lesson, and cracks his whip at the door three times; after which with much ceremony he binds the thong round the stock of the whip . . . he then ties to the top of the whipstock a small leathern purse containing two shillings (originally twenty-four silver pennies) and . . . marches into the church, where he stands in front of the reading desk until the commencement of the second lesson, he then goes up nearer, waves the purse over the head of the clergyman, kneels down upon a cushion, and continues in that posture, with the purse suspended over the clergyman's head, till the end of the lesson, when he retires into the choir.

No entirely satisfactory explanation of the ceremony has been put forward, and in 1846 it was suppressed, as unconforming to Victorian ideals of ecclesiastical etiquette.

Set in a depression among the high wolds, the large village of Binbrook comes as something of a surprise. The bare country around does not seem capable of having nourished such a large settlement, little smaller than such market towns as Caistor. Binbrook did indeed have some aspirations at one time to urban status. It had a market once, but this had more or less ceased to exist by the nineteenth century and 'before the rage for inclosure and destruction of warrens for rabbits some material trade was carried out here in the furr line, but now very little indeed'. It was as a reservoir of labour both for its own large parish and also for the farms of surrounding smaller settlements that Binbrook grew. No major landowner was to hand to control development of labourers' dwellings in the village, and nineteenth-century high farming demanded great numbers of workmen as well as the large number of shoemakers, dressmakers, shopkeepers, smiths, wheelwrights and other tradesmen called for to supply the needs of an isolated agricultural community.

One farmer of a thousand acres in Binbrook employed a foreman, shepherd, garthman, carpenter, blacksmith, seedsman and married head waggoner, as well as four or five young assistant waggoners who lodged with the foreman. All these were hired by the year. He also employed nine or ten day-labourers as well as young boys and women hired casually for such jobs as turnip lifting. Weeding and other tasks were contracted out to labour gangs. Binbrook was one of the centres for such gangs: the farmer paid the gangmaster for the job, and the gangmaster was responsible for paying the member of the gang. Victorian ideas of morality were shocked by some aspects of the gang system, which threw women and young children, with little supervision, into the company of men. Young farm servants, hired by the year, away from home and subject to all kinds of temptation with few checks upon their behaviour, were considered to be in equal danger. In 1900 a local clergyman quoted a sin map of England in which Lincolnshire was one of the two blackest counties. This he put down to the scattered parishes and the easy opportunities for wrong-doing attached to farm work. He could not resist a side swipe at the Wesleyans, whose revival meetings, after which the young people wandered home after dark, he considered to arouse sensuous just as much as religious emotions.

The country around Binbrook is an area of rolling cornfields, scattered clumps of trees and an enormous sense of distance. There is little hedgerow timber, in fact there are few hedges. It is a land almost empty of houses, though at harvest time it sometimes seems to be full of combine-harvesters, cutting a geometrical pattern in the banks of corn. The occasional farm-steads are substantial, sometimes enormous, groups of buildings like that of Great Tows, between Binbrook and Ludford. Nearly all are post-enclosure, nineteenth-century buildings.

All the settlements in the central area of the wold near Binbrook are in the valleys of a fan of streams which join to become Waithe Beck. The greenness of the valleys often contrasts strongly with the bareness of the surrounding tops – Stainton-le-Vale, for instance, when the road plunges down from a plateau into a bowl filled with water and trees, at Croxby where the stream broadens into fishponds surrounded by woodlands, or at Thorganby, which has 'a sylvan feature rarely met with on the wolds. The grounds behind the house are finely varied and the declivitous hillsides terminate in a narrow vale'. All these villages are small, even minute. Farther to the east, Wold Newton nestles in a similar narrow valley, while beyond the eastern edge of the wolds slopes gently down to the coastal plain. On these eastern slopes the valleys of streams descending into the marsh do not penetrate far into the hills, and each one has or had a small settlement: North Ormsby, which occupies the site of a Gilbertine priory, traces of whose fishponds can still be seen, and the sites of the lost villages of Cadeby and Beesby. The A16 from Louth to Grimsby follows a lowland route, but a minor road, the B1431, follows the lower contour of the wolds and gives extensive views across the Marsh towards Grimsby and the sea.

The gatehouse of Thornton Abbey, *c.*1800

Brocklesby's memorial arch

Alkborough: looking across the Humber

The Vale of Trent at Gate Burton, *c.*1800

Ironstone mining near Scunthorpe

Stow church, *c.*1800, before its Victorian restoration

The rood screen in the church at Cotes-by-Stow

Above left: Romanesque carving on Lincoln Cathedral's west front.
Above right: A cherub of Death, Snarford. *Below:* Effigies of Sir
George St Poll (d.1615) and his wife, Snarford

Above: Lincoln Cathedral dominating the lower town. *Below:* Arcading on the north-west tower of Lincoln Cathedral

Lincoln Cathedral: the western towers

Two views of Lincoln's Minster Yard. *Above*: The Chancery and other houses in Pottergate. *Below:* The Archdeaconry and the gateway to the Old Palace

Brocklesby Country

The whole of the northern wolds, and their borders of marsh and Humber bank, can be counted as 'Brocklesby country'. The Earl of Yarborough's hounds, the Brocklesby Hunt, which hunted the whole of this area, provided a great social focus. The Earls of Yarborough were in the early nineteenth century the county's great Whig magnates. Their estate of over fifty thousand acres was the largest in the county and one of the two or three largest in England, and for several decades Brocklesby was the political centre of North Lincolnshire.

A younger branch of the Sussex Pelhams appears to have settled at Brocklesby late in the sixteenth century. For two centuries they added to their estates by purchase and marriage, during the course of which the main line died out, before Charles Anderson-Pelham was raised to the peerage as Baron Yarborough in 1794. This peerage was later elevated to an earldom in 1837.

This estate, which was later to become a byword for high farming, was still unimproved in the early nineteenth century when Arthur Young saw near Brocklesby 'large tracts of excellent land under gorse; and at Cabourn and Swallow I passed through the same for miles. It is a beautiful plant to a fox-hunter. Lord Yarborough keeps a pack of hounds; if he has a fall, I hope it will be into a furze bush; he is too good to be hurt much, but a good pricking might be beneficial to the country.' Whether or not these words had any effect is uncertain, but it must have been at around this time that the long campaign of agricultural improvement on the estate was commenced. Already the Pelhams had started their tree-planting activities. Pelham's Pillar, between Brocklesby and Caistor, celebrates the first Baron's achievement in planting 12½ million before his death in 1823.

The improvements in farming were a long process involving considerable capital expenditure by both landlord and tenants, and by the middle of the century they had produced fame for the

estate in farming circles. In 1854 a *Stamford Mercury* correspondent records how twelve years earlier he had first seen the
area, 'then entirely unknown, its fine farm buildings on which
£150,000 have been spent . . . its 30,000 acres of good turnip land
divided by clipped hedges of thorn. I thought I had made a
discovery of a domain equal in the spirit, magnitude, and
rapidity of its improvement to the well-known estate of Holk-
ham.' The enormous outlay of the farmers in improving their
land was 'made by tenants-at-will (i.e. with no paper security of
tenure) who had true confidence in their landlord – most farms
passing from father to son as a matter of course'.

Most of the farms were large, averaging nearly a thousand
acres, and Brocklesby tenant farmers acquired all the gracious
living which would have gone with well-to-do owner occupiers
or squires in other parts. Like their lands, they improved, from
the 'grower of turnips and fat sheep and not unlike a sheep
himself' of the 1820s to the clientèle of Caistor market in the
1880s, when, it was said, a stranger would be surprised to see all
the smart traps and well-dressed men. 'The gentlemen in cloth
breeches and a London-cut coat . . . is not a proprietor . . . but a
tenant-farmer and the son of a tenant-farmer' who has probably
been to Oxford or Cambridge and has a brother in the Church or
at the Bar.

The nineteenth-century improvements have left indelible
marks on the landscape, in the plantations, shelter belts and
hedgerow timber as well as in the well-built farmsteads and
cottages of grey brick from the estate brickyards. Cottage building was in full swing in 1858 when a reporter visited some at
Swallow and found them not only pleasing to the eye but also
well laid out with spacious living-room, back kitchen, good
dairy, lobby and porch on the ground floor, three good-sized
bedrooms, courtyard, offices and large garden. These and many
more had been built to the Countess of Yarborough's design.
'Her Ladyship (God bless her) appears to know full well that the
first thing necessary to the virtuous behaviour and good morals
of this class is a comfortable and well-appointed dwelling.'

At the centre of the estate is Brocklesby Park itself, delightfully wooded, surrounding the house which was rebuilt following a disastrous fire in 1898. In Brocklesby church are impressive monuments to two Sir William Pelhams, the founder of the

family, one of Elizabeth's generals, who died in 1587, and his son, who died in 1629. The latter lies beside his wife on an impressive altar-tomb in the face of which a beautiful, and crowded, family group testifies to their fecundity. An even more splendid monument is to be found just inside the bounds of the park in the neighbouring village of Great Limber, where the mausoleum to the first lord's young wife, Sophia Aufrere, in the form of a classical temple, has been described as James Wyatt's masterpiece. John Byng, however, who saw it in the course of building, was more interested in the fact that, 'below it, for the sake of contrast and miserable comparison stands (for the reception of the living) an alehouse so bad as not even to afford cheese'.

North of Caistor the wolds narrow to reach a final point on the Humber bank between Barton and South Ferriby. Almost all its villages nestle comfortably along the steeper western edge looking out towards Brigg and the Ancholme valley. The large village of Barnetby, which acquired some importance as a railway junction, stands at a gap in the hills where the A18 carries heavy traffic from Yorkshire and Scunthorpe towards Grimsby. A little to the south Bigby and Somerby lie beneath plantations on the hillside; in the former's nineteenth-century church are a fine series of monuments to various Skipwiths and Tyrwhitts. In Somerby lies a rather cheerful-looking knight of the late thirteenth century, perhaps one of the Cumberworths who owned the manor in the medieval period. Later Sir Thomas Cumberworth, who died in 1450, was to direct that he should be buried here in the north aisle. He left his boots and spurs to 'my child of the stabull', his stockings to 'my child of the hale' and his gloves to 'my child of the kechyne'.

Beyond Barnetby the wold edge swings north-west. Elsham delighted at least one nineteenth-century picturesque tourist with its 'romantic situation', 'church on a bold projection' (with a splendidly ornate western doorway), 'hall embosomed in a woody park' and wide views over a vale 'richly ornamented with plantations'. It was the hall, owned by his friends the Elwes family, that Percy Grainger made his headquarters for expeditions into Brigg workhouse and elsewhere to collect Lincolnshire folk-songs.

At Elsham the Brigg to Barton-on-Humber road climbs steep-

ly to the top of the wolds, but another route, which skirts their
foot to South Ferriby on the Humber, passes a succession of
villages. Worlaby, with some Saxon survival in an otherwise
thoroughly restored church and with the 1663 brick almshouses
built by Lord Bellasis for 'the lodging and relieving of four poor
women', was celebrated in execrable verse by one of the most
enthusiastically incompetent of Lincolnshire's many bad poets,
Joseph Goodworth Bedford of Wrawby, in his *Poems* published
in 1872:

> O lovely village! highly favoured spot,
> Where many a snug and comfortable cot
> . . . .
>   May now be seen
>
> Above them on a rising eminence
> Stands Worlaby House, a villa residence
>   Midst ornamental grounds
> Its fishponds, shrubberies, lawn and gardens neat,
> Their state of cultivation seems complete
>   And peace abounds
> . . . .
>
> A splendid school has recently been built
> In order to supply a want long felt
>   A better education
> And now I think a village such as this
> With all its vast and grand facilities
>   Claims admiration.

(This claim would no doubt have been strenuously disputed by
members of the Brigg Drum and Fife Band who, when they
visited the village in 1869, 'were set upon and beaten . . . and
their instruments cut and damaged'.)

On the wolds above the line of villages there are in places
spectacular views over the Humber and the new, slender and in
its way beautiful Humber Bridge. The approach road from the
M180 to the bridge crosses the upland area, as have for centuries
the preceding routes to crossings at New Holland and Barton.
There is an air of bleakness and remoteness about the countryside; it is Lincolnshire's Ultima Thule with nothing beyond but
Yorkshire.

Humber Bank

Now, after decades of projection, planning and increasingly expensive construction, there is no barrier more formidable than the tolls to hold up communication between the two sides of the river. This must in course of time have a profound psychological effect on the life of the area, for the Humber had always been a formidable barrier. Defoe's dismissal of Barton has often been quoted but will bear quoting again: 'A town noted for nothing that I know of, but an ill-favoured dangerous passage, or ferry, over the Humber to Hull, when in an open boat, in which we had about fifteen horses, and ten or twelve cows, mingled with about seventeen or eighteen passengers called Christians, we were about four hours tossing about on the Humber before we could get into the harbour at Hull.' A hundred years later the crossing was described as 'sometimes very terrifying from the waves caused by the river and tide waters meeting'.

But Hull, so much larger than any of the Lincolnshire towns, was a great magnet. The introduction of steam packets in the early nineteenth century reduced the terrors of the crossing, and by 1826 there were a number of rival ferries: the *Elizabeth* steam packet from South Ferriby, the *Royal Charter* steam packet together with sailing boats from Barton, and a market boat from Barrow. All these were superseded later in the century by the opening of the ferry from New Holland with its easy access by railway. Henceforth, in the palmy days of the age of steam, the economic and social ties between the two sides of the river were probably much closer than they were to be in the 1970s when they were forcibly espoused in the new county of Humberside.

Most of the Humber bank settlements are populous enough to swallow up several of the tiny villages of the neighbouring wolds. Barton might, one feels, have gone on to greater things. Already in 1086 it had its ferry and a market, and it was a port of some importance in the Middle Ages, but Hull outstripped it.

Later the railway age rather disregarded it, and it did not develop much beyond the description in White's *Directory* of 1856: 'A great trade in corn, malt and flour is carried on here. There are several corn-mills; malt and lime kilns; brick and tile and tan and fellmongers' yards; a ship-yard; a coarse pottery; and manufactories of whiting, rope, sail-cloth, &c.'

Barton has been described as an 'uneventful little town'. However, its pleasant, predominantly Georgian and early Victorian streets, such as Fleetgate, Bargate, Beck Hill and Priestgate, are delightful to wander through on one of those rare days when summer pays a fleeting visit to the banks of the Humber, and, if the modest scale of the vernacular architecture bears witness to the limited ambition of the town in modern times, its two impressive medieval churches give some idea of its importance in earlier times. St Peter's is the older of the two, redundant now and under restoration by the Department of the Environment. Its most prominent feature is a fine Saxon tower whose lower stages are of the late tenth century, with round and triangular-headed blank arcading and small windows, again triangular and round-headed. The upper stage is, like so much Saxon work in the county, of the period immediately before, or even after, the Norman Conquest. The tower served in fact as the nave of the original church; to its east is a surviving forebuilding of an even earlier period than the tower; to its east was a chancel which gave way at a later period to a new aisled nave and chancel of considerable size. There is a lot of late thirteenth-century work here, with later additions such as the Perpendicular clerestory. Unless this replaces earlier post-Conquest work which has disappeared without trace, St Mary's Church, originally a chapel-of-ease of St Peter's, must have been considerably larger when built than its mother church, for there is a great deal of work surviving in St Mary's which cannot be much later than 1200.

East of Barton, Barrow-on-Humber and Goxhill are both large villages with good churches. In the former is the tomb of George Uppleby who died in 1816 and was: '... What most admire, A well-formed, good-like, comely, country squire,' or so says Robert Franklin, a native of Barrow, in his poem "The Justice of the Peace".'

As farmer he was chief among the rest,
His flocks and herds were of the very best;
The fine sleek ox around was seen to feed
And lambs disporting, of the Leicester breed;
The well-bred heifer, and the beauteous cow,
That might have graced an agricultural show!
The various feathered fowl around the place,
From peacock, turkey, to the bantam race;
The useful draught horse, and the choicest swine,
Departed Uppleby! – these once were thine.

A little to the south, on the almost imperceptible eastern slope of the wolds, Thornton Curtis has another fine church, mostly of the thirteenth century, which has, among other splendours, a font of black Tournai marble similar in design and period to that in Lincoln Cathedral.

But the principal glory of Thornton lies some distance to the east of the village along a narrow road of twists and turns with distant views of Humber bank industry. The ruins of Thornton Abbey, and especially its almost intact gatehouse (the largest in England), are one of Lincolnshire's most important monuments. It was founded in 1139 for canons regular of the Order of St Augustine by William le Gros, Count of Aumâle and Lord of Holderness, and prospered to become one of the wealthiest religious houses in the county. After its suppression in 1539 it was refounded for a mere six years by Henry VIII as a college of secular canons for the administration of the sacrament, the observance of good manners, the care of the aged and the instruction of the young.

All that is to be seen above ground of the monastic buildings is a beautiful fragment of the chapter house and some traces of adjoining buildings, together with a wall of the south transept of the church, the rest of which can be traced from its exposed foundations. These lie at some distance from the great gatehouse which so struck Abraham de la Pryme in 1696: 'I was amazed to see the vast stupendous fragments of the buildings that have been there. There is all the gait-house yet standing, of a vast and incredible biggness, and of the greatest art, ingenuity and workmanship that ever I saw in my life.' It is still a most impressive sight, looming above its surroundings like a pyramidal iceberg. There are stone facings in parts, but the

main material is brick – very early brick for this is a building of
the 1380s.

The approach to the gatehouse from the outside is through a
brick barbican, forty yards long and lined with loopholes, crossing a moat. Architectural authorities disagree as to whether
this is an original feature or a grandiose approach for a great
house added after the dissolution. Large figures of the Virgin, St
John the Baptist and other saints look down from the west front
of the gatehouse. The chief impression left by the interior is of
the impressive proportion of the principal rooms and the tor-
tuous inconvenience of the spiral staircase which links the
floors. Henry VIII, in his older, more portly days, stayed here for
three days in 1541 and must have run great danger of being
stuck for ever. The narrowness of the stair and the absence of
any surviving kitchens or domestic offices have led some scholars to doubt whether the gatehouse was, in fact, the abbot's
lodgings and quarters for distinguished guests. On the other
hand, there is no other rational function which this enormous,
prestigious building could have served.

Grimsby is the largest town in Lincolnshire. It is also a town
in which the picturesque tourist is unlikely to find much joy.
Only the fine, if heavily restored, parish church of St James
remains as a witness to its medieval prosperity. All the rest of its
former wealth of religious buildings have disappeared without
trace, and its present-day aspect is that of an undistinguished
Victorian town hacked apart by twentieth-century planning
and road construction. And that is virtually what it is. The early
medieval port where Scandinavian merchants came to carry on
their trade, and where they 'found no want of mud and mire',
was probably at the peak of its prosperity in the first half of the
thirteenth century. The gradual silting of the harbour led to
long centuries of obscurity. In 1697 Abraham de la Pryme found
'but a poor little town . . . scarce a good house in the whole' and
moralized upon this punishment for the horrible sin of sacrilege
in pulling down so many of the town's former religious establishments.

By the early nineteenth century a population of about fifteen
hundred was existing in sleepy decay stimulated by fierce and
corrupt local politics, hoping for great things from the new
harbour under construction by the Grimsby Haven Company.

But it was the mid-century works, resulting in the opening of the Royal Dock in 1852, combined with the construction of the Manchester, Sheffield and Lincolnshire Railway, providing easy access to all parts of the kingdom, which brought about the town's spectacular expansion from 3,700 people in 1841 to 63,000 in 1901. In its heyday Grimsby was, of course, a fishing port *par excellence*, one of the greatest in the world. Expansion in this direction, however, was first noticeable somewhat later than expansion in general trade and had few existing foundations to build upon. It is ironic that in 1800 there was such a lack of fish in the town itself that the corporation offered a bounty of one guinea 'to induce the masters of fishing cobbles to supply the town with fish during the ensuing winter'.

The countryside around Grimsby compasses both the flat coastal marshlands and the first pleasant undulations of the eastern wold. The industrial area has spread far beyond the town itself along the Humber bank to the port of Immingham and to the vast oil terminal and refinery of Killingholme. The river's deep-water channel swings close to the bank here; hence, when a new dock for Grimsby was projected early in the present century, the site was transferred on engineers' advice to Immingham, a transfer to which, after some hesitation, Grimsby gave its support.

In July 1906 the ceremony of turning the first sod was attended by nine hundred people, brought by four special trains, who broke into spontaneous applause when Lady Henderson (wife of the Chairman of the Great Central Railway), not content with a mere token performance, filled her silver-decorated barrow with her silver and ivory-handled spade, wheeled the barrow along the planking and dumped the contents in a workmanlike manner. Over the next six years before the completion of the dock, 'Tin Town' alias 'Humberville', the village of corrugated iron which housed the navvies, became an object of curiosity for the neighbours to visit. They admired its excellent sanitation, the large canteen as imposing as a mission hall, the remarkable cleanliness of the huge dormitory, where clean sheets and the use of the kitchen cost 6d a day, and, not least, the law-abiding nature of the inhabitants who were roused to indignation when it was considered necessary to erect a police station on the site.

Grimsby's advancing tide of brick has caused most of the nearby villages to expand out of all recognition in recent years. Stallingborough is comparatively little developed, and here the eighteenth-century brick church has some good sixteenth- and seventeenth-century monuments to the Ayscoughs, including an alabaster bust of a pensive and hirsute Sir Francis, who holds a baton with the authoritative air of a chairman about to impose order on the meeting. The nearby village of Healing, where the Mussendons' 'once fayre house', sacrilegiously built with stone of the demolished church of St Mary's in Grimsby, brought such a curse upon the family, according to Gervase Holles, that both house and family had disappeared by the mid seventeenth century, is very much a dormitory village. So is Laceby, though enough older building survives to show why Arthur Young, and a succession of copyists, described it as 'one of the prettiest villages in the county'. Aylesby and Riby are still entirely rural. At the latter, Denzel Holles set up house, following his marriage in 1558. His great-nephew Gervase described Riby as 'lying at the entrance upon the Woldes, a place happy in the sweetness of the ayre and very delectable by the pleasant hilles and dales . . . affording withall as good hawking and hunting and as good conveniency for trayning and ayring of young horses as is anywhere else to be found'. Riby Grove, the stately home of the Tomlines, has gone, but traces of its park are still to be seen.

Grimsby has almost entirely swallowed up the inner ring of its surrounding villages, Great and Little Coates, Bradley and Scartho. The latter has one of a further group of North Lincolnshire mid-eleventh-century church towers. Others can be found at Old Clee, Waythe and Holton-le-Clay. A little farther out Waltham is still just about a distinct settlement, although much overgrown, and the fields of Humberstone in which Young saw 'a marvellous exhibition of every sort of luxuriant weed' now sport mainly brickwork and suburban gardens.

8

West Lindsey

The Scunthorpe Area

The geology of Lincolnshire can be seen at its simplest in the north of the county. At the latitude of Grimsby the procession from coastal marsh to chalk wolds, to clay vale, to limestone heath, to the sands and clays of the Vale of Trent, each in well-defined strips, can be made in less than half the distance which these features cover at the latitude of Lincoln.

West Lindsey covers three of these geological divisions. In an unbroken line from Lincoln up to Winteringham, on the Humber, the Cliff rises steeply to about two hundred feet above the western lowlands and slopes more gently down towards the central vale on the eastern side. The three divisions are clearly defined in landscape, in building materials between the plentiful stone of the Cliff and the brick of the other areas, and even in communication, where the straight roads of the higher country contrast with the often winding lowland routes.

The spectacular rise of Scunthorpe in the late nineteenth century and the more limited earlier expansion of Brigg tend to obscure the fact that this was formerly one of Lincolnshire's most completely rural parts. Previously only Gainsborough had any importance as a town, even by county standards. The area served by small market centres, little more than villages, like Market Rasen and Kirton-in-Lindsay, of a very limited and localized significance. The River Trent has throughout historic times been a centre of trade and communication (Gainsborough owes its existence to this), and the Ancholme, once it had been canalized in the mid-eighteenth century, opened up a route from the central vale to the Humber and provided a stimulus to the expansion of Brigg. It was not entirely successful as a navigation, however, until it was improved in the 1820s, when several hundred men were at work along the whole length. Their lawless depredations were such that 'an inhabitant of the district round Brigg asserts that scarcely a duck or fowl of any size is to be found for some miles on either side of the Ancholme'.

A couple of miles to the west of Ferriby Sluice, where the Ancholme joins the Humber, the great Roman road, Ermine Street, also reaches Humber bank at Winteringham. Its northernmost section is no longer a major road; in parts it is merely an unmetalled track, for the A15 which follows much of its course swings away north-eastwards through Brigg towards Barton and New Holland. Abraham de la Pryme, who toured this area extensively in search of antiquities when he was curate of Broughton in the 1690s, puts this change of route down to the many robberies which took place in the extensive woodlands of the area,' So that travellers durst not pass but in whole caravans together'. As a result 'Broughton, Appleby, Winterton and Wintringham, that were great and populous towns formerly . . . soon decayed and came to nothing.'

Dormitory development for Scunthorpe has given Winterton and Broughton once more the appearance of 'great and populous towns'. On approach they can easily look to be pure housing estate, but each has a good historic core of brick and local stone around a fine church. Both have Saxon towers, that of Broughton having a rather peculiar circular staircase tower protruding from the herringbone masonry of the main tower, similar to the arrangement at Hough on the Hill in North Kesteven. As in de la Pryme's day, a great area around Broughton is covered with woodland, dark conifers forming a beautiful backcloth to the lightness of the local stone when it catches the sunlight. A little to the north Appleby is also well wooded and has escaped major development. Further north still the area between Winterton and the Humber is almost bare of trees; it is an open, lonely agricultural landscape of wide views and few reminders of neighbouring industry but for the great scars of ironstone quarrying, past and present, which run the whole way along the Cliff edge, and the ubiquitous pylons carrying power in all directions from the Trent valley power-stations. At Whitton, Lincolnshire's most northerly village, de la Pryme found nothing worth seeing, in spite of the advantageous situation, and proceeded to quote an outrageous local rhyme to the effect that

'At Whitton's town end, brave boys, At every door, There sits a whore, At Whitton's town end.'

Between Whitton and Alkborough, at Trent Falls, the Trent joins the Humber, and at the latter we enter the Trent valley at one of its most beautiful sections. Here, in contrast with the flat lands which border the river for most of its length, the action of the water has over millions of years of prehistory thrown up an enormous cliff of sandstone which for a few miles runs parallel to the limestone ridge further east. The hand of man has improved the face of nature with plantations, and it is possible to walk for several miles along the cliff through a screed of beech, sycamore, horse chestnut and even surviving elms, with broad views now and then over the enormous distances of the lowlands to the west. At Alkborough the view is spectacular; standing at the carefully preserved medieval turf maze (Julian's Bower), the whole area around the confluence of the Trent and Ouse spreads out like a map below. The local stone in some of the Alkborough houses is of a delightful colour, a sort of yellow, browny green, and the fine church has yet another Saxon tower.

At Burton-on-Stather the local stone combines with old brick of a sort of tobacco colour. Burton 'in ancient times was the metropolis of the busy Trent': such is the somewhat exaggerated claim in White's *Directory* of 1826. At that time it had some urban claims and still boasted a market. In 1695 de la Pryme had been scornful: 'but little and ill-built and the worst market place that ever I saw'. Like so much of the area it is now very much overgrown with housing development. At the neighbouring village of Flixborough the sandstone cliffs end, and there is industrial development on the river bank – notoriously, of course, the chemical plant which blew up to put the words 'Flixborough disaster' on everybody's lips a few years ago. Two centuries earlier a similar disaster struck when, 'On 22nd February 1777, the brig Phoenix . . . having twenty barrels of gunpowder on board, took fire in the Trent opposite Burton Stather and blew up; the explosion unroofed several houses in the town and was heard with terror at a distance of many miles.'

Just to the south of Burton-on-Stather the industry of Scunthorpe begins, but absolutely on its verge in the rural oasis of Normanby Park. The fine Regency house, designed by Sir Robert Smirke, formerly the home ʃ the Sheffields, and its grounds are now owned by Scunthorpe Corporation and are open to the public. Outside the park are some good examples of early nineteenth-century estate cottages, particularly interesting in a county where little of such building survives from earlier than the middle of the century. According to Arthur Young, the Sheffields were model landlords, providing labourers' cottages at low rents in which they had considerable security of tenure and restricting the number of public houses in the area. The fruits of this policy were absence of poverty, cleanliness, sobriety and regular church attendance. The men at least were very sober and industrious; they even milked the cows – they had to as the women he found to be very lazy: 'They do nothing but bring children and eat cake.'

The area which we now know as Scunthorpe is a conglomeration formed in very recent times from what had been a group of scattered villages and hamlets in a poor and sandy district. It takes its actual name from one of the most insignificant of these, the township of Scunthorpe in the parish of Frodingham. When Abraham de la Pryme first visited the area in 1695, he found nothing of note in the area 'but the barrenness of the country and the sandy commons that I passed over, which . . . brought into my mind the sandy deserts of Egypt and Arabia'. In 1800 Scunthorpe itself was 'a mean stud and mud village' and the other settlements of the area were little better. In 1842 the chief industry of the district was still the culture of rabbit warrens, the fine silver-grey rabbits of the area being in particular demand by furriers. Even as late as this there was no thought of any other riches which might lie beneath the infertile topsoil.

Yet, surprisingly enough, the ironstone of the area had been known and worked in Roman and prehistoric times, and there is considerable evidence of pre-Roman settlement. Examples of many of the artefacts from this early period can be seen in Scunthorpe Museum. These early industrial beginnings, however, had no continuing history in more modern times, and the rise of the area to fame was the result, so the story goes, of the sudden observation of ironstone made by Rowland Winn when he was out shooting on his estate, or, to be more exact, his father's estate.

The Winns of Nostell Priory, Yorkshire, had owned a large estate in this area since the seventeenth century but seem to have to a large extent neglected them. If de la Pryme is to be believed, they seem to have been regarded with no great love in the area. His contemporary, Sir Rowland, knighted ('or pretended to be so') by Charles II, he calls 'a mighty, mad, proud spark, exceeding griping and penurious and a great oppressor of the poor'. To be fair, these lands offered little opportunity for improvement without enormous outlay, and the owners appear to have regarded them, reasonably enough, as capable of producing only low rents and rough shooting. Perhaps it was the shooting which brought Rowland Winn to reside at Appleby, but he was alive to the possibilities inherent in a good bed of ironstone. Landowners up and down the Cliff from Lincoln to the Humber were alive to them in the late 1850s. That it was the Scunthorpe area which saw the potential turn into a reality was due to two factors: the closeness here of the ironstone to the surface and Winn's determination.

The first idea may well have been to mine the ore and sell it to iron-masters as far afield as Derbyshire and Staffordshire and even South Wales. North Lincolnshire was not ideally situated for any actual iron manufacture as it was some distance from the nearest coalfield. The large-scale export of ore was, however, as difficult as the large-scale import of coal until the transport of the area was improved. There was no railway, and the roads to the nearby Trent were abominable. Winn was the chief promoter of a new Trent, Ancholme and Grimsby Railway which was to join the Manchester, Sheffield and Lincolnshire at Barnetby (thus opening the way to Grimsby) and to run from there westwards through the ironfield before crossing the Trent to link up with the South Yorkshire Railway. The first stretch from Frodingham to the river was constructed at great speed, and by the end of 1860 it was possible to transport the ore to the Trent by rail for loading onto barges. But the extension to Barnetby and the bridging of the Trent took a much longer time to complete. The bridge at Gunness in particular, opposed by the port of Gainsborough and other river interests as an obstacle to the free passage of shipping, was a long and difficult job where construction was bedevilled by bad publicity of a whole series of accidents to river boats. It was late in the 1860s before the whole line was open for traffic. By this time the future of Scunthorpe as a manufactory, not a mere supplier of ore, was decided; the first blast furnaces started production in 1864. By 1873 the *New-castle Daily Chronicle* was reporting on this new rival to the north-east which was 'rapidly assuming the appearance and proportions of a second Middlesbrough'. The ore was more accessible, cheaper and better than Cleveland's; the only draw-back was the distance from which coal had to be transported. Three new works added their production to that of the original one in the 1870s, and housing, such as the industrial hamlets of New Frodingham and New Brumby, was run up to accommo-date a fast-expanding workforce. By the 1880s the landscape was one of large industrial pockets with associated housing, alternating still with large areas of undeveloped land. As ex-pansion continued and as associated industries sprang up along-side the furnaces, these open spaces have gradually been filled, and the scattered nuclei of settlement have joined into one sprawling mass. There is nothing picturesque about Scun-thorpe, and the somewhat anonymous face of modern industrial plant has even destroyed the appearance of demonic energy which the town once had when its labours clouded the face of day and lit up the night sky.

Almost lost among the Victorian and later architecture of Scunthorpe is Frodingham's medieval parish church and the seventeenth- and eighteenth-century work of Brumby Hall. And on the town's southern boundary is the very fine Early English parish church of Bottesford.

At Bottesford Scunthorpe's tide of bricks and mortar is halted, and rural Lincolnshire once more asserts itself. To the west, extensive woodlands clothe the sides of the Cliff and the former warrens at its foot. To the south, beyond the motorway the A159 crosses an area of flatlands and gentle sand slopes towards Gainsborough. On its western side Scunthorpe is fast expanding along the A18 towards the Trent. The road crossing the river, beside the railway, was opened at this point as late as 1916, and a further crossing on the M180 now also exists a little further south. This multiplicity of crossings has totally transformed the transport pattern of the area over the last century. Before that there was no bridge over the Trent below Gainsborough, and even there the bridge only dates from the late eighteenth century. The Trent was, therefore, in appearance at least, as formidable a barrier to east-west transport as it was an important route for traffic from north to south.

This idea of the Trent as a barrier, however, must be treated with some scepticism. It was certainly a hindrance to the passage to and from the west of heavy transport, but man and horse could and did find easy access to the opposite bank by one of the many ferries. The Trent was much less of a barrier to the inhabitants of the Isle of Axholme than were the marshes which, before drainage, cut them off from the neighbouring counties of Yorkshire and Nottinghamshire. It seems probable that this comparative ease of cross-river communication must have been a major factor in attaching this particular area to Lincolnshire rather than to one of the other neighbouring counties.

The Isle of Axholme

The Isle of Axholme is an area some fifteen miles long by less than ten miles wide. Its western boundary with Yorkshire follows the meandering course of the Old River Don, while to the south it is divided from Nottinghamshire by the River Idle. The whole of the countryside is criss-crossed by a palimpsest of channels put down by centuries of drainers, and the work of these men has resulted in Axholme losing in appearance its island nature. But the low, dreary expanse of Thorne Waste and Hatfield Chase, where counties merge imperceptibly together, indeed the whole of the area except the low central ridge where the villages are built, was once so waterlogged and liable to flooding that it formed an effective barrier.

Cut off thus for long periods from their neighbours, living an independent life based on the wealth of fish, fowl and grazing which their fens supplied, it is not surprising that the Islonians regarded strangers with suspicion and were, by them, looked upon with the same condescending contempt that can often be heard in descriptions of other fen-dwellers. 'It was a mighty rude place before the drainage, the people being little better than heathen, but since that ways have been made accessible unto them by land, their converse and familiarity with the country about them has mightily civilised them, and made them look like Christians.'

To them, as to fenmen everywhere, the land in its unredeemed state was a source of wealth. To Charles I, ever at a loss to raise revenue to match his expenditure, his Axholme manors were a source of potential profit. In 1626 the King entered into an agreement with Cornelius Vermuyden for the drainage of sixty thousand acres in Axholme and Hatfield Chase. Vermuyden was to receive one-third of the drained land; the remaining two-thirds was to go to the King, who undertook to 'treat and deal, agree and conclude' with all those who claimed common rights.

What followed, for at least a quarter of a century, was the

county's first taste of fenland guerrilla warfare. To some extent this arose from objections to the drainage itself, both to the fact that it was carried out at all and to the fact that it was at first far from efficient. But the major cause of outrage was the enormous amount of land kept by the Crown in its own hands, which reduced the commoners' share to pitifully small proportions and cut down drastically the amount of stock for which they could find pastures. After a period of rioting and unrest they were forced into agreement in 1636. Then Civil War provided them with an opportunity to take back what they considered to be theirs. Parliament, like the King, could not look favourably upon such high-handed actions, but the commoners were persistent. They interspersed riots and legal actions and accepted any help which was available, including that of John Lilburne and the Levellers. It took thirty-one 'set battles' to 'subdue these monsters' under the Commonwealth, and still they fought on in the law courts for years – not without success for, when the legal proceedings finally came to an end in the early eighteenth century, the commoners were in possession of several thousand acres more than had originally been allocated to them.

Success such as this, even limited success, against the power of the Crown, Parliament and the 'undertakers', betokens organization and considerable wealth as well as determination. The site was on the whole an area not of major landowners but of men of small and moderate-sized holdings who could draw a reasonable fortune from the wealth of its fens and, after drainage, the wealth of its soil. This was one of the areas of the country where the multiplicity of ownership kept strip cultivation in existence until a very late period; signs of it can in fact still be seen here and there in the landscape. It is not now, however, a classical open-field landscape of narrow strips (or 'selions') all of which grow the same crop. It is a landscape in which an owner has perhaps consolidated three or four strips into one. There are no fences between one of these pieces of land and the next group of strips, but a varied pattern is imposed upon the ground by the varying crops which are grown. The greatly sloping fields of Haxey are a good example of this. It must be emphasized, too, that this is a post-enclosure landscape where, because of the large number of owners and the nature of the soil and the crops, the enclosure allotments were often as small as the normal unenclosed strips of other areas.

Axholme's villages, too (in fact many of them have the size and historically the status of small towns), show, like the countryside, the widespread prosperity of its inhabitants and the untidy building patterns of a sort of haphazard democracy. There are no tidy and beautified estate villages here and few attempts at beautification for its own sake. Everyone seems to have built to suit his needs, whether a substantial farmhouse or a small cottage, as and where he needed, in the universal red brick of the Isle.

The land of Axholme was, like that of the Holland fens, so good that, if well cultivated, a reasonable holding almost guaranteed a reasonable living. 'The crops there of every kind are almost universally good,' says Arthur Young. 'I never yet saw any lands so well weeded, so well attended to, and kept so generally clean . . . the whole country is like a garden.' Onions were one of the crops which he particularly noticed, and a contemporary comments also on the importance of hemp, flax and potatoes in the economy of the district. The hemp and flax crops gave rise to a thriving manufacture of sacking and canvas at Epworth in the nineteenth century.

Most of the settlements in the Isle are situated along a low but in places surprisingly undulating ridge which runs up its centre. The A161 from Gainsborough crosses a corner of Nottinghamshire, then follows this ridge through the villages on its way towards Goole. Haxey, the first Axholme village one reaches, is in many ways typical, a large and somewhat straggling settlement, brick-built with a few earlier houses interspersed with the predominant Victorian, and with its outlying hamlets of Craiselound and Westwoodside. From below, the eyes follow the strip pattern of the fields up to a skyline dominated by the church and the water-tower. The churches of Axholme, though not on the level of the superb ones of the Holland fenland, include several large and splendid buildings, and Haxey, mainly fifteenth-century Perpendicular but with some earlier bits, is one of the best.

West of Haxey near the Yorkshire border is the much smaller village of Wroot, 'situate on low grounds remarkable for a kind of Knott Fly, the sting so sharp that people, not used to the country, mowing meadows are not able to bear with it and leave their work – they call them "little men of Wroot"'. One of the best Lincolnshire tales, related by de la Pryme, is of the servant who left his master at Wroot to seek his fortune as a highwayman. He took up station on the Great North Road and attempted to stop a very genteel horseman who turned out to be a highwayman himself and told the tyro that he was doing it all wrong. The learner thanked him kindly, knocked him over the head and stole his horse and £50; returning then to his master, he said, 'Tush, master, I find this a very hard trade as you said it would prove, and I am resolved to go no more, but be contented with what I have got.'

North of Haxey the main road follows an undulating course along the ridge with wide views to either side. Spurs of higher land descend from the ridge into the flat fens; water-towers and the towers of disused windmills act as focal points for the eye. On the edge of the fens, close to the settlements, the names of Haxey and Epworth Turbaries on the map remind us of what was once the principal fuel of the area, for these are the diggings which were allotted to each parish to cut peat. Epworth is less scattered than Haxey and has a distinctly urban air, with its market-place, large church (like Haxey's mainly Perpendicular) and, of course, the Old Rectory which is a centre of pilgrimage for Methodists from all over the world. John Wesley was born at Epworth in 1703 – not, however, in the existing rectory, for his birthplace was burnt down in 1709 by a mob of angry Islonians, who were at odds with John's father's Tory and High Church principles.

Belton-in-Axholme is a large village with one of the Isle's best churches, again mainly fifteenth-century work, with tower gargoyles and angels on the porch. Northwards the road passes the grounds of Hirst Priory, a pleasant area of timber in an area often somewhat bare of trees, and descends to the lowlands to cross the Stainforth and Keadby Canal. Crowle, standing on a very gentle elevation above the surrounding form, is urban with a nice little market-place, the buildings around it mainly Victorian, and a church with considerable survival of Norman work and a fragment of a Saxon cross, on which one can see dragons, a man on horseback and a conversation piece of two figures in profile.

At Eastoft the A161 reaches the Yorkshire boundary. A minor

road branches eastward to the Trent past Luddington, whose church stands lonely in the middle of a great plain. On the banks of the broad and winding Trent one feels that Axholme really is an island. To the north and east are the river and the wooded slopes between Burton-on-Stather and Flixborough; to the south and west stretches the enormous plain of Axholme, hedge-less, full of corn, with only the ubiquitous pylons to give a vertical contrast to the vast horizontal expanse. The air is full of the sound of the wind in the reeds by the river. A little further south the village of Amcotts provides an oasis of green in the otherwise rather monotonous landscape; in contrast the view across the river is now an industrial one, over to Flixborough and distant Scunthorpe.

It is now possible to follow the Trent and the line of settlements along its bank most of the way back to Gainsborough, through Althorpe, whose church is almost all a 1483 rebuilding, West Butterwick and Owston Ferry. Impressive river façades in several of these villages bear witness to the former importance of the river as a means of transport.

Gainsborough and the Vale of Trent

Most of the settlements on the west bank of the Trent have their counterparts on the east bank, and numerous ferries plied between the two sides in former times. As on the west, a road follows the east bank of the river linking these settlements, from Gunness opposite Althorpe to Walkerith near Gainsborough. It passes through Burringham, East Butterwick and Susworth, which in the early nineteenth century was 'a very extensive mercantile situation lately erected by Mr Frankland – Mansion, Granarys, etc.' surrounded by 'some remarkable fine orchards'. East Stockwith, which in earlier days had rivalled Gainsborough as a port, was now 'a nice genteel-built village', while a few miles to the south Morton was another 'considerable genteel village'. Morton is now a northern suburb of Gainsborough but retains an air of gentility from the substantial villa residences built there by the Gainsborough merchants in the nineteenth century.

These Trentside villages used the natural tidal rise and fall of the river to produce the rich agricultural land which we now see along its banks. The process was called 'warping' and is described by Arthur Young who saw it in progress at Morton and other parishes. The method was to cut a canal to take off some of the river water with a series of lateral cuts into the surrounding land; the level of water could be controlled by a sluice at the river end. When the river rose, the land under warping was flooded, and as the water retreated, a thick layer of river mud was left behind. 'Thus a soil of any depth you please is formed, which consists of a mud of vast fertility.' The process could be a very quick one, for the river carried an enormous amount of mud; near Gainsborough Young was shown a spot where warp was left to a depth of ten inches in eight hours.

Gainsborough was the main port on the Trent and the most important centre for the river trade in the eighteenth and nineteenth centuries. Its shipbuilding yards are gone, as are most of its wharves and many of its warehouses, but the view of its river frontage from the flat lands on the west bank is still an impressive one.

The town's importance as a port may well have arisen as a result of its position at the limit of river navigation for sea-going vessels. At Gainsborough goods were trans-shipped to or from smaller craft which could negotiate the higher reaches of the Midlands, and through Gainsborough came pottery from Staffordshire, cheese from Cheshire, lead and iron from Derbyshire, ale from Burton-on-Trent, corn, coal and manufactured goods. During the Napoleonic Wars three hundred tons of munitions passed through the port each week on its way from Butterley Works in Derbyshire. The same firm sent the sections of Vauxhall Bridge by this route in twenty-seven ships in 1815. Up river came foreign timber and raw materials for the Midland manufactories and large quantities of luxury 'London goods' for the shopkeepers of Midland towns.

From at least the seventeenth century boatwrights and shipbuilders were carrying on their trade in Gainsborough. There were three shipyards here in 1826; some of the vessels they built were of considerable size, the *Brailsford* of 465 tons in 1811, the *Elizabeth* of 700 tons in 1812. They built their first paddle-steamer in 1815, the *John Bull*, which commenced a regular service between Gainsborough and Hull. The introduction of steam led to an immediate increase in passenger transport on the river, for it now took only a few hours for a trip which had taken anything up to a week by sail. By the 1860s it was even possible to take a day trip to the seaside at Cleethorpes or Scarborough by steamboat.

The prosperity of the port reached its zenith early in the nineteenth century; from mid-century onwards it was in decline. There was a sharp fall in the river trade in the early 1850s and further decline thereafter. The competition of the railways was blamed, but there was also perhaps a gradual deterioration in the navigability of the Trent itself. By 1908 only a few sea-going vessels dared to venture as far as Gainsborough.

Fortunately for the town's prosperity, it did not rely solely on its river trade. The 1856 *Directory* mentions 'four extensive mills for crushing linseed, three breweries, several large malt kilns ... five brass and iron foundries', in addition to the warehouses, rope-walks and shipyards. The impressive buildings of Marshall's, the largest of its iron foundries, still line one of the town's main streets for more than a quarter of a mile. As a result of the growth of engineering, the population rose rather than fell as the river declined in importance, from 4,500 in 1801 to 8,600 in 1871, 12,300 in 1881 to 19,200 in 1901. The twentieth century has seen a static, even declining, population and has witnessed the clearance of many of the crowded courts run up on building land which has made available in what had been the back gardens of the larger eighteenth-century houses. In 1881 over half the inhabitants lived in 121 of these 'yards'. The combination of these crowded living conditions with the miasmic influence of the Trent waters, 'more fertilizing than transparent', was no doubt responsible for Gainsborough's suffering more severely than any other Lincolnshire town in the cholera epidemic of 1849.

Few travellers have had anything complimentary to say about Gainsborough; Pevsner's *Buildings of England: Lincolnshire* describes it as 'one of the dreariest of the Midland red brick towns', surely an exaggerated claim: the Midlands can produce towns far drearier than this. Gainsborough is relieved, if by nothing else, by its comparatively small size, by its river, by the wooded hills of Thonock at its back, by one or two streets which preserve enough Georgian façades to make up for the deplorable dreariness of many of the modern buildings which have replaced former slums. It also possesses in its Old Hall a piece of domestic architecture of supreme interest and importance.

The two building periods represented here are the late fifteenth century, when Sir Thomas Burgh erected a house to replace one destroyed by the Lancastrian army in 1470, and the 1590s, when William Hickman made extensive additions. The external appearance is of three surviving ranges around a central courtyard, partly timber framed, partly of brick. A fourth range including a gatehouse must once have existed, but all trace is now gone. The main surviving medieval portions are the fine hall with its soaring roof timbers and a wonderful example of a medieval kitchen with two enormous fireplaces. The Old Hall fell on hard times in the eighteenth and nineteenth centuries and was put to such diverse uses as slum tenements, a linen manufactory and a theatre, but now, with extensive restoration in progress and with its occupation as a museum by the county museum service, its future seems secure.

Close to the Old Hall is the parish church of St James, an interesting marriage of a medieval tower with a classical eighteenth-century body which gave rise to the rhyme:

> Gainsborough's proud people
> Built a new church for an old steeple.

The market-place lies a little to the south of the church, and from here a road curves down towards the river bank and to the bridge erected in 1790 to replace the somewhat dangerous ferry where in 1760 six people had been drowned when a man leaped his horse into the boat and overturned it.

North and south of Gainsborough the valley of the Trent stretches to some ten miles in width before the limestone ridge of the Cliff is reached. The soils vary between hungry sand and deep clay, and the villages, now almost entirely brick built, presented formerly that array of stud and mud-built hovels which was universal in those areas of the county where stone was not easily available. To the north the A159 to Scunthorpe crosses a good deal of what was once 'sandy poor ling land' and is now, at Laughton Forest and Scotter Common, Forestry Commission plantations. It passes Blyton and Scotton with its late thirteenth-century church, and the large village of Scotter with attractive vistas of brick and colourwash. Messingham is the last village before the road reaches the M180 and the spreading tide of Scunthorpe. The church is interesting for the fragments of medieval glass, unconsidered trifles snapped up from many sources in his archdeaconry by Archdeacon Bayley who was the incumbent here in the early nineteenth century.

Bayley's curate, John Mackinnon, was encouraged by his vicar to write an account of the village as he knew it, together with what he could gather about its earlier state from oral evidence. The result, produced in 1825, is a fascinating description which is doubtless as applicable to many more villages in the area as it is to Messingham itself. Mackinnon speaks of the village's retired situation and the inevitable bad roads of former days, of pre-enclosure fields which 'yielded but little and that principally rye, which was cultivated for home consumption'. 'Here dwelt a peasantry rude in manners and uncultivated in mind', who made up for the poorness of their crops by the riches in fish and fowl of the abundant stretches of water and reed beds. Their amusements included Shrove Tuesday cock-fights and football matches, dancing at Easter and at the village feast, 'pat aback, dip o' the kit and blindman's buff' on May Day and telling stories around their peat fires in the winter. All of them kept sheep which, with the hemp which they grew in their backyards, supplied all the materials needed to produce their clothing and domestic linen.

Such was the village and its inhabitants before enclosure and drainage, which Mackinnon considered to have brought not only agricultural improvement founded by a great rebuilding of the previously poor housing but also an improvement in the people, their manners and their knowledge of the world.

From Gainsborough eastward the A631 climbs the steep bank of sandy soil which rises here above the flat lands by the Trent and passes the village of Corringham on its way towards Market Rasen. It is an area of neat fields and hawthorn hedges with distant views of the Cliff and the stone villages which climb its slopes. Scattered among the fields are the large farmsteads erected at a cost of £2,000 each for his tenants by Sir Thomas Beckett after the enclosure of Corringham in the late 1840s. The passing motorist can easily miss Corringham, and this would be a pity, as its village street runs off the main road at right angles, a pleasant street with the fine parish church of St Laurence at the end of it, with Anglo-Saxon tower, Norman arcade and further work of varying periods, including Bodley's painted ceilings and organ case and screen of 1883–4. In the chancel are monuments to several members of the Beckett family and also to Robert and Thomas Broxholme erected in 1681 by their still surviving brother and sister:

> Though to be four in person they were known,
> Yet both in will & minde they were but one.
> One father on one mother them begot,
> And they made up one fourefold true-love-knot.
> They kept one family and which is rare,
> They had no jarrings neither discords there.

Two lines of villages run south from the Gainsborough to Corringham road. One follows the line of the river to reach the

Nottinghamshire border at Newton-on-Trent; a minor road meanders southward from Corringham village to link the other, finally reaching Saxilby on the Foss Dyke. We will deal first with the riverside group, which follows the Trent through one of its most attractive stretches, an area picked out by Arthur Young as one of the county's finest pieces of landscape: 'Near Gainsborough there are very agreeable scenes . . . the view of the windings of the Trent, and its rich land plain of meadow, all alive with great herds of cattle, are features of an agreeable country.'

The agreeableness of the country made it a popular one for the gentry of the area to build their seats, and the parks and plantations of the Andersons of Lea, the Daltons of Knaith and the Huttons of Gate Burton make a great contribution to the beauty of the scene. The main road from Gainsborough to Lincoln follows a winding course through this civilized landscape past the grounds where Lea Hall once stood, past the wall which conceals Knaith's hall and church down by the river and through the oaks of Gate Burton where the massive neo-Classical hall dominates the scene from the east side of the road. To the west the parkland continues down towards the Trent near whose bank among the trees a Grecian temple stands in picturesque decay. It is a fitting scene for Watteau's lovers to embark if not for Cytherea at least for Hull.

At Morton, where the Roman Tillbridge Lane once forded the Trent, there are some good eighteenth-century brick houses and a fine eleventh-century herring-boned tower to the charmingly battlemented church. Torksey has an oil terminal, a golf course, the junction of the Foss Dyke with the Trent and one towered wall of an Elizabethan mansion, Torksey Castle. There is little else to show of the former importance of a settlement which was outstripped in importance only by Lincoln and Stamford in Domesday Lincolnshire.

The low but steep range of hills of sand which has closed in the valley from Gainsborough southward has now given way to a plain whose slopes are relieved only by the gentlest of undulations. Long views open out to the east as far as the Cliff and Lincoln Cathedral. Following the road south, we are soon on the Nottinghamshire border. The villages are built of a good dark eighteenth- and nineteenth-century brick. At Kettlethorpe the

gatehouse remains of the fourteenth-century house of the Swyn-
fords.

Brick is also the building material of the line of small villages
which runs south from Corringham through the clays. The
churches at Heapham and Springthorpe have two more of
Lincolnshire's Saxon towers, but the two main delights of this
area are the churches of Stow and Cotes-by-Stow. The former is
one of the most monumental pieces of Saxon architecture surviving in England. It dwarfs the small village which surrounds
it and dominates the countryside. What we now see is in fact a
mixture of Saxon and Norman construction, but it seems likely
that the original Saxon church was already of the present size.
The Saxon work is in the crossing and transepts, the crossing
arches giving an impression of enormous strength. This is all
early eleventh-century work though there are traces of the
tenth-century church in the bottom courses of masonry. After
the Conquest, we are told, Bishop Remigius found the church in
ruins, and the nave is probably more or less as he rebuilt it. The
chancel is later but still Norman. The whole of the church,
whether viewed from outside or in, is magnificent.

A total and delightful contrast is to be seen a couple of miles to
the east of the village where, perhaps even as Stow church was
being first built, a small settlement was growing up around the
cotes where the shepherds of the parish gathered their flocks.
Cotes is a tiny hamlet: a small church, a vast farmyard and little
more, but the church is a gem. It is a mixture of Norman, Early
English and fifteenth-century work and has, in a county which
is on the whole so poorly endowed in this respect, its medieval
rood screen in an almost complete state of preservation. Bench
ends and pulpit add to the wealth of woodwork, and the six-
teenth- and seventeenth-century memorials to Hansards and
Butlers complete the picture.

Stow's former hamlet, Sturton, which has now outgrown its
parent, stands on Tillbridge Lane, the Roman road which branches off from Ermine Street a little to the north of Lincoln and
runs down to the Trent. East of Sturton a solitary farmstead
marks the site of Stow Park, one of the medieval houses of the
bishops of Lincoln and a favourite residence of the saintly and
ultimately sainted Hugh of Avallon who governed the see from
1186 to 1200. He celebrated his installation by the slaughter of

three hundred of his deer from Stow Park to provide a feast for the poor, and it was at Stow Park that the bishop was adopted by a swan of marvellous strength and size which thrust its company upon him at every opportunity and greeted him upon his returns to Stow with great joy.

The whole of the Wapentake of Well which covers this part of the county was subject to the episcopal manor of Stow. The life of the medieval peasant springs vividly to life in a survey of the holdings, rents and services of this manor drawn up in 1283. In return for their holdings of land, his tenants owed to their lord works of ploughing and harvesting, thatching for his farm buildings, forage for his horses and hens for his table. Some carried out carriage works for his goods, some acted as his messengers, one as his carpenter, some as his brewers. Some were responsible for going to the Trent or the Isle of Axholme in the bishop's ship to fetch timber or peat turves for fuel. On the days when they were carrying out ploughing works for the lord, he was to provide them with their food, four loaves of wheat, barley or rye, and eight herrings.

The low-lying ground to the east of Stow and Sturton where the little River Till now flows in canalized propriety supported little population in earlier times owing to the marshy nature of the ground and the frequent overflowings of the river. Broxholme is one small settlement on rather higher ground, a village which has slightly shifted its position, for the marks left by the original houses and village street can be seen in the fields near to the present site. Saxilby, near the junction of the Till with the Foss Dyke, grew in Victorian times from the importance of its canal traffic and has now grown larger still from the extensive housing estates put up for people who work in Lincoln.

The Cliff

The limestone ridge running from the Humber south to Lincoln is called 'the Cliff', as opposed to the name of 'the Heath' which is usually given to its continuation to the south of the county capital. The geology and resultant landscape of both areas are very similar.

The Cliff itself is almost completely bare of settlement, but it provided ample limestone to construct two rows of villages which lie along the spring lines on its eastern and western sides. The western scarp is steep, and the settlements here nestle below it or climb the lower contours; to the east the slope is a much more gentle one. The parish layout is one of rectangles which stretch several miles from east to west to take in both limestone land on the top and some of the clay land at the foot of the slope; north to south, however, the parishes do not stretch very far, and the villages lie close together. Ermine Street provides the boundary between the eastern and western groups of parishes. From Ermine Street there are enormous views to the east over the lowlands to the distant wolds. Along the western edge Middle Street, which follows the upper contours, provides even broader panoramas to the Trent valley and beyond.

All these parishes, with scarcely an exception, were enclosed in the classical period of enclosure between about 1770 and 1820. Here and there signs of the enclosure layout of fields remain, but there has been a great tendency to throw field after field into one to produce vast, rolling areas of corn or beet or potatoes. The plentiful stone was used in some parishes to produce dry stone walls instead of hedges, and some survive, though there is little or no sign that the art is being kept alive. It is a bare, often cold and windswept landscape, often almost treeless, though a number of good parks and plantations relieve the eye from time to time. This was never an area of much woodland and is probably less bare now than it was in the pre-enclosure period when Lord Yarborough could ride across country from Manby near Brigg to Harpswell without having more than three hedges to negotiate. The Cliff is also less bare of habitation now than it was before enclosure. Houses are still few enough in the views on either side of Ermine Street, but scattered over the scene are the substantial stone farmhouses and their surrounding buildings put up when the farmers moved out of the villages to live among their enclosure allotments in the early to mid nineteenth century.

It was a landscape which aroused the admiration of Cobbett on his rural ride from Barton to Lincoln: 'Generally speaking the land is excellent; easily tilled, no surface water, the fields very large . . . and innumerable flocks of those big, long-woolled sheep, from one hundred to a thousand in a flock. One of the finest sights in the world is one of these thirty or forty acre fields, with four or five or six hundred ewes, each with her one or two lambs skipping about upon the grass.'

Anyone who travels north of Lincoln in a hurry will follow Ermine Street, absolutely straight for mile after mile except where it now does a long curve to allow a long enough runway for the Vulcan bombers of Scampton RAF station. The road follows an up-and-down course through the gentle undulations of the limestone, passing near to the parklands of Hackthorn Hall where the eighteenth-century poet John Langhorne was for a time tutor to the Cracroft family. In his verse he celebrated the beauties of 'Hackthorn's flower-filled vale'; he also celebrated other beauties in a most practical way and eloped with the daughter of the house. But all was forgiven; a due and proper marriage settlement was made, and the poet dedicated his *Country Justice* to Robert Wilson Cracroft.

At regular intervals other parks relieve the bareness of the land. The grounds of Fillingham Castle stretch from the edge of the Cliff across to Ermine Street with screeds and clumps of trees and an ornamental gateway to the main road. A little farther north the woods of Norton Place lie on the east side of the road. At this point, where Ermine Street crosses the A631 from Gainsborough to Market Rasen, is the only ancient settlement to be found on this long stretch of road, the picturesquely named hamlet of Spital-in-the-Street. This grew up around a hospital founded in the fourteenth century. It is very small; its former coaching inn now a farmhouse, a few cottages, a small chapel, an almshouse and a former Sessions House, now a potato store, but its position near an important crossroads gave it for centuries an importance much greater than its size. Coaches from London to Barton Waterside stopped at the Spital Inn; magistrates, jurors and delinquents from a wide area attended Quarter Sessions. Here, for instance, on 21st December 1383 Robert de Willough-by and other justices sat to deal with cases presented to them by jurors from the whole of West Lindsey, cases such as that of Thomas de Holm who on the Vigil of St Andrew's Day preceding had at night feloniously killed Johanna and Beatrice Skowt of Spital and stolen their goods and chattels to the value of £20. Thomas was, it was said, a known thief, but the family of his victims was not above reproach. John Skote from nearby Bishop Norton, probably a relative, was accused of three separate offences: the theft of twelve sheepskins worth 2s, of 18d in the purse of Robert Williams' wife and of four bushels of grain worth 2s.

A more leisurely traveller can set off from Lincoln along Middle Street on the Cliff's edge, dropping down almost at random into any or all of the villages of light-coloured lime-stone, bright when the sun shines on it, which line the foot. In all of them the larger houses, usually seventeenth or eighteenth century, are the pre-enclosure farmhouses deserted by the far-mers when they moved out later to their enclosure allotments. Burton has the parkscape and hall of the Monsons and one or two fine smaller houses; North and South Carlton each have good manor houses, and in the short distance between the two the lost village site of Middle Carlton shows up as cropmarks. The elevation of the road above these villages gives a panoramic view of them.

At Scampton the needs of the RAF station have forced Middle Street as well as Ermine Street into a detour, and the road descends to the lowlands for a few miles before ascending once more. At Fillingham a wooded landscape marks the western edge of the park of Sir Cecil Wray's eighteenth-century Gothic castle, which can itself be seen through the trees. Below the ridge the parkscape continues in an ornamental lake beside the village. The next village, Glentworth, was the Wrays' home in the Elizabethan period, but what we can see forlornly rotting away at the foot of the hill is the remains of a grandiose house designed by James Paine for the Earl of Scarbrough in 1753. Less poignant to see is Glentworth's fine church tower and the great monument to Sir Christopher Wray, Elizabeth's Lord Chief Justice. Also buried here is Dame Elizabeth Saunderson, of 'great virtues and a greater desire of concealing them ... humble without meanness, liberal but not profuse, devout without ostentation'. She was the last of the direct line of the Wrays, and at her death in 1714 Glentworth went to James Saunderson, Lord Castleton, and ultimately to the Lumleys, Earls of Scarbrough, as heirs of her husband, and Fillingham to the nearest heir male of the Wrays, Sir Cecil, 'who out of respect and gratitude has caused this monument to be erected'.

At Harpswell the park-like nature of the landscape continues, though all trace of the hall of the Whichcotes is now gone and a farmhouse stands on the site. Many traces of this family, which owned the parish for several centuries, can be found, however, in the church where there are memorials to George, who died in 1720, and his son Thomas Whichcot, MP for the County of Lincoln from 1740 to 1774, whose loyalty to the Hanoverian succession was such that he gave the church its clock as a memorial to the defeat of the Jacobite rebellion of 1745 in the hope that whenever it struck it would remind the parishioners of their deliverance.

At Harpswell the A631 from Gainsborough ascends the Cliff; the vast buildings of the former RAF station at Hemswell are set in a wide, bare landscape. Hemswell itself, followed by Willoughton, Blyborough and Grayingham, continues the attractive line of villages. Kirton-in-Lindsey is much larger: a small market town which has after some painful reappraisals reconciled itself to becoming a large village. A few years ago it had a somewhat forlorn air, with a number of derelict buildings around its market-place devoid of commerce, bringing to mind words intended for quite a different town far away from Lincolnshire:

> Below the down the stranded town,
> What may betide forlornly waits.

All this was a far cry from the hopeful days of the 1850s when, just as the ironstone boom was about to hit Scunthorpe, it was forecast that Kirton would become a centre for mineral extraction and would rival in its size and importance 'not only the humble towns of Brigg and Gainsboro' but perhaps Birmingham'.

Kirton was never destined, however, to take off as an urban centre, although it retained throughout the nineteenth century some importance as a local market and as an administrative centre. It succeeded Spital as the home of the Quarter Sessions and also had the House of Correction for West Lindsey, where the Reverend David Wayland was somewhat anxious, in taking up his appointment as prison chaplain, to find two pistols ready cocked beside the prayer book and to be given the instruction, 'If one of them should spring at you, shoot him instantly.'

Kirton's narrow streets of stone houses spreading up the hillside are pleasant to wander through, and the church with its imposing tower is evidence of its aspiration to urban status.

The line of villages along the eastern verge of the Cliff presents features very similar to those on its western flank. All are stone built; all have their attractive features. An early nineteenth-century description of one of the best of them could have stood, and could still stand, for them all: 'rather a neat village standing on a dry rocky situation; houses stone and neat; there is rather a comfortable village inn, and the property of the lordship divided by white-thorn hedges'. North of Glentham, Waddingham has its stream and its village green; Redbourne has the house and parkland of the Duke of St Albans, with ducal estate building and the ducal coat of arms here and there in its street. Hibaldstow is a large and attractive village with some good houses.

Brigg and the Central Vale of Lindsey

Cobbett found Brigg 'a delightfully pretty town'. In this he is unique. Other observers of the same period ventured no further than 'a neat place' or, more expansively, 'The town is well built and paved and enjoys the benefit of a good trade in corn, coal and timber. Here are also several manufacturers of fur, with tanners and fell-mongers who give employment to a considerable portion of the inhabitants; and it is said that more hands are employed here in dressing rabbit skins than in any other provincial town in the kingdom.'

It was the bridge over the Ancholme here, after which the main route swung north eastwards away from Ermine Street, combined with the possibilities inherent in a navigable river, which brought about the rise to urban status of Brigg, or Glandford Bridge as it was originally called. By 1669 it was an important enough centre for Sir John Nelthorpe to found a grammar school here, and when Abraham de la Pryme in 1696 gives us a description of 'Brigg . . . that I go so oft to, to see the newse', it was already a pretty large town with a good trade. It had no church, however; Wrawby, at over a mile's distance, was the main parish, but different parts of the town were actually parts of three others as well. As a result it became a great haven for dissenters and 'a seminary for all such like cattel the whole county over'.

A chapel of ease was erected first in 1699, but the present parish church dates only from the 1840s, built in a style which has been described as neo-Early English. Signs of the importance of the river trade can still be seen where the main road enters the town over the river lined with nineteenth-century warehouses. It then broadens out into a rather narrow market-place, at whose northern end Bigby Street and Wrawby Street diverge at an acute angle. Brigg is not a major architectural experience; like so many of Lincolnshire's market towns, it is predominantly nineteenth-century brick, relieved by a few survivals of merchants' town houses from Georgian times and, in the present case, a number of rather cheerful-looking town inns.

In the 1820s the Ancholme was made navigable for vessels of sixty tons as far as Bishop Bridge in the parish of Glentham, about a dozen miles south of Brigg. This resulted in an increase of trade and population in the villages along the valley and provided an avenue of transport for the crops now growing on the recently drained lands. The horse-boat from Bishop Bridge and Kelsey brought the country folks in to Brigg market every Thursday. But the valley remained liable to flooding in particularly wet seasons: within the last year or two the eastward view from Waddingham Cliff towards the distant wolds took in what appeared to be a vast lake along the Ancholme lowlands.

The twin villages of North and South Kelsey lie some half-dozen miles south of Brigg. In South Kelsey church are monuments to the Hansard family, prominent in the county in the late medieval period. Charles Tennyson d'Eyncourt, ever conscious of ancestry, asked the parliamentary reporter of that name whether he claimed any descent and was most put out to be informed that Mr Hansard was probably related but was more interested in present achievements than in noble forebears. As was so often the fate of the inhabitants of the more remote areas of Lincolnshire, the inhabitants of Kelsey had their critics. In 1872 the *Stamford Mercury* described the village as 'dirty drunken and disreputable'. 'An Old Ratepayer' sprang at once to the defence: 'The genuine Kelseian is a stout, robust fun-loving fellow, rather noisy sometimes, hence he is sometimes called a tippler, but he is generally a good neighbour and loves to associate with his fellows and laugh.'

Between the former marshes of the Ancholme valley and the wolds is a stretch of sandy 'moorish' ground. Ancient settlements are sparsely scattered, and the land often lay uncultivated until the early nineteenth century. The roads were abominable. When the Elmhirst family moved to Usselby in 1821, they had to dismount from their carriage and walk for the last few miles through the deep sand. The great tracts of moors and common were covered with gorse, heather and fern and, in times of flood, with small lakes and pools. The area was alive with wildfowl, game and vermin of all kinds. The gradual reclamation of the land has totally changed the face of this country. Large areas have been afforested. At Moortown House is the small-scale parkscape of the Skipworth family and the home of G. B. Skipworth, a benevolent landlord, a rabid opponent of vaccination and clerical magistrates, and one of the Tichborne claimant's most fervent supporters. He was imprisoned for a while for contempt of court over the affair; on his return home the church bells rang, the bands played and triumphal arches were erected along his route. A mile or two to the south of Moortown are the more extensive park and plantations of the Dixons of Holton-le-Moor with the late eighteenth-century hall and the charmingly laid out village. A pleasant and unusual touch is the placing of the actual names of the tenants (around 1900 perhaps) on a number of the estate cottages.

The small town of Market Rasen lies near the foot of the wolds between moors and the 'cold clay country' which stretches southwards towards Lincoln. The main street, the greenstone church tower and an imposing Ionic portico to its Methodist chapel, and good pieces of Georgian domestic architecture scattered here and there, make it a good place to while away an hour or two. The neighbouring village of Middle Rasen has impressive Norman work in its church, and at West Rasen the church, trees, farm and fourteenth-century packhouse bridge over the miniscule River Rase combine beautifully.

South of Market Rasen a network of roads pursue eccentric courses in the general direction of Wragby. Linwood, with fine fifteenth-century brasses in the church to members of the Lyndewode family, lies in this direction. A little further west the A46 to Lincoln crosses first Lissingley Field, which before its enclosure late in the nineteenth century was 'a common meadow in the several parishes of M. Rasen, Buslingthorpe, Lissington etc. . . . as soon as the hay is cut and carried by 12 Augt, it becomes an open common for the scramble of the whole country'.

Apart from a few stretches of woodland the area between Market Rasen and Lincoln is a bare, open, gently undulating and sometimes rather dreary corn plain. The one thing which no traveller should miss is Snarford church which lies about half a mile off the main road with only a single farmhouse for company. The church is small, plain, high roofed, rather barn-like. On the fifteenth-century font are the head of Christ and the instruments of the passion. But what one comes to see is the chapel with its monuments to members of the St Poll (or St Paul) family, monuments which are not only sumptuous by any standard but also a total contrast to the simplicity of the building in which they stand. The canopied tomb of Sir Thomas St Paul, who died in 1582, is enormous, with six bulbous posts, fantastic decorative devices and kneeling children upon the canopy. Near it is the standing wall monument to Sir George St Paul, who 'lived in great honour and died in much comfort' in 1613. His widow married Robert, Lord Rich, who was created Earl of Warwick, and their busts adorn a third monument nearby.

The monuments seem to fill the chapel almost to bursting, yet, oddly enough, it was used as a school in the 1820s, and here in the evenings the schoolmaster, Joseph Pacy, sat desperately reading in an effort to keep ahead of his scholars, while his friends made ghostly howlings outside in an effort to frighten him.

9

Lincoln

The city of Lincoln lies at the point where a gap in the Cliff allows the River Witham, which has flowed for thirty miles and more in a northerly direction, to swing south-east and reverse its course towards Boston and the sea. To the north and south is limestone heathland while to the east and west are low-lying tracts of what was once fen and sandy waste. The cathedral stands out for miles around in the eye of travellers from nearly every direction. To Robert Southey, approaching from the west, the nearer he came, the more dreary was the country around him and the more majestic the building in front. Another tourist in 1801 saw the slopes with the castle and cathedral on top rising above 'several miles of level waste nearly half of which was a succession of lakes, from which were rising at that instant myriads of water birds which . . . formed an infinity of bright flickering spots on the sombre background'.

The Romans founded a legionary fortress on the level ground at the top of the northern slope some two hundred feet above the valley floor. Its original extent is marked by a few stretches of wall which have been uncovered but principally by the known sites of its four gates. The northern one, Newport Arch, still survives intact despite the occasional attentions of absent-minded lorry drivers; part of the eastern gate has been excavated and can be seen in the forecourt of the Eastgate Hotel; the west gate is known to exist under the western wall of the castle, while the site of the southern one is known to have been near the top of Steep Hill. As Lindum Colonia prospered, it expanded down the slope of the hill towards the river and the Foss Dyke, the canal which the Romans built to connect the Witham and the Trent.

As with most towns, the fate of Lincoln in the centuries which immediately follow the fall of the Roman Empire and the arrival of the Germanic tribes is obscure. Bede's description of the visit of Paulinus to preach Christianity and his conversion of the 'prefect of the city' suggests the continuation in some degree of urban life and organization. Lincoln was certainly of sufficient importance to become one of the centres of Scandinavian rule in the Danelaw, and Domesday Book records that there were about a thousand households here in 1066. It also records that 166 of these houses were demolished to make way for the building of the castle. At about the same time the centre of the enormous diocese which included Lincolnshire was transferred from Dorchester-on-Thames to Lincoln, and work on the construction of the cathedral was started.

These two buildings were to dominate the spiritual and administrative life of the area, just as they were to stand out over the surrounding countryside. The castle was one of the keys of the kingdom, its importance shown by the battles which were waged around it between 1140 and 1144 during the anarchy of Stephen's reign and again in the confused times which followed the death of King John in 1216. After the thirteenth century it was militarily less prominent, apart from a brief and inglorious siege during the Civil War, but it remained a judicial and administrative centre for many centuries.

Lincoln's great days were during the Middle Ages, when its position as fortress, centre of spiritual and temporal government, and important trading town joined both inland and seaward by a network of navigable waterways, combined to make it one of the greatest cities in England. By the early sixteenth century it was in decay, its trade sadly reduced, many of its host of churches falling into ruin and being sold for building stone. The corporation seized upon the opportunity presented by a visit of Henry VIII in 1541 to clear the town of dunghills and other rubbish and array the aldermen in gowns of scarlet and crimson and such other citizens as could afford it in gowns of russet, to wait upon the King with a gift of twenty fat oxen and a hundred fat sheep and to lay their sad case before him. They were seeking some relief of taxation, without which 'most part of the citizens will be compelled in short time to forsake the city, to its utter desolation'.

Lincoln continued to impress visitors with its air of decay and desolation, below hill at any rate, throughout the seventeenth and eighteenth centuries. Defoe found it 'an ancient, ragged, decayed, and still decaying city'. Even in the early nineteenth century it was credited with 'the mere appearance of an overgrown village' whose rude and uncultivated lower classes had no enjoyment except in an alehouse and no conversation except arguments over hangings and electioneering. But if trade below hill was a picture of decline, the area above which centred on the Minster Yard was going through a period of fashionable boom in the eighteenth century. Many of the gentry built houses on Dean and Chapter leaseholds; here dowagers could be relegated to gossip and play gentle games of cards with the canons in residence and their wives, and here the country landowners could come to attend assizes, assemblies, Lincoln Races and the annual 'Stuff Ball', founded to promote the wearing of native woollens. It was an eternal round of 'bells ringing, clocks striking, men drinking, women talking and children dancing', as the Dean's wife said in 1771.

Whatever may have been its appearance to visitors, throughout the eighteenth century the town was undergoing a slow revival as a commercial centre, almost imperceptible perhaps in the early years of the century but speeding up with improvements to the navigation of the Foss Dyke and the Witham between the 1740s and 1770s. The increase in trade is shown by the rise in the tolls collected on the canal from an average of little over £100 a year in the 1720s to about £1,000 in the 1760s, about £4,000 at the beginning of the next century and £8,500 in 1830. The increased productivity of the surrounding countryside which was a result of drainage and enclosure also contributed; there were more goods to be moved as well as easier means of moving them, and greater wealth produced. The population of Lincoln in 1801 was nearly seven thousand, probably double that of 1700, and it was to double again by 1841. The arrival of the railways in 1847 gave impetus to an infant engineering industry. White's *Directory* of 1856 reported that already 'one of its iron foundries and machine works has grown into an immense establishment for the manufacture of patent portable steam engines, agricultural implements and machinery'. The firm, Clayton & Shuttleworth, employed a force of seven hundred at their Stamp End works. Other firms had also been set up, and before the end of the century Lincoln became one of the great centres of heavy engineering, the home of threshing machines, excavators and enormous steam-navvies and the birthplace of the tank.

The rather unhandsome sprawl of the lower city is a result of this industrial expansion. Outwards from the thin belt of eighteenth- and early nineteenth-century building along the enormously long High Street, pasture closes and waste ground were given over to the construction of the factories and the houses of their work-people. Other development took place along the river to the east of the town centre and on the slopes above it, and on open ground westwards towards the race-course. Later still, in the present century, Lincoln has, in the way of all towns of any size, spread out much farther, over a great swathe of countryside to the south and south-west and also on the northern, above-hill, side which had been less touched by earlier expansion.

Entering the city from the south, along High Street, the churches of St Botolph, St Peter at Gowts and St Mary le Wigford and the remaining range of the hall of St Mary's Gild survive as reminders of Lincoln's medieval expansion in this direction. The rest is much more modern; a great deal of Victorian building, much undistinguished twentieth-century rebuilding and some graceful relics of the Georgian age in upper storeys which surmount the sort of shop fronts which nowadays seem designed to make every town look like every other. The street crosses the river at the High Bridge, which carries sixteenth-century timber-framed buildings on its western side and medieval vaulting, restored of course, below. Also much restored is the fifteenth-century guildhall which incorporates one of the town's medieval gateways, the Stonebow.

A little way to the west of the High Bridge is Brayford Pool, a wide expanse of water where the River Witham meets the Foss Dyke. In the eighteenth and early nineteenth centuries it was the hub of Lincoln's activity as an inland port, with numerous boats plying to and fro between here and the Midland and Yorkshire towns, laden most likely with corn or flour in one direction and coal in the other. Some of the vessels were constructed by local boatbuilders such as the one named Talks who built a sloop for Alderman Thomas Greaves, a timber and coal merchant. Being 'in needy circumstances and a drinking man', Talks had to be kept going with frequent advances of cash, more in fact than the total sum originally contracted for. This did not prevent the boatbuilder suing Greaves' heiress for the whole amount after the alderman's death. Brayford is bereft now of its thriving commercial traffic; the pleasure boats which it houses are a poor substitute, as are the unappealing office blocks for the mills and warehouses which once surrounded it.

The motorist is likely to have almost unlimited time to admire the beauties of selected areas of downhill Lincoln. In its road network the city is wasp-waisted; great fans of highways to the north and south of the river are drawn together for the crossing. To make matters worse, in a moment of aberration the nineteenth-century city fathers allowed the construction of two level-crossings within a couple of hundred yards of each other in the High Street. Even at the time this was viewed with some concern, and it has since become a recipe for total chaos. To make matters worse, it often seems that everyone who lives to the south of the town works on the north side of it and *vice versa*. In traffic jams, therefore, Lincoln can compete with honour at the very highest level. A bypass is projected; a speedy start on construction is promised, even a completion date suggested; most of the inhabitants will believe in it when they see it.

Unfortunately Lincoln's best traffic jams usually strand the traveller near its worst architecture. There is a lot of this. The lower town centre has been pretty thoroughly hacked about since the war; multi-storey car parks abound, concrete boxes of many sizes but all too little shape, chain stores the vilest of their vile race. Over all a new City Hall, malevolently brooding on the scene, is thoroughly worthy of its surroundings, while the nearby city police headquarters seems to have been designed to stand a siege of indefinite length. Beside these the restrained administrative neo-Georgian of the 1930s county offices is a positive relief. Here and there Georgian and Victorian survivals bear witness to what the city centre was once like, together with occasional survivals from even earlier periods, such as the early Tudor Cardinal's Hat at the top of High Street and the medieval Greyfriars' building which houses the City and County Museum.

But if the lower town presents comparatively little to give pleasure to the eye, the hill slopes and the historic core which surrounds the castle and cathedral at the top provide ample compensations. Domestic architecture of all periods from the twelfth century onwards can be seen on Steep Hill, through Bailgate and in the other streets and narrow lanes which immediately surround the close. The earliest is to be found on the Steep, in Jews' Court and Jews' House near the bottom and in the so called House of Aaron the Jew near the top, all of them reminders of the large Jewish community which flourished in the city in the two centuries after the Norman Conquest. In the close the fourteenth and fifteenth centuries are represented by the Chancery on the east side and the Vicar's Court on the south, near to which are extensive remains of the medieval bishop's palace. This whole area suffered considerably when the castle was besieged during the Civil War, and many houses survive which were rebuilt during the century which followed it. Many were not rebuilt right from the ground, however, and there are numerous survivals of earlier buildings behind the seven- teenth- and eighteenth-century fronts. In Bailgate the predomi- nant architectural periods are Georgian and Victorian, with some relics, however, of the houses put up by well-to-do trades- men in the Tudor and Stuart era, such as the fine timber-framed one on the corner of Castle Hill.

The public buildings of the area are mainly Georgian, the former Blue Coat School on Christ's Hospital Terrace, the nearby Theological College, erected as the County Hospital in the 1770s, the stock brick Judges' Lodgings on Castle Hill and the Assembly Rooms in Bailgate, where the scene of eighteenth- and nineteenth-century routs, assemblies and Stuff Balls is concealed behind a twentieth-century front. Inside the walls of the castle the first sight which faces the visitor at the far end of the grounds is the County Hall built to Sir Robert Smirke's design in the 1820s to house county meetings and the assize courts. Should it be described as mock-Gothic or mock-Tudor? In either case it is an attractive building with a slender colonnade, battlements and graceful towers, the whole brilliant red with Virginia creeeper in autumn. Also in the grounds is the county gaol, the front wing of the 1780s and the rear of the 1840s.

Whatever medieval buildings there may have been within the six acres of the castle yard, and it is likely that these were few and impermanent, no traces of them now remain. The whole strength of the place lay in its magnificent curtain wall, set on a high embankment and once further protected by deep, dry ditches outside the walls, and in the twin keeps and other towers along the outer circuit. There were two Norman gateways at the east and west ends; the western one is now blocked, and the eastern one now provides evidence both of the original work and of the thirteenth-century rebuilding. Cobb Hall is an angle-tower at the north-east corner of the curtain also added in the thirteenth century. The Observatory Tower, south of the gateway, consists of fourteenth-century work on top of one of the Norman keeps, itself crowned with an early nineteenth-century turret. It was built by one of the prison governors. It is said that he built it to study the stars, hence its name; the reason he gave to the magistrates who approved the expenditure, however, was that it was needed as a look-out to prevent the prisoners from escaping. A little farther west is the second mound, crowned by the Lucy Tower, a twelfth-century shell-keep.

Although there are many traces of Norman masonry in the outer wall and the herringbone coursing is conscientiously renewed where it appears during the restoration work which is now gradually taking place, the impressive curtain owes as much to the nineteenth century as to any other. It certainly owes a great deal to the importance of the security of the place when it was used as a prison. In the eighteenth century the walls were in considerable decay; the moat had been filled in and houses built over it. The county magistrates were responsible for their prison but had no control over the castle as a whole, which belonged to the Duchy of Lancaster. In 1831 they bought it from the Duchy, and throughout the 1830s a programme of restoration was carried on under the supervision of their surveyor, Edward James Willson. That he was an architectual historian as well as an architect and devoted to recording and preserving traces of his county's past, was a stroke of luck.

There was no hope by now of recovering the moat; many parts of it were occupied by beer shops and houses of ill fame which carried on a thriving trade in scandalous proximity to the cathedral. Willson concentrated on rebuilding the walls and on repelling all attempts by the owners of surrounding properties to dig into the embankments which were their foundation. Phillip Ball, the owner of the Strugglers Inn, was a particular thorn in Willson's flesh. He dug into the bank to construct gardens and a bowling-alley, accidentally uncovering the Roman west gate in the process; it stood just long enough to be admired and sketched before collapsing. The castle wall was in considerable danger of doing the same. Warnings were of no avail, nor was a court injunction; only imprisonment for contempt of court finally stopped Ball. At this point the local Liberal Press discovered that he was politically sound, and a martyr was born: 'poor Radical Phillip' was lauded for his resolute stance in face of the tyranny of Tory magistrates. Thus anyone who likes to think of castle walls as symbols of medieval repression can take pleasure in the thought of Lincoln's being symbols of nineteenth-century repression as well.

And so we come to the cathedral, echoing William Cobbett's words, 'To the task of describing a thousandth part of its striking beauties I am inadequate.' It was, he thought, 'the finest building in the whole world'. The beauty of the building is enhanced by the dominance of its setting. It towers above the town below in a manner unrivalled by any other English cathedral except perhaps Durham.

Three main building periods are represented: the Norman work of Remigius and his successors survives in the west front; surrounding it up to the lower courses of the towers; and dominant throughout the rest of the minster is the Early English rebuilding which started under St Hugh in about 1190 and culminated in the completion of the Angel Choir in 1280. All that was left for later generations was to preserve the building and to gild the lily. This they did with the addition of large numbers of chantry chapels and the upward extension of the towers in the fourteenth and fifteenth centuries. All three were originally crowned with spires; that on the central tower collapsed in 1548; the western ones were removed, to the riotous fury of the inhabitants of Lincoln, in the eighteenth century.

The description of Lincoln takes up about fifty closely printed pages in Pevsner's *Buildings of Lincolnshire*. Anyone who wants to look at the building properly should carry that book around with him, not this one. All that I can do here is to make idle reference to a few of its delights, such as the view of the exterior by floodlight. The lighting is not bright and garish; it bathes the whole building in a soft glow, picking out details of pinnacles and niches, columns and arcading and the hundreds of statues which adorn the building. One of these, on a buttress of the retro-choir, east of the Galilee Porch, was universally famous throughout the eighteenth century. It portrays the devil astride a witch's back and is referred to by, among others, Alexander Pope. 'The Devil looks out o'er Lincoln' became quite a catch-phrase. Less neck-cricking is the splendid Romanesque decoration of the Norman west front. Beasts, birds, foliage and geometric decoration climb the jambs of the arches; above them a frieze of Old and New Testament scenes includes the expulsion of Adam and Eve from Paradise, Noah's Ark, the reward of the blessed and the torments of the damned. Inside the building the magnificent details of the carving on the choir-screen can also be studied close at hand and without discomfort; there are innumerable tiny figures among the lovingly carved foliage, owls and bishops and grotesques. There is more neck-breaking work, unfortunately, needed when one looks at the marvellous company of angels which gives the Angel Choir its name. All of them are different; many play musical instruments, such as the viol, the pipe and tabor or the trumpet; one is engaged in the strictly secular occupation of holding a falcon with its lure, while others are at the more normal angelic business of displaying books and scrolls.

In the north choir aisle is the cathedral treasury, which has a display of church plate from the diocese. Beyond here a door opens to the cloisters and the thirteenth-century chapter house. Over the northern range of the cloisters is the library designed for Dean Honeywood by Christopher Wren. At its eastern end is the one remaining bay of the medieval library, complete with some survivals of its original furnishings. This room is used for the exhibition of material from the library, and it is here that the Lincoln copy of Magna Carta may be seen.

During the Middle Ages this enormous building was the centre of worship for the whole of the diocese. People came from far and wide to reverence the shrine of St Hugh during their life, and at their death it was as natural to leave a legacy to the upkeep of the fabric as it was to make arrangements for their own funerals. Many left funds for the saying of Masses in one of its many chapels; the wealthy sometimes bequeathed part of their wealth for the building of new chantries and the endowment in perpetuity of chantry priests. It has been estimated that, when the services which took place at all these minor altars are counted, as well as the major cathedral services, thirty-seven Masses were being said here each day in the early sixteenth century.

All this demanded an enormous number of clergy. The principal members of the chapter were supported in the performance of services by a small army of vicars, 'poor clerks', choristers and chantry priests. It was an army which sometimes caused problems of discipline; young vicars were attracted by the flesh pots of the city and returned late, drunk and naked having gambled away their clothes; poor clerks went pigeon-hunting up the tower and almost set it on fire with a burning torch; a chorister accused Mr Treasurer of womanizing and said that Mr Subdean with his long crane's neck had a good face to look out of a halter. In all matters of discipline the close was the separate jurisdiction of the chapter, its separation from the city visually and practically reinforced by the close wall which they had royal licence to erect. Some substantial stretches of this survive, notably the one which can be seen from Winnowsty Lane, to the east of Minster Yard. Opposite the west front Exchequer Gate was once another part of the circuit, as was Pottergate.

Pottergate now stands stranded on a traffic island, a symbol of the sad fate which has befallen the cathedral and its close, which is not a close. For the main road through the city now brings a thundering, grinding procession of lorries within a few yards of the east end of the building, shaking it to the foundations. All that can be said in favour of this is that it provides the picturesque traveller, who may have been fuming and crawling at the bottom of the hill for half an hour, with a traffic jam which is architecturally rewarding. Unless the Church suddenly becomes militant enough to set up road blocks or, better still, a missile defence system, he seems likely to be able to enjoy the view from his car for some time to come.

Postscript

'In Lincolnshire, a very large county, there is little for curiosity; but a few gentlemen's seats, and the sea-coast is flat and unpleasant.' Such, jaundiced by bad inns and worse food, were the concluding thoughts of John Byng in 1791. The county has in fact tended to suffer at times from a rather bad Press. Only agriculturalists have been unstinting in their praise. Cobbett left 'this noble county, having never seen one acre of waste ground'. Arthur Young, more judiciously, considered it 'a better country than general ideas have permitted some to esteem it'. Other tourists flitted round, seeking out a few scattered areas which abounded in 'that inequality of surface, that diversified interchange of hill and dale, wood and lawn, which constitute the picturesque and beautiful in natural scenery'.

I hope that I have shown in the preceding pages that Lincolnshire has abundant and varied attractions both in landscape and in buildings, including many places where the two combine into the most obvious picture-postcard beauty, plain for anyone to behold who bothers to look. It also has a magnificent road system, comparatively lightly used, where motoring can still be a pleasure unknown in more heavily populated areas. The unfortunate corollary to this is that getting about the county by public transport is, to say the least, a challenge to one's ingenuity, especially in the remoter parts where a village is lucky if it has a market-day bus to the nearest town. Railways too, with which the author of Murray's *Handbook for Lincolnshire* in 1903 found the county 'admirably served', are sadly curtailed, and there can be little confidence in the future of several of the few lines which remain.

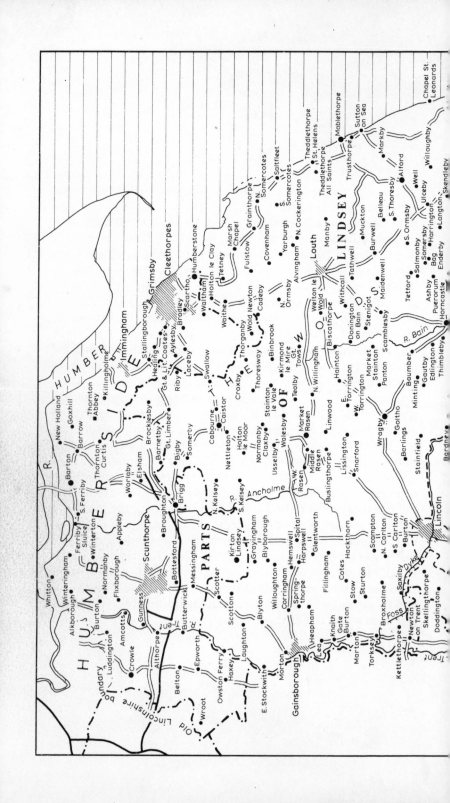

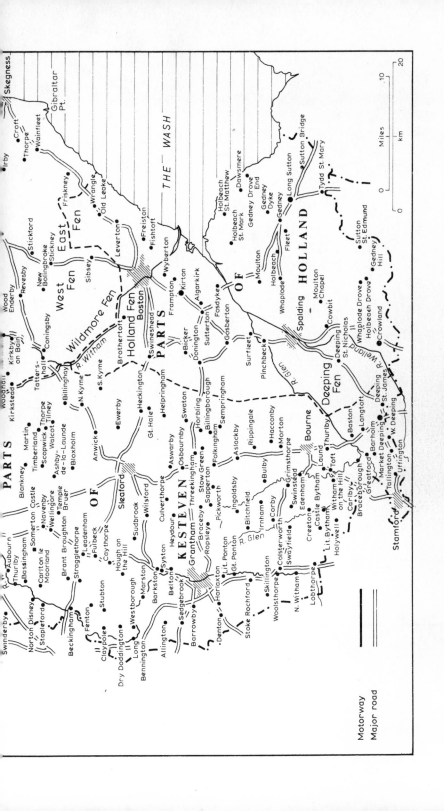

Index